UGA.
7 April 88

SOCIAL WORK PRACTICE WITH CHILDREN AND ADOLESCENTS

SOCIAL WORK PRACTICE WITH CHILDREN AND ADOLESCENTS

By

JOHN S. WODARSKI, Ph.D.

Director, Research Center
Professor, School of Social Work
University of Georgia
Athens, Georgia

CHARLES C THOMAS • PUBLISHER
Springfield • Illinois • U.S.A.

Published and Distributed Throughout the World by

CHARLES C THOMAS • PUBLISHER
2600 South First Street
Springfield, Illinois 62717

© *1987 by* CHARLES C THOMAS • PUBLISHER

ISBN 0-398-05371-5

Library of Congress Catalog Card Number:87-10128

Printed in the United States of America
SC-R-3

Library of Congress Cataloging-in-Publication Data

Wodarski, John S.
  Social work practice with children and adolescents.

  Bibliography: p.
  Includes index.
  1. Social work with children—United States.
2. Social work with youth—United States. I. Title.
HV741.W68   1987   361.7'042   87-10128
ISBN 0-398-05371-5

PREFACE

Whether one's orientation is psychiatry, psychology or social work, professionals are united in their sentiment that all is not well in the area of therapeutic service provision for children and adolescents. Recent reviews of literature evaluating the empirical data to support the effectiveness of therapeutic services to children and adolescents indicate no substantial improvement, and even more disheartening, deterioration in many instances (Feldman, Caplinger, & Wodarski, 1983; Parloff, London, & Wolfe, 1986).

Perhaps it is time that we pause and attempt to isolate why therapeutic services are not fulfilling our expectations. In a typical example, Johnny, a ten-year-old fourth grader, is referred for counseling because he exhibits the following behaviors at school: hitting other children, damaging physical property, running away, climbing and jumping out of windows, making noises and aggressive or threatening verbal statements, and throwing objects such as paper, candy, erasers, chairs and so forth. The teacher and the school social worker meet to discuss Johnny's presenting behaviors. At the same time a psychologist is brought in to assess these difficulties through testing. The parties agree that Johnny should be sent to a child guidance clinic for therapeutic services. Upon arrival at the clinic, Johnny is given a diagnostic workup, i.e., a battery of psychological tests, an interview with the chief psychiatrist, and a social history secured from the parents by the social worker. The psychiatrist's dictation indicates that Johnny has conflicts with his parents stemming from his early childhood experiences, his teacher and his peers, and that these can be resolved through psychotherapy. The psychiatrist asks the social worker to work with the parents and teacher in an effort to reduce some of the conflicts. A year later Johnny's behavior at school has not changed. However, the psychiatrist and the social worker feel that Johnny, his parents and his teacher are making progress.

Several deficiencies can be identified in this example of service provision. The major problem is the failure to establish clear treatment

v

goals for Johnny, his parents and teacher. The questions, "Who is the client?" "What should be changed?" "How should this be achieved, where, and by whom?" were not addressed by the three professionals who would influence Johnny's future. Even when goals are set the literature indicates that no clear criteria are specified for determining whether or not the goals had been achieved. Unfortunately, this example typifies the protocols of many organizations providing therapeutic services for children and adolescents.

Another deficiency in typical service provision is the tendency for treatment to take place in a context other than where problematic behaviors are exhibited. Even when problematic behaviors change in the presence of a psychiatrist, the chances are slim that behavioral changes will generalize to the classroom. There are other dysfunctional aspects in offering services at a mental health center or another specialized treatment agency such as a child guidance clinic, family service agency, and so forth. The provision of services at a specialized agency increases the probability that: (1) as the child receives services along with others who are so defined, he/she is likely to acquire a negative and stigmatizing label and this may initiate the establishment of a self-concept of deviance; (2) the child is less likely to be provided the opportunity to view adequate role models in such settings as interaction with normal peers is severely constrained; and (3) role models provided in segregated treatment milieus may be more deviant than those provided in other treatment settings, thus diminishing the likelihood of positive reinforcement from peers for prosocial behaviors. Thus, the provision of services in the environment where the problematic behaviors originally occur would eliminate many of the dysfunctional aspects of specialized and segregated treatment agencies.

Few would deny the controversy surrounding the efficacy of the present-day therapeutic services aimed at changing the child's and adolescent's behavior. Many issues pertain to where the services should be provided and by whom, the proper duration of services, and appropriate criteria for evaluation. Thus the purpose of this text is threefold: (1) to deliberate relevant issues in terms of assumptions, rationales, and empirical support, and to propose issues for future research directed toward providing therapeutic services to children and adolescents; (2) to provide guidelines for structuring services from an organizational perspective; and (3) to review procedures involved in evaluating therapeutic services provided to children and adolescents. The intention is to provide practitioners with an inventory of items to be considered prior to the initiation of services to children and adolescents and to evaluate services currently provided in order to improve them.

The text is geared toward preparing a variety of professional change agents to provide therapeutic services to children and adolescents. It is applicable for courses dealing with behavioral change in children and adolescents, which are offered in medical schools, schools of social work, and departments of sociology, psychology and education. The assumption is made that all helping professions perform a variety of similar tasks when working with children and adolescents. The key variable differentiating professional change agents is the context of training and/or practice. That is, the difference is organizational rather than behavioral.

REFERENCES

Feldman, R. A., Caplinger, T. E., & Wodarski, J. S. (1983). *The St. Louis conundrum: The effective treatment of antisocial youths.* Englewood Cliffs, NJ: Prentice-Hall.

Parloff, M. B., London, P., & Wolfe, B. (1986). Individual psychotherapy and behavior change. In M. Rosenzweig & L. Porter (Eds.), *Annual review of psychology* (pp. 321–349). Palo Alto, CA: Annual Reviews Inc.

CONTENTS

Page

SOCIAL WORK PRACTICE WITH CHILDREN AND ADOLESCENTS

Chapter 1

SOCIAL WORK PRACTICE WITH CHILDREN AND ADOLESCENTS

The existing literature indicates demand for accountability in the delivery of social services. The call for definite criteria of change, delineation of change methods and evaluation of the effects of the change methods will increase the quality of social services provided. With limited exceptions, however, there have been few efforts to conceptualize and formulate the aspects of social work practice common to children and adolescents. Moreover, virtually all such endeavors have been rather limited since they have shown a pronounced tendency to conceptualize social work practice in terms of specific techniques, practice in certain agencies, fields and/or client groups (Wodarski, 1985).

The literature has no single widely recognized or generally accepted statement regarding the aims and purposes of the professional practice of social workers with children and adolescents. The purpose of this chapter is to propose a consistent conceptualization and formulation of social work practice through the identification of the common elements of practice. Thus will be ensured the provision of social work services on a more rational basis to children and adolescents and a more adequate empirical evaluation of the services provided to clients.

Social work practice with children and adolescents can be conceptualized in terms of common relationship factors such as indications of interest, concern, respect, encouragement, model provisions, and so forth. The concepts of social work goals, knowledge, and methods are interrelated and form a common basis for social work practice with children and adolescents. It is stressed that social work practice is a highly abstract concept bridging together many other concepts of descending levels of abstraction. The concepts of social work values, goals, knowledge, and methods, all a part of the concept of social work practice, are conceptualized at a lower level. Social work practice formulated on a lower level of abstraction consists of the behaviors which occur between a person or system of persons defined as clients and a person

3

defined as a worker. It is elaborated how these factors influence the delineation of what occurs between the worker and client in terms of the specification of the client's behavior, the worker's interventive attempt, where treatment will take place, and so on. Finally, issues involved in the conceptualization of social work practice with children and adolescents are reviewed.

Interpersonal Skills: Common Base

The empirical foundation of social work practice can be based on a social psychological model of interpersonal helping (Wodarski, 1981). This conceptualization of professional practice is based upon the premise that effective interpersonal helping can be learned through the successful mastery of a variety of hierarchically ordered and complexly interrelated *interpersonal and interventive skills* and *perceptual/conceptual-cognitive abilities.* The concepts of hierarchy and developmental progression are central to this conceptualization of practice because the acquisition and mastery of more complex skills and abilities later in the practice are dependent upon the worker's ability to acquire and master basic helping skills and perceptual/conceptual abilities during the initial stages of preparation for practice. The progression from one level of interpersonal and theoretical expertise to the next is dependent upon the learner's ability to master critical interpersonal and cognitive tasks at each level of development.

It is important to keep in mind that the training model allows for maximum flexibility in the preparation of individual students, because it recognizes the uniqueness of each one's needs and expects that each will develop at his/her own rate. As a result, students are not expected to reach and obtain each developmental task at the same time.

Successful completion of each task at each particular level of development is assessed by a variety of *objective* and *standardized measures* and and *evaluation procedures* (for an elaboration see Wodarski, 1985a). Students, themselves, are allowed to decide when they believe they have gained the necessary skills and abilities to move to the next level of training. Evaluation, therefore, is a joint effort which involves the student and the instructor. When the student demonstrates that he/she has achieved the maximum competency requirements, he/she is permitted to move on to more advanced levels of training. If a student fails to achieve minimal levels of competency in one or more areas of interpersonal skills development or cognitive abilities, he/she is not permitted to advance to the next level until he/she successfully masters all skills and abilities at the present level. Initial clinical competencies in this model should be developed at the bachelor's level of instruction with advanced competencies developed at the master's level.

Beginning Conceptual Skills

Essential to social work practice are the various theories employed in assigning causation to the client's behavior (Brieland, 1977; Minahan, 1981; Wodarski, 1983). It is essential to illustrate how practitioners' theoretical conceptualizations of their clients can influence: (1) how they will predict and explain a client's behavior; (2) how much change they believe can take place in the client; and (3) the selection of the types of methods, techniques, and interventions they will use in working with the client. Thus, students should develop the following competencies which provide the rationale for the social-psychological approach to interpersonal helping.

Students will:

1. Have current knowledge of the effectiveness of contemporary approaches to interpersonal helping in social work practice and behavior change.
2. Understand the theoretical relationship between theories of human behavior, the genesis of deviant behavior patterns in children and adolescents, the interpersonal helping process, and outcome evaluation procedures.
3. Understand and be able to articulate the basic axioms of the social-psychological approach as they relate to the helping process. For example:
   (a) That interpersonal helping is an active, developmental process that transpires between two intimately involved individuals who mutually influence each other.
   (b) That the course and outcome of this process are dependent upon factors which are inherent to the development of the relationship system as well as factors that are external to it.
   (c) That the helper's behavior and practice competencies are central to positive therapeutic outcome.
   (d) That the reciprocal exchange of positive behaviors is an impor-

tant factor in accounting for the continued progression of the helping relationship toward its final goal.

(e) That there are three types of empirically validated, universal interaction patterns and sequences of human communication, and that the conscious influences of these communication-relational patterns by the helper are central and critical to positive service outcome. These communication-relational patterns are: symmetrical, complementary and parallel patterns of interaction (Carson, 1969; Thibaut & Kelley, 1959; Wodarski & Bagarozzi, 1979).

(f) That effective interpersonal helping skills and patterns can be learned and mastered through systematic and rigorous training.

(g) That the interpersonal helping process requires mutual effort, cooperation, joint decision making and problem solving.

(h) That the evaluation of therapeutic outcome is an essential component of the helping process.

(i) That in order for evaluation to be valid it must encompass at least four domains of personal and interpersonal functioning: behaviors, cognitions, attitudes, and affects.

Establishing and Maintaining a Positive Helping Relationship

Proponents of different therapeutic approaches disagree on many points. There is general consensus, however, that one potent treatment variable is the relationship formed between worker and client (Goldstein, Heller, & Sechrest, 1966). Many theorists have conceptualized this crucial treatment variable at a high level of abstraction but few have been able to conceptualize "relationship" in an operational and discrete manner. From a social learning perspective, however, Rosen (1971) has viewed the relationship between two or more individuals as an interactional situation that consists of a series of behavioral exchanges or, more specifically, of stimulus-response exchanges. At any point during their ongoing interaction either participant can draw upon a large pool of potential behaviors. Every behavior enacted by the worker or the client is considered to have certain cost and reward characteristics for each participant, and consequently, the interaction between any two behaviors results in its own unique cost and reward outcomes for each participant (Thibaut & Kelley, 1959). Likewise, any prolonged series of behavioral exchanges produces differing new cost and reward balances for the therapist or client(s). Although these outcomes or differential results of social interaction may vary for each individual, they influence crucial facets of treatment such as relationship formation, continuance, and involvement in the therapeutic process. The following skills are considered critical in the establishment, maintenance, and termination of therapeutic relationships.

1. Know the basic interpersonal skills (and the empirical data that support their use) required for the successful formation of a helping alliance.
2. Know the basic interpersonal skills (and the empirical data which support their use) required to successfully maintain the therapeutic alliance throughout the course of the helping process.
3. Understand the importance of maintaining a positive therapeutic alliance by avoiding the use of negative coercive strategies such as the threat of punishment, retribution, ridicule, and shaming.
4. Understand the importance of reciprocity in the exchange process, the client's perceptions of equity, fairness, rewards, costs, alternatives available, etc., in maintaining the therapeutic alliance.
5. Understand the theoretical and practical significance of interpersonal attraction and perceived similarity in the initial states of relationship formation.
6. Understand the theoretical and practical significance of reducing the helper's anxiety in the initial stages of relationship formation.
7. Understand the theoretical and practical significance of conveying the core conditions of nonpossessive warmth, genuineness and accurate empathic understanding which strengthen interpersonal involvement and the maintenance of a positive therapeutic relationship.
8. Understand the importance of conveying respect to the client throughout the therapeutic relationship.
9. Understand the importance of conveying professional competence and expertise to the client and the role that they play in enhancing the helper's ability to influence the client.
10. Recognize the uniqueness of each client and their difficulties and that each client will progress at their own speed and rate of development.
11. Understand the importance of both verbal and nonverbal be-

haviors in the formation and maintenance of the therapeutic relationship.

Development and Mastery of Nonverbal Interviewing Skills

Congruent nonverbal skills are considered essential to effective communication. A recurring theme throughout the research in nonverbal communication in interpersonal helping is the degree of consistency between verbal and nonverbal channels of communication (Barrett-Lennard, 1962; Graves & Robinson, 1976; Tepper & Haase, 1978). Congruence is operationalized as consistency of response between verbal and nonverbal behavior. If some persons are more skilled than others in interpreting and communicating nonverbal messages, then this has implications for the selection of practitioners for training and perhaps for the selection of clients for specified types of interpersonal helping.

The following are considered to be critical nonverbal interviewing skills. For an elaboration of these see Chapter 10 of *Rural Community Mental Health Practice* (Wodarski, 1983).

1. Attending skills
2. Core conditions of helping
   (a) Appropriate and effective use of physical distance in the helping interview
   (b) Forward lean toward the client
   (c) Appropriately relaxed posture which communicates attentiveness, interest and concern
   (d) Appropriate and regular eye contact, looking at the client as the client speaks, spontaneous eye movements, etc.
   (e) Allowing an appropriate amount of time to elapse before responding verbally or nonverbally, sharing time with client, etc.
   (f) Open and accepting body posture, i.e., legs, feet, arms, hands, etc., being careful not to create a physical barrier between the helper and the client
   (g) Appropriate and fluid hand and arm movements which are spontaneous
   (h) Appropriate physical contact with the client such as a handshake when first meeting, aiding a handicapped person, etc.
   (i) Elimination of physical barriers that may interfere with the

helping process, e.g., furniture, room arrangements, external noise, interruptions

(j) Appropriate and alert arousal level which conveys involvement

(k) Use of appropriate face and head movements, e.g., affirmative head nods, relaxed facial expression, appropriate use of facial expressions which mirror client's affects and indicate empathic understanding (e.g., helper does not burst out laughing when client expresses sadness or relates a painful experience)

3. Helper should demonstrate the ability to incorporate important socio-cultural considerations into the helping process which influences initial relationship formation and enhances the helper's attractiveness and credibility in terms of physical appearance.

(a) Appropriate dress for the context in which the helping relationship takes place

(b) Appropriate dress for the particular client group, racial or ethnic population with whom one is working

Development and Mastery of Verbal Interviewing Skills[1]

Requisite to implementation of micro and macro practice technologies are adequate verbal skills, that is, the ability to communicate to the client the steps involved in the practice endeavor, to building the relationship, and to facilitate the influence attempt (Shulman, 1984). A significant variable seems to be the worker's ability to convey credibility regarding his or her abilities and treatment techniques. Studies indicate that workers can show credibility through being organized, providing structure in the client's and worker's role in therapy, suggesting appropriate topics for beginning discussions, and engaging in proper verbal and nonverbal communication (Corrigan et al., 1980; Schmidt & Strong, 1970).

A number of researchers have found repeatedly that certain interpersonal skills help facilitate positive changes in their clients while a substantive proportion of professionally trained therapists are either ineffective or cause their clients to deteriorate (Bergin, 1966, 1967a, 1967b, 1971, 1975). The following interpersonal skills have been isolated that are characteristic of effective therapists and are referred to as "core conditions" (Truax & Mitchell, 1971). For a discussion of these core conditions see Wodarski and Bagarozzi (1979). They not only influence the client's continuation in treatment, but increase the probability of behavior change when applied with the appropriate intervention technique. These core conditions are:

(1) Accurate empathic understanding

(2) Nonpossessive warmth — unconditional positive regard

(3) Genuineness — congruence

(4) Respect

(5) Self-involvement — the ability to make appropriately self-disclosing statements which indicate to the client that the helper is with them. These essential relationships build conditions that are elaborated in the helping process (e.g., "It makes me feel sad when you feel all alone and that your friends avoid you.") Self-involving statements are feeling statements made by the helper about the client, him/herself or the relationship. They are not beliefs or thoughts but are direct reports of emotional experiences. They are not intellectualizations, rather they serve as models for the client's self-explorations.

(6) Self-disclosure is different from self-involvement in that it involves sharing personal information as well as feelings.

Assessment

In recent years accountability has become a primary issue in the social services (Wodarski, 1981). Although the profession has responded well to many community needs through the use of paraprofessionals and volunteers, there continues to be a most serious allegation that intervention methods lack demonstrated effectiveness in achieving positive client change. Accurate assessment of client, worker, and agency attributes are essential for effective practice (Kutchins & Kirk, 1986; Wodarski, 1981, 1985a). Unfortunately, until recently there were few accurate assessments of clients available to professionals (Streever, Wodarski, & Lindsey, 1984).

The goal of this aspect of training is to equip the student with the fundamental tools necessary for accurate assessment, an essential element of effective intervention at all levels of social work practice, whether it be at the individual, group, organizational, or societal level (Gingerich, Feldman, & Wodarski, 1976). Rigorous training in assessment is considered to be a sine qua non for qualitative training and social work practice. Insufficient time spent on this process, no matter what powerful techniques the change agents possess, results in ineffective or irrelevant intervention since an accurate assessment of the client's difficulties has not occurred. The following assessment skills are requisites for effective practice.

1. Develop a rationale for a problem solving approach to interpersonal assessment in terms of how one uses this paradigm to solve personal and interpersonal difficulties. For example:
   (a) Problem identification
   (b) Elucidation of the problem in specific terms which allow for the application of standardized intervention procedures
   (c) Generating a list of possible intervention strategies which seem appropriate to the case at hand, conceptually linking assessment to the rationales for intervention
   (d) Selecting a treatment approach (individual, family, and group) which is the most appropriate for the child or adolescent and his/her unique situation
   (e) Implementation of the treatment
   (f) Monitoring the treatment
   (g) Modifying treatment when necessary due to elucidation of barriers
   (h) Evaluating whether treatment goals have been achieved, i.e., has the problem been resolved
   (i) Planning for the maintenance of gains once formal intervention has been discontinued
   (j) Implementing procedures that will aid in the maintenance of gains made in treatment
   (k) Conducting periodic follow-ups to determine to what extent treatment gains are being made
2. Understand the relationship between accurate assessment and the development of a viable treatment plan
3. Understand that in order for intervention areas to be successful and comprehensive it must consider the following areas of human functioning: behaviors, attitudes, cognitions, and affects
4. Understand that behaviors have symbolic meaning and significance and that for certain clients, understanding these symbolic meanings may facilitate the behavior change process
5. Understand that behaviors are exhibited in particular environments, with certain individuals and within specific contexts, and that in order to obtain accurate information, assessment should be con-

ducted in those environments and contexts and with those individuals who are intimately involved with the client and the problem.

Primary Diagnostic Skills

The clinical interview can provide a suitable setting to observe the client's reaction to certain stimuli. The client's reaction, i.e., how the client presents him/herself physically and verbally, handles stress, and so on, gives the social worker a cue as to how the client approaches various life situations and provides the opportunity to gather information about reinforcement preferences, and possible antecedents and consequences that control the behaviors chosen for modification, how motivated the client is to change, and finally, who would be the best mediators of change (Holland, 1970; Kanfer & Grimm, 1977; Kolko, 1986; Thomas, 1974; Wahler & Cormier, 1970; Wolpe, 1970, 1973).

In the last decade, a number of scales have been developed to facilitate obtaining information necessary for workers to make adequate assessments of children and adolescents (Achenbach & Edelbrock, 1984; Levitt & Reid, 1981; Newmark, 1985). This aspect of preparation should review the measurement instruments and procedures currently available for assessing and documenting child and adolescent change during the helping process. All the materials are designed to provide ongoing feedback on the attainment of service goals.

1. Requisite information gathering skills:
   (a) Appropriate questioning of the client that does not arouse defensiveness and helps the client clarify and focus on the problem at hand
   (b) Paraphrasing and summarization statements which enable the client to think about and reflect upon the issues under consideration
   (c) The appropriate use of open-ended, semistructured and closed questions
2. Appropriate use of concreteness—the ability to help the client place structure on his/her life situation

Skills in Behavioral Observation

Behavioral assessment is based on three essential operations: (1) the analysis of target behaviors chosen for modification in terms of observable events; (2) definition of the behaviors in a manner that enables two persons to consistently agree that the selected behavior has occurred; and (3) the systematic collection of data to determine if selected antecedent or consequent events (behaviors) significantly influence the rate of the client's behavior chosen for modification (Wodarski, 1981). Thus, alteration of behavior is attempted from (1) events that occur before a client's behavior (antecedents), or (2) events that occur after a client's behavior (consequences). Depending on the client's behavior, the context of therapy, characteristics of the change agent, and so forth, techniques for the modification of behavior are chosen from either or both categories. Thus, the following assessment skills are necessary.

1. Ability to make accurate behavioral observations which provide the helper with the essential information necessary for baseline data analysis and treatment planning
2. Ability to use a variety of assessment instruments, procedures, and questionnaires which can be used to evaluate the client's behaviors, attitudes, cognitions, and affects
3. Securing the following information:
   (a) The presenting problem in behaviorally specific terms which identify the following:
      1) behavioral deficits
      2) behavioral excesses
      3) behaviors to be acquired
      4) behaviors to be maintained
      5) behaviors to be altered
      6) behavioral assets
   (b) History of the presenting problem
      1) duration
      2) frequency
      3) locations, environments, contexts, and persons involved
      4) which persons and environments facilitated desired behaviors, thoughts, attitudes, feelings, etc.
      5) which persons and environments hinder desired behaviors, thoughts, attitudes, feelings, etc.
      6) how undesirable behavior, affects, etc., are maintained

　　　　7) persons clients can depend upon to help with treatment
　　　　8) individuals that should be involved in treatment
　　　　9) environments and contexts in which interventions should be attempted
　　　10) what client and others have done in the past to modify or correct problems
　　　11) techniques, people, etc., that have been helpful
　　　12) techniques, people, etc., that have not been helpful
　(c) Situational analysis of the problem
　　　　1) In what situations does the problem behavior occur?
　　　　2) In what situations is the problem behavior most severe?
　　　　3) In what situations does the problem behavior never occur?
　　　　4) What are the antecedent cues, stimuli, people, thoughts, feelings, etc., that set off the problem?
　　　　5) How does the client respond?
　　　　6) What behavior, feelings, thoughts, stimuli, occur immediately following the behavior which tend to reinforce and maintain it?
　　　　7) What are the behaviors, feelings, thoughts, people, stimuli, etc., that immediately follow the behavior which tend to reduce the probability of its occurrence in the future?
　　　　8) How does the client think, feel, behave, etc., after he/she has had time to think about the consequences of his/her behavior?
　　　　9) What additional factors does the client believe are related to the initiation and maintenance of the problem behaviors, thoughts, feelings, etc.?
　　　10) What are the discriminative stimuli, and schedules of rewards and punishments for the behavior?
　(d) Client's expectations for change
　　　　1) Help client outline in behaviorally specific terms what he/she hopes to accomplish, how he/she expects to feel, think and behave as a result of coming for treatment.
　　　　2) Help clients evaluate whether their goals and aspirations are realistic and attainable given their age, physical and intellectual capacities, their sex, race, and social position, their educational and vocational experiences, etc.
　　　　3) Set appropriate expectations for change and for ability to change.

(e) Self-control consideration
   1) In what situations can the client control the problem behaviors, thoughts, feelings, etc.?
   2) In what situations can the client not control the problem behaviors, thoughts, feelings, etc.?
   3) Have any of the problem behaviors been followed by aversive consequences that have reduced their frequency?
   4) Has the client developed or does the client possess the capacity to develop a means of self-control which will enable the avoidance of those situations where problem behaviors usually are exhibited?
   5) Has the client developed or can the client be helped to develop alternative, more functionally appropriate behaviors which will be instrumental in overcoming the problem?

(f) Motivational assessment (reward-cost analysis according to the client's perception)
   1) What satisfactions (rewards) would continue if the client's behavior remained the same?
   2) If the client's behavior worsened?
   3) What disadvantages (costs) would the client suffer if the problem remained the same?
   4) If the client's problem worsened?
   5) Does the client believe that the effort he/she will have to make to change (client investments) plus the inherent costs involved in making that change will be worth the rewards (outcome, profits) he/she hopes to receive? (i.e., is the exchange considered fair and equitable?)
   6) What advantage does the client believe will occur for significant others if his/her behavior improves?
   7) If it worsens?
   8) What disadvantages does the client believe will occur for significant others if his/her behavior improves?
   9) If it worsens?
   10) All in all, does the client perceive that changing his/her behavior for the better will prove to be more rewarding than costly in the long run?

(g) Additional areas of assessment
   1) What are the cultural conditions (social norms and envi-

ronmental forces) which contribute to maintaining the problem behaviors, thoughts, feelings, attitudes, perceptions, etc.?

2) Can the congruence of several environments be increased or can the client be helped to remove him/herself from those environments where he/she is most likely to exhibit problematic behavior?

3) Does the client's environment encourage or discourage self-evaluation, self-improvement, and beliefs that change is possible?

4) Does the client's milieu regard psychological procedures as appropriate for helping solve his/her problems?

5) Is there enough support in the client's milieu to maintain changes in attitudes, behaviors, feelings and cognitions that successful intervention will produce?

Relationship Development

The development of a therapeutic relationship is conceptualized as not much different from the development of interpersonal relationships in general because all interpersonal relationships are believed to proceed toward greater cohesiveness only if both participants experience their interpersonal exchanges as more rewarding than existing alternatives (Altman & Taylor, 1973; Levinger & Snoek, 1972). From the initial attraction between client and therapist in the first meeting and the mutually negotiated contractual agreements between the two participants, the relationship escalates to a point where communications are open and both parties make positive evaluations of each other based upon mutual satisfaction with the exchanges experienced thus far. Such an evaluation fosters continued interaction and the cohesion produced is the basis for successful therapeutic progress. Both therapist and client should see this relationship as a mutually cooperative endeavor which is characterized by increased intimacy, self-disclosure, and empathic understanding if the client is to reach the final stage of the therapeutic process, i.e., attainment of the desired behavior changes previously negotiated, continued ability to resolve behavioral problems by employing the skills learned in therapy, and an increasing capacity to achieve desired goals with minimal help from professional sources.

1. Decide whether the helper has the skill, ability and the resources to treat the client effectively or whether referral to another professional or agency is required.
2. Decide upon the treatment context.
3. Decide upon the treatment model.
4. Decide upon what significant individuals, small system group and so forth should be involved in the treatment process and what their roles will be.

Treatment Intervention: Conceptualizing the Change Process and Its Facilitation

Practitioners should not only be trained in crisis intervention, the task-centered model, and basic interventive strategies for work with individuals, groups and families, but should have the opportunity for training in advanced interpersonal treatment technologies. These consist of empirical approaches to the solution of interpersonal problems. Numerous data-based technologies are available for workers to use in helping clients acquire necessary behaviors to operate in their environments. These will be elaborated in this chapter's section on treatment components.

Foundation Requisites of the Intervention Process

1. Understand that the client's perceptions play an extremely important role in determining practice outcomes, i.e., does the client believe he/she has the ability to change.
2. Understand that change is facilitated through the helper's skill and ability to maintain the previously developed therapeutic relationship.
3. Understand the importance of negotiating a viable treatment contract with the client.
4. Understand that as the treatment progresses, the therapeutic alliance may be influenced by a variety of forces which are external to it as well as forces which are inherent in the relationship.
5. Understand that as the relationship develops over time, the client may perceive that the efforts (inputs) he/she must make in order to achieve the desired goals (outcome) are more costly than had been anticipated. Such perceptions may result in the client becom-

ing uncertain as to whether to continue the therapeutic endeavor (i.e., the client becomes resistant). Such perceptions may hinder therapeutic progress.

6. Recognize resistance when it occurs.

Identifying Sources of Resistance

1. The ability to accurately identify the sources of resistance
2. The ability to decenter, reverse perspectives and role take in order to understand the client's sources of resistance
3. The ability to step back, observe, and process one's own involvement in the helping process and how one's behavior might be contributing to the development and maintenance of the client's resistance
4. To know a variety of techniques that can be used to create and strengthen the client's expectations of personal efficiency which will help the client overcome resistances

Treatment Process

A substantial body of research indicates that a worker can influence a client's future verbal behavior, such as the number of utterances, pauses between verbal exchanges, rates of speech, number of interruptions, length of silence between verbal exchanges, and length of verbal statements. Hence, if a worker wishes to increase any of these behaviors, he or she should model them (Matarazzo & Saslow, 1968; Matarazzo & Wiens, 1977; Salzinger, 1969) and engage in other behavioral increasing activities, such as shaping and selective reinforcement, that is, reinforcing the client's closer approximation to the desired behaviors. For example, if a relevant treatment goal is to increase the client's rate of utterances the worker can reinforce the client's appropriate verbal responses to achieve this objective and model such behavior. However, virtually no investigators have looked at the pattern of an interview. Thus, a crucial aspect of the training program consists of the general category of skills called higher order communication skills. These are:

1. Timing of specific verbal communications
2. Appropriateness of the intervention
3. Managing course of treatment, that is, how and when to increase

or decrease the intensity of treatment and appropriately planning for termination based on accurate assessment

Negotiating a Treatment Contract

Recent research results indicate structure and goal-setting are characteristics of effective intervention which favor behavioral change (Butcher & Koss, 1978; Feldman & Wodarski, 1975).

1. The ability to patiently and cooperatively develop and negotiate a treatment contract that both the client and the helper perceive to be equitable, fair and attainable
2. The ability to specify the duration of the contract
3. The ability to behaviorally outline specific roles, responsibilities, behaviors, etc., that participants are expected to exhibit in order to fulfill their part of the contract
4. The helper's ability to maintain and fulfill his/her part of the contract by being consistent and fulfilling negotiated expectations
5. The ability to revise the contract when necessary

If one fully understands interpersonal helping in terms of a sociopsychological model of relationship development, one realizes that the helper's responsibility to meet contractual agreements in a reliable and consistent manner is crucial to the further development of the therapeutic relationship. If the helper is inconsistent or fails to fulfill contractual obligations, he/she demonstrates a lack of respect for the client and becomes a model for similar behavior by the client. As a result, a negative reciprocal exchange process can be set in motion.

Overcoming Resistance in its Initial State of Relationship Development

1. The ability to use verbal and nonverbal techniques of subtle influence to overcome initial resistances; for example:
   (a) Nonverbal, minimal encouragers such as head nods, body postures, smiles, eye contact, etc., that are consciously used to reinforce cooperative behaviors and positive attitudes, affects and cognitions on the part of the client
   (b) Verbal, minimal encouragers such as responses that reinforce the continuation of client's verbalizations, cooperative behaviors, positive affects and cognitions (e.g., reflection of con-

tent and affect, rephrasing client's statements in ways which influence the client's thinking and behavior, etc.)

Overcoming Resistance in Later Stages of Relationship Development

1. The ability to use persuasion effectively; for example:
   (a) suggestions
   (b) interpretations
   (c) giving directions and assignments
   (d) using paradoxical injunctions
   (e) confrontations
   (f) immediacy
2. The ability to modify communication-relational patterns so that cooperation between the helper and the client is achieved
   (a) the conscious and appropriate usage of alternative patterns of interaction (i.e., symmetrical, complementary and parallel forms of exchanges)
3. The ability to communicate about the client-helper relationship in a way which facilitates further positive relationship development
4. The judicious and appropriate use of emotional arousal techniques which serve as incentives for overcoming resistances and promote individuals and relationship development and maintenance (e.g., relaxation techniques which reduce anxiety, repeated exposure to anxiety producing stimuli which ultimately lose their potency after continued presentation, cognitive relabeling of affective responses in ways which facilitate the client's responding such as when a fear response is relabeled as excitement)
5. The ability to successfully involve clients in performance tasks which will increase their personal mastery (e.g., participant modeling, performance desensitization, performance exposure, self-instructed performance)
6. The ability to successfully expose the client to vicarious experiences through the use of various modeling procedures which enable them to adopt a more cooperative response and lessen their resistance

Evaluation

The practitioner's repertoire of clinical intervention skills involves the systematic application of treatment techniques derived from behavioral science theory and supported by empirical evidence to achieve behavior change in clients. The practitioner must possess both theoretical knowledge and empirical perspective regarding the nature of human behavior, the principles that influence behavioral change, and the empirical data that provide the rationale for the interventions. The worker also must be capable of translating this knowledge into concrete operations for practical use in a variety of clinical settings and choose the appropriate intervention foci. In order to be an effective practitioner, therefore, the social worker must possess a solid behavioral science knowledge base as well as a variety of research skills. Moreover, a thorough grounding in research methodology enables the clinician to evaluate therapeutic interventions, a necessary requisite of scientific practice. Because the rigorous training of social workers with scientific perspective equips them to assess and evaluate any treatment procedure that has been instituted, there is continual evaluation providing corrective feedback to practitioners. For the scientific social worker, theory, practice, and evaluation are all part of one intervention process and the arbitrary division of theory, intervention, and research, which does not facilitate therapeutic effectiveness or improve clinical procedures, is eliminated (Wodarski, 1981).

Conceptual Skills for Evaluation

1. Develop a rationale for the scientific study and evaluation of the helping process.
2. Develop a working knowledge of a wide variety of research designs, experimental approaches and statistical procedures which can be used to evaluate treatment outcome.
3. Develop a working knowledge of a wide variety of reliable and valid assessment instruments, questionnaires, rating scales, behavioral and observational procedures that can be used to evaluate treatment outcome.
4. Develop an understanding and a rationale for conducting follow-up evaluations.
5. Develop an understanding of the relationship between the type

of presenting problem, the treatment process, the evaluation procedures, the assessment instruments and the length of follow-up.

6. Understand the formal aspects of the social psychological theory of human behavior, deviance and behavior change:
   (a) to develop a thorough understanding of the theoretical concepts, axioms, propositions and their logical relationships as they relate to assessment and subsequent interventions.
   (b) to be able to evaluate the conceptual soundness of the theory.
   (c) to be able to determine whether the treatment strategies that have been developed follow logically from the theory's formal structure.
   (d) to be able to revise poorly constructed theories so that they are rendered more logical and internally consistent.
   (e) to be able to revise poorly conceptualized treatment procedures and intervention strategies so that they become more consistent with the theoretical formulations concerning the nature of human behavior, the development of problem behaviors and planned behavior change.

Methodological Evaluation Skills

1. The ability to select and use appropriate research designs, experimental approaches and statistical procedures to evaluate treatment effectiveness and outcome
2. The ability to determine an appropriate time frame for conducting valid and reliable follow-ups
3. The ability to be objective in one's evaluations
4. The ability to objectively assess one's treatment strategies and to modify them or revise them when necessary

Evaluation of the Intervention Process

Analysis of the Intervention Process

1. The ability to systematically retrace the treatment process
   (a) to determine whether a standardized treatment approach has been followed

(b) to determine whether the approach used was effective in producing the desired outcome

(c) to assess whether the instruments and measurement procedures used to evaluate change were appropriate to capture the changes that actually did take place

(d) to evaluate the reasons for a treatment's ineffectiveness (e.g., it did not address the true cause or source of the problem, treatment was not potent enough to produce desired results, interventions were too global, interventions were too specific, interventions were poorly timed, interventions were based on inadequate conceptualization of the client's situation in terms of variables affecting it, and procedures were employed which were inadequate for this particular client)

(e) to be able to revise the treatment process so that it is more accurate in alleviating the cause of the problem

(f) to select appropriate assessment instruments which will accurately reflect changes in the client's behaviors, affects, attitudes, and cognitions

Choosing the Interventive Foci

This chapter has elucidated the basic requisite skills in providing effective services to children and adolescents. Practitioners must choose interventions based on a variety of factors. These are:

(a) the level of intervention (i.e., individual, group, or family)

(b) the theory (theories provide us the conceptual requisites and rationales for assessment and intervention)

(c) the appropriateness of the theory and intervention to the developmental issues clients face, such as the issues of development of social and academic competencies, trust, self-esteem, dealing with sexuality, substance abuse, their ethnicity, and so forth

(d) populations to be served—children and adolescents: neglected, physically and sexually abused, developmentally disabled, violent, pregnant, unemployed, substance abusers, depressed and suicidal, and so forth

(e) institutions served by the focus of practices—mental health, families, health, schools, and so forth

Implementation of Change Strategy: Level of Intervention

Social work has been characterized historically as a profession that emphasizes a one-to-one relationship with clients in order to achieve behavioral change (Glenn & Kunnes, 1973; Ryan, 1971; White, 1984). However, the profession has seldom addressed itself adequately to the appropriateness of the various service delivery mechanisms for certain types of clients. Few empirical studies have delineated the parameters or criteria for determining whether one-to-one, group, or family level treatment is best for achieving behavioral change in a given situation.

Individual, Group and Family Treatment. Recent years have witnessed a growing emphasis on group and family treatment as a result of various conceptualizations, particularly social systems, that place a heavy emphasis on the roles that the client's peers and significant others play. Relatively few clients, however, are treated in this manner as compared to those treated individually. Yet, there are a number of obvious deficiencies in placement of clients in casework services. The casework relationship is unlike most situations faced in daily interaction and cannot provide the worker data on the client's interactional patterns with significant others. In contrast, the provision of services in groups and families offers the following benefits. The group interactional situation more frequently typify many kinds of daily interactions. Services facilitating the development of behaviors that enable people to interact in groups and families are likely to better prepare them for participation in larger society, that is, to help them learn social skills necessary to secure reinforcement (Feldman & Wodarski, 1975). For example, training in the following life skills which adolescents at risk need are: cognitive anger control, interpersonal, relaxation, systematic desensitization, and problem solving, and can all occur in one-to-one contexts. From a social learning theory perspective, however, it is posited that if a behavior is learned in a group context it is likely to come under the control of a greater number of discriminative stimuli; therefore, greater generalization of the behavior can occur for a broader variety of interactional contexts.

There are additional substantiated rationales for working with individuals in groups and families. Peer group experiences create a learning situation in which the performance of each group member furthers the attainment of overall group goals. This increases individual members' support for group performance, strengthens performance under a variety of similar circumstances, and further enhances the attainment of group goals. Group reward structures capitalize on peer influence and peer reinforcement. These are considered to be some of the most potent variables in the acquisition, alteration, and maintenance of prosocial norms among youths (Buckholdt & Wodarski, 1978). Groups provide a context where new behaviors can be tested in a realistic atmosphere. Clients can get immediate peer feedback regarding their problem solving behaviors. In groups clients are provided with role models to facilitate the acquisition of requisite social behavior. Groups provide a more valid locus for accurate diagnosis and a more potent means for changing client behavior (Meyer & Smith, 1977; Rose, 1977). Lastly, the provision of services through groups and families greatly increases the number of children and adolescents that can be served by an effective treatment program.

These theoretical rationales indicate that treating children and adolescents in families and groups should facilitate the acquisition of socially relevant behavior. However, criteria need to be developed concerning who can benefit from group and family treatment. Such knowledge will only be forthcoming when adequately designed research projects are executed in which clients are assigned randomly to individual, group and family treatment to control for confounding factors such as type of behavior, age, sex, income level, size and academic abilities.

In instances where an individual does not possess the necessary social behaviors to engage in family or group treatment, a one-to-one treatment relationship may provide the best treatment context. For example, many antisocial children would be quickly lost in a group simply because they do not have the essential social behaviors for interaction. Likewise, with hyperactive children, it may be necessary to work on an individual basis until their dysfunctional behaviors are controlled enough to allow them to participate in a group context. However, as soon as they develop the necessary social skills, therapeutic changes are likely to be further facilitated and maintained if they can be placed in small group treatment (Jacobs & Spradlin, 1974).

Treatment Components

Length of Therapy

A substantial number of evaluative studies have been produced in the last three decades that have had a profound impact on traditional therapeutic practice. Major changes have come about as a result of these studies. One of these changes concerns the length of therapy (Fischer, 1978). In the past, therapy was considered to be a long and involved process. Current research, however, indicates that the optimal number of visits is between 8 and 16. Reid (1978), Stuart (1974), and others are providing a rationale for the development of a short-term model of therapy for social work practice.

Behavior Acquisition

A second current major focus involves helping clients learn new behaviors to deal with their specific situations. This emphasis is in opposition to that of changing attitudes or motivation first and positing that behavioral change will follow. Research evidence is accumulating to indicate that if clients are taught behaviors that enable them to influence their environments, both external and internal (e.g., self-management procedures, appropriate assertive behavior, and problem solving), their social functioning increases.

Development of new behaviors is believed to occur optimally in structured therapeutic contexts; that is, where intervention procedures follow a sequential pattern to develop and maintain new and socially relevant behaviors. Such patterns usually consist of mutually agreed upon contracts that include goals, methods, termination criteria, and the rights and responsibilities of client and worker. Two examples of empirically based treatment technologies are task-centered casework and behavioral approaches.

Task-Centered Casework. Task-centered casework is a theoretical system of short-term intervention that emerged in 1972 with the publication of *Task-Centered Casework* by Reid and Epstein. Reid and Epstein (1977) published a follow-up book, *Task-Centered Practice,* and Reid (1978) has another book, *The Task-Centered System,* which nicely elucidates the relevant aspects of the task-centered approach. Task-centered casework is unique in development since researchers and practitioners have worked together to specify its constructs and have tested various aspects of the total intervention package (O'Connor & Reid, 1986; Reid, 1985).

In 1975, Reid took a major step in placing task-centered casework on firm empirical grounds by operationalizing the variable of task performance in a five-step plan called task implementation sequence (TIS). TIS is a progressive treatment sequence including "enhancing commitment, planning task implementation, analyzing obstacles, modeling, rehearsal, guided practice, and summarizing" with the goal being to elicit specific client behaviors. The introduction of "operational tasks" was part of a beginning effort to specify the model's constructs and thereby place the paradigm on firmer scientific ground by specifying the unit of attention, the task, in more measurable terms. One of the keys to the success of task-centered casework may be the structural elements of the model, its emphasis on short-term service, and the specification of goals to be achieved by the client in concrete steps.

Behavioral Approaches. Along with the development of the task-centered approach, corresponding and enhancing treatment technologies have been developed. These consist of behavioral approaches to the solution of interpersonal problems. Numerous data-based behavioral technologies are available for workers to use in helping clients acquire necessary behaviors to operate in their environments. Every year more data support the successful history of behavior modification practice with children classified as hyperactive, autistic, delinquent, retarded, antisocial, neurotic, and psychotic. For an elaboration of the extensive data base see Hersen and Van Hasselt (1986).

The following is a categorization of the areas of possible application of behavioral technology in social work practice. Each application has substantial empirical support. A further elaboration of theory, research, and illustrations of the application of the techniques is available in *Behavioral Social Work* (Wodarski & Bagarozzi, 1979).

Children

1. *Foster care.* Development of behavioral management programs and appropriate parenting skills for both natural and foster parents. Training parents of children to use contingency contracts, stimulus control, and time-out procedures to facilitate their development of social skills needed for effective adult functioning.

2. *Schools.* Helping decrease absenteeism, increasing appropriate academic behavior such as reading comprehension, vocabulary development, and computational skills, increasing interpersonal skills such as the

ability to share and cooperate with other children and adults, and decreasing disruptive behaviors.

3. *Juvenile courts.* Helping decrease deviant behavior and increase prosocial behavior by contingency contracting, programming significant adults to provide reinforcement for prosocial behavior, developing programs for training children in those behavioral skills that will allow them to experience satisfaction and gain desired reinforcements through socially acceptable means.

4. *Community centers.* Helping children develop appropriate social skills, such as working together, participating in decision making, making plans, discussing, and successfully carrying plans through.

5. *Outpatient clinics.* Helping clients reduce anxiety, eliminate disturbing behavioral problems, control anger, define goals in terms of career, increase self-esteem, gain employment, solve problems (both concrete and interpersonal), develop satisfying life styles, and learn skills necessary for successful adult functioning in society.

Adolescents

1. *Family service.* Helping in the development of family interactional skills for effective problem-solving, negotiation skills and goal-setting behaviors, development of prosocial behaviors, and development of clearer communication structures to facilitate interaction among family members.

2. *Community mental health centers.* Helping adolescents reduce anxieties through relaxation and stress reduction techniques. Teaching self-control to enable adolescents to alter certain problem-causing behaviors. Offering assertiveness training as one means of having personal needs met. Helping in the acquisition of behaviors to facilitate interaction with family, friends, and co-workers.

3. *Psychiatric hospitals.* Using interventions to help adolescents acquire necessary prosocial behaviors for their effective reintegration into society. Structuring adolescents' environments through provision, by significant others, of reinforcement for the maintenance of appropriate social behaviors such as self-care, employment, and social interactional skills. Analogous emphasis indicated for working with the retarded in institutions.

4. *Public welfare.* Helping adolescents achieve self-sufficiency, learn effective child management and financial management procedures, and develop social behaviors, parenting skills, and competencies needed to gain employment.

5. *Juvenile corrections.* Using interventions to increase prosocial behaviors,

to learn new job skills, and to develop self-control and problem-solving strategies that are not antisocial.

Macro Level Interventions

If, following an assessment, a practitioner decides that a client is exhibiting appropriate behaviors for their social context but that a treatment organization or institution is not providing adequate reinforcers for appropriate behaviors, or that it is punishing appropriate behavior, the practitioner must then decide to engage in organizational or institutional change. This may involve changing a social policy, changing a bureaucratic means of dealing with people, or other strategies. In order to alter an organization, the worker will have to study its reinforcement contingencies and assess whether or not he or she was the power to change these structures so that the client can be helped.

Even broadly defined social policy decisions can directly affect the behaviors that will be exhibited by children. For example, certain economic policy decisions (e.g., those pertinent to teenage employment, child care policy and other social phenomena) have a determinant effect on behaviors that children will exhibit in the future. A decision to adopt a full employment policy will obviously affect children. Additionally, a national children's rights policy would ensure that each child is provided with adequate housing, education, justice, medical and social services, and so forth.

In social work practice, the primary focus has been on changing the individual. Practitioners must restructure their thinking. "Inappropriate" behavior exhibited by a client must be examined according to who defined it as inappropriate and where requisite interventions should take place. Future research should provide various means of delineating how human behavior can be changed by interventions on different levels, thus providing the parameters for micro and macro level intervention (Wodarski, 1985). The obvious question that will face social workers is how to coordinate these multilevel interventions.

Generalization and Maintenance of Behavioral Change

Interventions at the macro level are increasingly more critical, since in a now classic study, follow-up data collected 5 years later on antisocial children who participated in a year-long behavioral modification program which produced extremely impressive behavioral changes in the children, indicated that virtually none of the positive changes were maintained (McCombs, Filipczak, Friedman, & Wodarski, 1978; McCombs, Filipczak, Rusilko, Koustenis, & Wodarski, 1978). Possibly, maintenance could be improved when change is directed also at macro levels.

Considerable study is needed to delineate those variables that facilitate the generalization and maintenance of behavior change. These may include substituting "naturally occurring" reinforcers, training relatives or other individuals in the client's environment, gradually removing or fading the contingencies, varying the conditions of training, using different schedules of reinforcement, and using delayed reinforcement and self-control procedures (Kazdin, 1975). Such procedures will be employed in future sophisticated and effective social service delivery systems and will provide the rationale for more clients to be treated in small group systems (Wodarski, 1980).

Summary

This chapter provides the basic requisites for the foundation of social work practice. It is essential that students master these foundation skills and attributes. After such mastery, students can develop skills in the highly complex treatment technologies that must necessarily be implemented to help clients change. We have tended to conceptualize social work practice at a very elementary level. For this reason treatment programs may not have produced many significant results nor have prevention approaches been effective. The future will witness not only the practitioners' mastery of these elementary skills but their ability to implement comprehensive treatment strategies that will insure that children's and adolescents' behavior can be changed. The development of comprehensive treatment strategies will require, of course, that clinical social work educators engage in more research to isolate the relevant parameters of practice.

Requisites for the establishment, implementation and evaluation of social work treatment programs for children and adolescents are presented in Chapter 2. Chapter 3 centers on the essentials of assessment and the significance this has for social work practice with children and adolescents. Viewing social work clientele from various theoretical perspectives (a historical overview) are presented with a case illustration in Chapter 4. Chapter 5 covers the relevancy of the life span developmental perspective for practice with children and adolescents. Procedures for the maintenance and generalization of achieved behavioral change are reviewed in Chapter 6. Chapter 7 discusses the childhood problems of developmental disabilities, physical and sexual abuse, and violent behavior that require the major attention of social workers. Chapter 8 elaborates adolescent difficulties of teenage pregnancy, unemployment, running away, substance abuse, and depression and suicide that require a major focus of social work. Preventive services for adolescents, an idea whose time has come, are elaborated in Chapter 9. The final chapter covers emerging practice trends.

Endnote

1. For elaboration of these skills see John S. Wodarski and Dennis A. Bagarozzi, "A Review of the Empirical Status of Traditional Modes of Interpersonal Helping: Implications for Social Work Practice." *Clinical Social Work Journal*, 1979, 7(4), 231-255.

REFERENCES

Achenbach, T. M., & Edelbrock, C. S. (1984). Psychopathology of childhood. In M. Rosenzweig & L. Porter (Eds.), *Annual review of psychology* (Vol. 35). Palo Alto, CA: Annual Reviews, Inc.

Altman, I., & Taylor, D. A. (1973). *Social penetration: The development of interpersonal relationships.* New York: Holt, Rinehart and Winston.

Barrett-Lennard, G. T. (1962). Dimensions of therapist response as causal factors in therapeutic change. *Psychological Monographs, 76* (43, Whole No. 562).

Bergin, A. E. (1966). Some implications of psychotherapy research for therapeutic practice. *Journal of Abnormal Psychology, 71,* 235-246.

Bergin, A. E. (1967a). An empirical analysis of therapeutic issues. In D. Arbuckle (Ed.), *Counseling and psychotherapy: An overview.* New York: McGraw-Hill.

Bergin, A. E. (1967b). Further comments on psychotherapy research and therapeutic practice. *International Journal of Psychiatry, 3,* 317-323.

Bergin, A. E. (1971). The evaluation of therapeutic outcomes. In A. Bergin & S. Garfield (Eds.), *Handbook of psychotherapy and behavior change.* New York: Wiley.

Bergin, A. E. (1975). When shrinks hurt: Psychotherapy can be dangerous. *Psychology Today, 6,* 96-104.

Brieland, D. (1977). Historical overview: Special issue on conceptual frameworks for social work practice. *Social Work, 22*(5), 341-346.

Buckholdt, D., & Wodarski, J. S. (1978). The effects of different reinforcement systems on cooperative behavior exhibited by children in classroom contexts. *Journal of Research and Development in Education, 12*(1), 50-68.

Butcher, J. N., & Koss, M. P. (1978). Research on brief and crisis-oriented psychotherapies. In S. Garfield & A. Bergin (Eds.), *Handbook of psychotherapy and behavior change: An empirical analysis* (2nd ed.). New York: Wiley.

Carson, R. (1969). *Interaction concepts of personality.* Chicago: Aldine.

Corrigan, J. O., Dell, D. M., Lewis, K. N., & Schmidt, L. E. (1980). Counseling as a social influence process: A review. *Journal of Counseling Psychology, 27*(4), 395–441.

Feldman, R. A., & Wodarski, J. S. (1975). *Contemporary approaches to group practice.* San Francisco: Jossey-Bass.

Fischer, J. (1978). *Effective casework practice.* New York: McGraw-Hill.

Gingerich, W. J., Feldman, R. A., & Wodarski, J. S. (1976). Accuracy in assessment: Does training help? *Social Work, 21*(1), 40–48.

Glenn, M., & Kunnes, R. (1973). *Repression or revolution.* New York: Harper Colophon Books.

Goldstein, A. P., Heller, K., & Sechrest, L. (1966). *Psychotherapy and the psychology of behavior change.* New York: Wiley.

Graves, J. R., & Robinson, J. D. (1976). Proxemic behavior as a function of inconsistent verbal and nonverbal messages. *Journal of Counseling Psychology, 23,* 333–338.

Hersen, M., & Van Hasselt, V. B. (Eds.). (1986). *Behavior therapy with children and adolescents: A clinical approach.* New York: Wiley.

Holland, C. J. (1970). An interview guide for behavioral counseling with parents. *Behavior Therapy, 1*(1), 70–79.

Jacobs, A., & Spradlin, W. W. (1974). *The group as agent of change: Treatment, prevention, personal growth in the family, the school, the mental hospital and the community.* New York: Behavioral Publications.

Kanfer, F. H., & Grimm, L. G. (1977). Behavior analysis: Selecting target behavior in the interview. *Behavior Modification, 1*(1), 7–28.

Kazdin, A. E. (1975). Recent advances in token economy research. In M. Hersen, R. Eisler, & P. Miller (Eds.), *Progress in behavior modification* (Vol. 1). New York: Academic Press.

Kolko, D. J. (1986). Depression. In M. Hersen & V. Van Hasselt (Eds.), *Behavior therapy with children and adolescents: A clinical approach* (pp. 137–183). New York: Wiley.

Kutchins, H., & Kirk, S. A. (1986). Reliability of DSM–III: A critical review. *Social Work Research & Abstracts, 22*(4), 3–12.

Levinger, G., & Snoek, J. D. (1972). *Attraction in relationship: A new look at interpersonal attraction.* New York: General Learning Press.

Levitt, J. L., & Reid, W. J. (1981). Rapid-assessment instruments for practice. *Social Work Research and Abstracts, 17*(1), 13–19.

Matarazzo, J. D., & Saslow, G. (1968). Speech and silent behavior in clinical psychology. In J. Shlien, H. Hunt, J. Matarazzo, & C. Savage (Eds.), *Research in psychotherapy.* Washington, DC: American Psychology Association.

Matarazzo, J. D., & Wiens, A. N. (1977). Speech behavior as an objective correlate of empathy and outcome in interview and psychotherapy research: A review of implications for behavior modifications. *Behavior Modification, 1,* 453–480.

McCombs, D., Filipczak, J., Friedman, R., & Wodarski, J. S. (1978). Long-term follow-up of behavior modification with high-risk adolescents. *Criminal Justice and Behavior, 5*(1), 21–34.

McCombs, D., Filipczak, J., Rusilko, S., Koustenis, G., & Wodarski, J. S. (1977, December). *Follow-up on behavioral development with disruptive juveniles in public schools.* Paper presented at the 11th Annual Meeting of the Association for the Advancement of Behavior Therapy, Atlanta, Georgia.

Meyer, R. G., & Smith, S. S. (1977). A crisis in group therapy. *American Psychologist, 32,* 638–643.

Minahan, A. (1981). Introduction to special issue. *Social Work, 26*(1), 5–6.

Newmark, C. S. (Ed.). (1985). *Major psychological assessment instruments.* Rockleigh, NJ: Allyn and Bacon, Longwood Division.

O'Connor, R., & Reid, W. J. (1986). Dissatisfaction with brief treatment. *Social Service Review, 60*(4), 526–537.

Reid, W. J. (1975). A test of a task-centered approach. *Social Work, 20*(1), 3–9.

Reid, W. J. (1978). *The task-centered system.* New York: Columbia University Press.

Reid, W. J. (1985). *Family problem solving.* New York: Columbia University Press.

Reid, W. J., & Epstein, L. (1972). *Task-centered casework.* New York: Columbia University Press.

Reid, W. J., & Epstein, L. (Eds.). (1977). *Task-centered practice.* New York: Columbia University Press.

Rose, S. D. (1977). *Group therapy: A behavioral approach.* Englewood Cliffs, NJ: Prentice-Hall.

Rosen, S. (1971). Client-worker relationship: A conceptualization. *Journal of Consulting and Clinical Psychology.*

Ryan, W. (1971). *Blaming the victim.* New York: Vintage Books.

Salzinger, K. (1969). The place of operant conditioning of verbal behavior in psychotherapy. In C. Frank (Ed.), *Behavior therapy: Appraisal and status.* New York: McGraw-Hill.

Schmidt, L. D., & Strong, S. R. (1970). Expertness and influence in counseling. *Journal of Counseling Psychology, 17*(1), 81–87.

Shulman, L. (1984). *The skills of helping: Individuals and groups* (2nd ed). Itasca, IL: Peacock.

Streever, K., Wodarski, J. S., & Lindsey, E. W. (1984). *Test instruments for assessing client change, worker ability, and general agency function in human service agencies* (manual distributed statewide to Department of Human Resources personnel). Athens: University of Georgia School of Social Work.

Stuart, R. B. (1974). *Trick or treatment.* Champaign, IL: Research Press.

Tepper, D. T., & Haase, R. F. (1978). Verbal and nonverbal components of facilitative conditions. *Journal of Counseling Psychology, 25,* 35–44.

Thibaut, W., & Kelley, H. H. (1959). *The social psychology of groups.* New York: Wiley.

Thomas, E. J. (Ed.). (1974). *Behavior modification procedure: A sourcebook.* Chicago: Aldine.

Truax, C. B., & Mitchell, K. M. (1971). Research on certain therapist interpersonal skills in relation to process and outcome. In A. Bergin & S. Garfield (Eds.), *Handbook of psychotherapy and behavior change.* New York: Wiley.

Wahler, R. G., & Cormier, W. H. (1970). The ecological interview: A first step in outpatient child behavior therapy. *Journal of Experimental Psychiatry and Behavior Therapy, 1,* 279–289.

White, B. W. (Ed.). (1984). *Color in a white society.* New York: National Association of Social Workers.

Wodarski, J. S. (1980). Procedures for the maintenance and generalization of achieved behavioral change. *Journal of Sociology and Social Welfare, 7*(2), 298–311.

Wodarski, J. S. (1981). *Role of research in clinical practice.* Baltimore: University Park Press.

Wodarski, J. S. (1983). *Rural community mental health practice.* Austin, TX: PRO–ED.

Wodarski, J. S. (1985a). An assessment model of practitioner skills: A prototype. *Arete, 10*(2), 1–14.

Wodarski, J. S. (1985b). *Introduction to human behavior.* Austin, PRO–ED.

Wodarski, J. S., & Bagarozzi, D. (1979). *Behavioral social work.* New York: Human Sciences Press.

Wolpe, J. (1970). Transcript of initial interview in a case of depression. *Journal of Experimental Psychiatry and Behavior Therapy, 1*(1), 71–78.

Wolpe, J. (1973). *The practice of behavioral therapy.* New York: Pergamon.

Chapter 2

REQUISITES FOR THE ESTABLISHMENT, IMPLEMENTATION AND EVALUATION OF SOCIAL WORK TREATMENT PROGRAMS FOR CHILDREN AND ADOLESCENTS

Many social work researchers, theorists, and practitioners have called for the establishment of social work services on a more rational basis and for the empirical evaluation of services in order to assess whether needs of children and adolescents are being adequately met (Brown, 1968; Fischer, 1973a, 1973b; Geismar, LaGay, Wolock, Gerhart, & Fink, 1972; Handler, 1975; Henderson & Shore, 1974; Lipton, Martinson, & Wilks, 1975; Meyer, Borgatta, & Jones, 1965; Mullen & Dumpson, 1972; Lundman, 1976; Lundman, McFarlane, & Scarpitti, 1976; Reid & Shyne, 1969; Sarri & Selo, 1974; Schinke & Gilchrist, 1984; Schwartz, 1966, 1971; Voit, 1975; Wodarski & Pedi, 1977). A review of the literature, however, reveals little consideration of steps involved in the planning and implementation of treatment programs and their subsequent evaluation. It is more unfortunate that steps involved in the evaluation of treatment programs tend to be elaborated without regard to the procedures involved in establishing and implementing them. Indeed, implementation and evaluation are interrelated. Adequate evaluation of services is not practicable without meeting key requisites for the establishment and implementation phases of social work treatment programs. Thus, the central aim of this chapter is to discuss basic requisites for planning, implementing and evaluating social work treatment programs for children and adolescents.

Recent research investigations provide data to suggest that many treatment contexts are inappropriate for the provision of services (Feldman, Caplinger, & Wodarski, 1983). For example, in most treatment programs for children and adolescents there occur crucial dysfunctions as a result of homogeneously grouping antisocial children together for the purposes of treatment. Moreover, most programs provide treatment in social contexts other than those where the problematic behaviors first, or most frequently, occur. Thus, even if prosocial behaviors are learned during the course of treatment, the capacity to generalize such learned behaviors to the open environment is unduly limited. Likewise, in such treatment contexts the labeled client typically receives services along with others who are similarly defined, thereby increasing the likelihood that the child will acquire a more negative and stigmatizing label. As some researchers suggest, this may lead toward establishment of a deviant self-concept and/or deviant identity. Also, in such settings the client is less likely to be provided the opportunity to view adequate role models. Interaction with normal peers is severely constrained and role models provided in segregated treatment milieus may be more deviant than those provided in other treatment settings, thus diminishing the likelihood of positive reinforcement from peers for prosocial behaviors (Feldman et al., 1983).

This presentation focuses initially on a series of major treatment considerations. What is the appropriate context for behavioral change? Who should act as the change agent? What characteristics should he/she possess? What are the rationales for service provided? How long should treatment continue? How does one prepare for the termination of treatment? How does one ensure that behaviors acquired in treatment are maintained; and so forth? The discussion also will focus on the organizational factors of contexts of treatment which are pertinent to the creation of services, structural components and the training of staff. Finally, the chapter reviews the characteristics of efficacious therapeutic programs for children and a number of requisites for the adequate evaluation of these programs. Specific items discussed are: securing an adequate pretreatment baseline of behaviors, specifying the behaviors to be changed, specifying workers' behaviors in terms of relationship formation and intervention, measures of worker and client behavior, specification of criteria for evaluation of treatment efficacy, monitoring of treatment implementation, reliability of measures, designs and statistics applicable to clinical evaluation, follow-up, implementation of findings, and so forth. Throughout the chapter relevant future research issues are reviewed.

Implementation of Change Strategy: By Whom, Why, and How Long?
Context of Behavioral Change

Unfortunately, if a child exhibits a problematic behavior in a social context such as a school, the behavioral change strategies all too frequently are provided in another social context, such as a child guidance clinic, family service agency, community mental health center, and so forth. Such procedures create many structural barriers to effective intervention (Kazdin, 1977; Stokes & Baer, 1977). Therapeutic change should be provided in the same contexts where the problematic behaviors are exhibited. If therapeutic strategies are implemented in other contexts the probabilities are reduced that newly learned behaviors can be sufficiently generalized and maintained. Considerable study is needed to delineate those variables that facilitate the generalization and maintenance of behavior change. These may include substituting "naturally occurring" reinforcers, training relatives, peers or other significant individuals in the client's networks, gradually removing or fading the contingencies, varying the conditions of training, using different schedules of reinforcement, using delayed reinforcement and self-control procedures and so forth (Kazdin, 1975). Such procedures will be employed in future sophisticated and effective social service delivery systems.

By Whom Should Change Be Delivered?

We have little evidence to suggest what personal characteristics of change agents facilitate the delivery of services to children. One could propose some general hypotheses, e.g., workers should be reinforcing individuals with whom children can identify; they should possess empathy, unconditional positive regard, interpersonal warmth, verbal congruence, confidence, acceptance, trust, verbal ability, physical attractiveness; and so forth (Carkhuff, 1969, 1971; Carkhuff & Berenson, 1967; Corrigan, Dell, Lewis, & Schmidt, 1980; Fischer, 1975; Suinn, 1974; Truax & Carkhuff, 1967; Wells & Miller, 1973; Vitalo, 1975; Wodarski, 1985). Likewise Rosenthal (1966) and Rosenthal and Rosnow (1969) have suggested the worker's expectations of positive change in clients is also necessary. Additional research suggests that a behavioral change agent should have considerable verbal ability, should be motivated to help others change, should possess a wide variety of social skills, and should have adequate social adjustment (Berkowitz & Graziano, 1972; Garfield, 1977; Gruver,

1971). Even though other social science disciplines are beginning to gather preliminary data concerning the attributes and skills of helping agents, there is virtually no literature in the field of social work to indicate what type of characteristics a worker should possess in order to help children. Presently such decisions are made quite arbitrarily. The notion that professional training enables all workers to be equally effective in producing behavioral change is yet to be substantiated. Much more research is needed to delineate the characteristics of effective change agents. Thereafter, hopefully, schools of social work will be able to develop more appropriate selection measures and to create more effective educational technologies to facilitate the acquisition of requisite skills and attributes.

If a worker chooses to employ a child's parents, teachers, peers, or others as change agents he will have to assess at the very least how motivated these individuals are to help alleviate the dysfunctional behavior, how consistently they will apply change techniques, what means are available to monitor the implementation of treatment to ensure that it is appropriately applied, and if the chosen change agent possesses characteristics such as similar social attributes, similar sex, and so forth that could facilitate the client's identification with the worker (Bandura, 1969, 1977; Tharp & Wetzel, 1969).

Rationale for Service Provided

The rationale for offering a program should be based primarily on empirical grounds. The decision making process should reflect that the change agents have considered what type of agency should house the service, that they have made an assessment of the organizational characteristics of the treatment context, and that the interests of agency personnel have been considered in planning the service. A number of additional questions also should be posited. How can the program be implemented with minimal disruption? What new communication structures need to be added? What types of measurements can be used in evaluating the service? What accountability mechanisms need to be set up? What procedures can be utilized for monitoring execution of the program (Wodarski & Feldman, 1974)?

Duration

No empirical guidelines exist regarding how long a service should be provided, that is, when client behavior has improved sufficiently, in terms of quality and quantitity, to indicate that services are no longer necessary. Such criteria should be established before the service is to be provided and these should indicate how the program will be evaluated. The criteria should enable workers to determine whether or not a service is meeting the needs of the client. Moreover, they should help reveal the particular factors involved in deciding whether or not a service should be terminated. The more concrete the criteria, the less this process will be based on subjective factors.

Organizational Factors Pertinent to the Creation of Therapeutic Services for Children

Structural Components

Few agencies have considered the key organizational requisites for the evaluation of therapeutic services. In fact, most agencies are physically structured in a sub-optimum manner for the delivery or evaluation of treatment. For example, few agencies provide observational areas with *one-way mirrors* where therapists can observe each other and isolate effective techniques for working with a child or his family unit. Viewing areas enable the unobtrusive gathering of samples of a child's behavior and facilitate the recording of interaction between parents and the child. They can facilitate training programs where parents learn to change interactional patterns with their child, and they can provide a means by which parents can view and model behaviors which the therapist exhibits in working with the child. These features also may enable workers to secure necessary data for the systematic evaluation of therapeutic services. The provision of such feedback to workers enables them to sharpen their practice skills, adds to practice knowledge, and provides another vehicle for teaching practice skills.

Another technological advance that will be of considerable help in evaluating the services provided to children is the use of *videotapes*. Videotapes can document many verbal and nonverbal interactions. They can provide a more effective and reliable medium through which therapeutic services can be evaluated. Likewise, with proper analysis they can help to sharpen practice skills and lead to a better understanding of how verbal and nonverbal behaviors exhibited by clients and workers influence their mutual interactions (Wodarski, 1975).

Training of Change Agents

Literature is just beginning to accumulate on the procedures that should be utilized in the training of change agents. One relevant training program has been developed on a pilot basis by the author (Wodarski, 1974). It has evolved as part of an evaluative research project regarding the assessment of a community-based treatment program for antisocial children. The training program consisted of initially presenting to students the basic rationale for using a social learning model in training change agents, that is, it permits objectives to be clearly operationalized and measured. During the training process the students gained an indepth knowledge of behavior modification principles through extensive reading. Second, three essential elements were reviewed which form the foundation of the training process: the operationalization of treatment interventions (behaviors to be exhibited by the change agent), and the acquisition of data to determine if the isolated events chosen to modify the client's behaviors (antecedents and consequences) have influenced the rate of the child's behavior. Next students were exposed to observational scales used to measure client and change agents' behaviors and to experimental designs that they could implement to evaluate their practice behavior. The incorporation of this knowledge in their subsequent training was emphasized. Role playing by various professional change agents was used to demonstrate such techniques as reinforcement, punishment, and so forth. Videotapes of professionals and students simulating small group interaction where they practiced the application of treatment techniques were used in order to help the change agents acquire requisite practice behaviors. It also was emphasized how periodic feedback from practitioners and students can enhance learning and practice skills. Before work with a client was initiated the students were required to review a tape of clients interacting in a group, to make a diagnosis, to design a corresponding intervention plan, and to specify how the success of the intervention would be determined (Wodarski, 1985).

Evaluation and Characteristics of an
Efficacious Therapeutic Program for Children and Adolescents

Adequate Specification of Behaviors and Baselines

An adequate treatment program must take into account the need for reliable specification of target behaviors; that is, those behaviors which are to be changed. For example, a treatment program to alleviate antisocial behavior might employ behavioral rating scales where the deviant behaviors are concretely specified. These could include such observable behaviors as hitting others, damaging physical property, running away, climbing and jumping out of windows, making loud noises and aggressive or threatening verbal statements, throwing objects, such as paper, candy, erasers, chairs, and so forth.

A prerequisite for the adequate evaluation of any therapeutic service is to secure a baseline prior to implementation of treatment. This enables the investigator to assess how his treatment interventions compare with *no* treatment interventions. The best type of baseline measure is secured by behavioral observers, who generally have learned to establish reliability on behavioral categories through an extensive training procedure. If observations of behaviors cannot be secured by trained observers, there are other less desirable data sources, such as baselines taken by the client himself or by significant others in his environment. Even though less reliable, these baselines many times are necessary due to various organizational or other environmental constraints. Some of these constraints may involve lack of money for trained observers or the investigation of a behavior that occurs at a time when it is not readily observable by others. When the researcher uses baseline data not secured by a trained observer, the data should be obtained from two or more independent sources in order to check on consistency.

The following are various practical considerations that should be addressed before a researcher decides on the exact procedures for securing a baseline. The first consideration involves where the baseline should be taken. A context should be chosen in which the individual's behavior occurs at a high frequency. If the behavior occurs in more than one context, baselines may be secured for the various contexts. This enables the assessment of a broader range of contexts where the behavior occurs, contributes to the determination of whether or not behavioral changes in one context are analogous to those in another, and provides a more accurate measure of behavior. Additional considerations pertain to where the behavior occurs. If the behavior is readily accessible to observation, there will be no problem. If it is inaccessible, such as a behavior that occurs late at night or in contexts where observation is not possible, the investigator will have to use reports by the client, or others who are present when the behavior occurs, to secure the data. As previously mentioned, it is preferable to have a trained observer secure data. In any case, an individual who is consistent and reliable should be chosen, and data should be collaborated in instances where this is possible. Finally, whether the person who secures data is a trained observer or someone else, a necessary requisite for evaluation of the service is the execution of periodic reliability checks to ensure that the data being provided are consistent (Nelson, Lipinski, & Black, 1975).

Conceptualization and Operationalization of Treatment

Appropriate conceptualization and operationalization of treatment interventions are imperative for the development of effective programs. A worker must be able to specify what behaviors he/she will implement in order to apply a given treatment strategy. This represents a difficult requirement for many, if not most, theoretical frameworks. Usually therapeutic services are described on a global level and are assigned a broad label such as transactional analysis, behavior modification, family therapy, and so forth. However, such labels are valuable only so long as they specify the operations involved in implementing the services. For instance, the global label of behavior modification can be separated into the following distinct behavioral acts: directions, positive contact, praise, positive attention, holding, criticism, threats, punishment, negative attention, time out, application of a token economy, and so forth (Wodarski, Feldman, & Pedi, 1974; Wodarski & Pedi, 1978). Moreover, essential attributes of the change agent that facilitate the implementation of treatment should be delineated.

Measures of Therapist and Client Behavior

Various measures, such as checklists filled out by children and/or significant others (e.g., group leaders, parents, referral agencies, grandparents, and so forth) and behavioral time sampling schedules, can be utilized to assess change in children. Likewise, behavioral rating scales can be used to assess the behaviors exhibited by a change agent. There are excellent texts available which describe the various measures that can be used.[1] They specify particular items measured and the appropriate clientele, types of data provided, reliability, and procedures involved in administration. The type of measurement process selected generally will depend upon the behaviors chosen for modification, the availability of technical equipment, the cost of securing various types of data, the context of measurement, and the frequency, duration, and intensity of the target behavior (Bijou, Peterson, Harris, Allen, & Johnston, 1969).[2]

The literature over the last decade has called for the utilization of multicriterion measurement processes for the evaluation of therapeutic services. However, the few investigators who have utilized multicriterion measurement indicate that many changes secured on certain inventories do not correspond necessarily with results of other measurement processes utilized. For example, in studies by Wodarski et al. (1975, 1976a, 1976b,) it was found that little correlation exists between self-inventory and behavioral rating scales. In many instances, a change can occur on one of the measurements and not on another. The strongest data are derived from behavioral observation scales simply because observers are trained for long periods of time to secure reliable and accurate data. If an appropriate behavioral observation scale is not available, then the investigator can develop his own scale by observing children systematically and then accurately defining the relevant behaviors so that two people can consistently agree that they have occurred.

Both self-inventories and behavioral scales have certain drawbacks. Self-inventories have low reliability but they cost less; also, they may measure behavioral tendencies that behavioral scales do not measure. Behavioral scales provide highly reliable data but are more costly and, depending on the breadth of observation, they may provide data that are limited to a specific social context. The decision to utilize a particular measurement process rests on the aims of the research project.

Specification of Criteria for Evaluation of Treatment Efficacy

Any therapeutic program should specify the criteria by which the service will be evaluated. This should be done *before* the treatment is implemented. For example, evaluation may occur by means of behavioral observations provided by trained observers and/or through the use of checklists filled out by children and significant others. In view of the multidimensional nature of human behavior it seems necessary for professionals to evaluate more than a single criterion in order to develop a comprehensive and rational basis for the provision of services. Moreover, highly sophisticated treatment programs will endeavor to quantify the extent of behavioral change targeted and actually achieved and the social relevance of changes that have occurred; that is, do they really matter in terms of the client's ability to function in his environment (Kazdin, 1977).

Treatment Monitoring

Having met all prior prerequisites, it then becomes necessary to monitor the implementation of treatment. Such monitoring should take place throughout treatment so that necessary adjustments can be made over time if the quality of treatment varies. If behavioral change is obtained and if the investigator can provide data to indicate that treatments were differentially implemented, the change agents can claim with confidence that their treatment has been responsible for the observed modifications in behavior. However, if such data cannot be provided when client change has occurred, many rival hypotheses can be postulated to account for the results (Wodarski & Pedi, 1977).

Reliable Measures

Reliability must be secured for all measures utilized in evaluating a program. Without this basic scientific requisite, evaluative efforts may be ill-spent and there can be no assurance of consistency in the data secured. The reliability requirement often is disregarded in evaluative research thus allowing for the postulation of rival hypotheses to account for the findings (Wodarski & Buckholdt, 1975).

Designs

Frequently it has been assumed that the only way that therapeutic services can be evaluated is through the employment of classical experimental designs, e.g., those where participants are assigned randomly to one or more experimental or control groups. However, such designs may have many deficits and may not be the most appropriate for the evaluation of services. They may be expensive in terms of money, energy required to implement them and administration (Wodarski & Buckholdt,

1975). Moreover, the criterion of random assignment of subjects is usually hard to meet in the evaluation of services provided to children. New designs, however, are emerging from social learning theory literature. These can be easily implemented in social work; they are economical in terms of money, energy required to implement them, and administrative execution. Above all, they provide data which will enable a worker to determine if his interventions have had an effect on client behaviors.

It is interesting to note that the emphasis in the evaluation of services in social work has been on the use of traditional experimental designs which involve grouping clients into experimental and control groups. This research philosophy is diametrically opposed to a basic practice assumption, namely that every individual is unique and needs to be considered in his own gestalt. The *single case* study, which has been championed in recent behavior modification research, may alleviate many of the measurement problems discussed. In this approach the client serves as his own control, and a client's change is evaluated against data provided by himself during a baseline period which precedes the application of treatment. This type of methodology also alleviates the moral and legal aspects of placing a client in a no-treatment control group. It is too early to predict the effects of various legal decisions on the use of traditional control groups in evaluative research. The use of these may be challenged in the future on two legal bases: (1) denial of the right to treatment, and (2) denial of equal protection (Wodarski, 1980).

The data provided in Figure 1 provide an example of a time-series design used to evaluate group work service provided to 10 five- and six-year-old antisocial children. In this figure percentage frequencies of prosocial, nonsocial and antisocial behavior are graphed for a group of children who met for two-hour sessions over a period of 14 weeks at a community center. This classical design in social learning theory consists of four basic phases and is commonly referred to as the ABAB design. In the first phase the children are exposed to a *baseline period.* During this period the group worker does not rationally plan interventions that are likely to influence the prosocial, nonsocial, or antisocial behavior within the group. This is analogous to a traditional diagnostic technique postulated by Sallie Churchill (1965) where the group worker refrains from interventions so that he can more accurately determine the treatment needs of the group. After the children's observed incidences of antisocial behavior have stabilized, treatment is begun (Phase II). Behaviors are considered stabilized if the average variance of the last session is within ten percentage points of the mean of the previous two or three sessions. Members' behaviors are monitored until they once again stabilize, whereupon a baseline condition is reintroduced (Phase III, or the reversal period). The procedure enables the therapist and others who evaluate the treatment program to determine whether the treatment itself was responsible for the various changes in behavior. Immediately after it becomes evident that the treatment has been effective in reducing antisocial behavior the treatment procedures are applied once again.

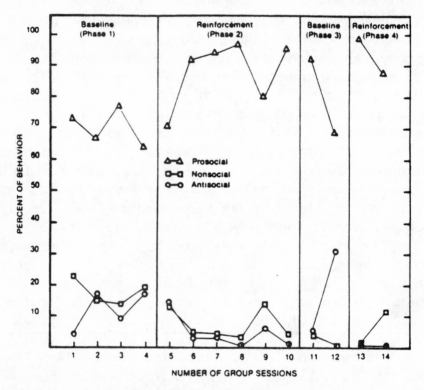

Figure 1. Average percentage of prosocial, nonsocial, and antisocial behavior exhibited by 10 children, according to number of group sessions.

In some situations the ABAB design may not be feasible due to the types of behaviors being modified and/or for various ethical reasons. The primary reason for utilizing an alternate design is that in the ABAB design the modified behavior usually will not reverse itself and, in many instances, reversals would be too damaging to the client or significant others. For example, when fighting is brought under control in a home it would not be feasible to do a reversal of this behavior since, in the past, undue physical harm may have been inflicted on others. A design that may be utilized in lieu of the ABAB design is the multiple baseline design, where a series of behaviors for modification are operationalized. Predictions are made regarding how the various techniques will affect different behaviors. Each behavior is then modified according to a time schedule. Usually one or two behaviors are modified at a time. For example, the worker might want to decrease such behaviors as yelling, fighting, throwing objects, or straying from the group, and to increase prosocial behaviors, such as task participation, appropriate verbal comments, and so forth. The worker in this instance might choose first to ignore the yelling and to use positive reinforcement to increase appropriate verbal comments. Once the yelling decreases and the appropriate verbal comments increase he would sequentially modify the second, third, and fourth behaviors. In Table 1 an outline is provided regarding how such a process operates. The technique being employed becomes more efficacious each time the behaviors change in the direction predicted for each child. This replication of results increases the practitioner's confidence in his techniques and is necessary in evaluative research since the conclusions gained from any one study or interventive attempt are always considered tentative.

TABLE 1
Multiple baseline design according to phases.

Communication Problem	Day					
	1	4	8	14	19	109
Name	Baseline	Intervention			Follow-up I	Follow-up II
Function	Baseline	Baseline	Intervention		Follow-up I	Follow-up II
Command	Baseline	Baseline	Baseline	Intervention	Follow-up I	Follow-up II

Another design which can be used is the AB design. In actuality it is the first half of the ABAB design. It involves securing a baseline and introducing treatment after the behavior to be altered is stabilized. This is a minimum prerequisite for evaluating the effectiveness of interventive attempts.

In summary, all of these designs can be easily implemented in social work. Above all, they provide data which will enable a worker to determine if his interventions have had an effect on client behaviors (Wodarski

& Buckholdt, 1975). It is not practicable to indicate what particular designs should be used at a given time because this depends on the context of the social work practice situation, the behaviors to be modified, time considerations, administrative concerns, and so forth.[3]

Statistics

Evaluation will involve several means of assessing whether or not significant change has taken place. Evaluation of therapeutic services will entail the construction of tables and graphs of client and therapist behaviors. Usually graphs are constructed from measures of central tendencies such as the mean, mode, or the median. A common error in social work practice is to focus solely on what is to be changed in the client and to proceed only to measure that. Sophisticated evaluation programs will measure the behaviors of the client and the change agent simultaneously in order to enable the assessment of what effects the change agent's behavior has had on the client. Guidelines regarding acceptable levels of change are being developed. They will indicate whether or not a program has had a positive effect in terms of the investment of professional effort, financial resources, and significance for the client (Gottman & Lieblum, 1974; Wodarski, Hudson, & Buckholdt, 1976). To aid in the evaluation endeavor, computer programs are now available that will summarize, graph, and place data in tabular form.[4]

Follow-Up

The proper assessment of any therapeutic program with children involves follow-up, a procedure employed by surprisingly few investigators. Crucial questions answered by follow-up include whether a therapeutic program has changed behaviors in a desired direction, how long were these behaviors maintained, and to what other contexts did they generalize. Pertinent questions remain as to when and where a follow-up should occur, for how long it should last, and who should secure the measurement. Empirical guidelines for these are yet to be developed. Failure to provide an adequate follow-up period is a major deficiency of many evaluative studies executed in the social sciences.

Implementation of Findings

It is necessary for evaluators to relate their results to practitioners if social work practice knowledge is to be advanced. Formal and informal channels of communication can be employed to communicate the evaluation of therapeutic services. Formal channels may consist of professional newsletters, conferences, and journals. However, research indicates that these channels are not utilized frequently, or that they do not influence practice behaviors as much as informal channels, e.g., indigenous leaders and peer relationships (Kolevzon, 1977; McNaul, 1972; Rosenblatt, 1968; Weed & Greenwald, 1973). Thus, the social work evaluator must assess indigenous leaders in the profession and determine what peer relationships influence practice behaviors most. They must then utilize these to communicate their research results and thereby influence practice.

Summary

The establishment, implementation, and evaluation of social work treatment programs for antisocial children is an interrelated process. It has been emphasized that considerable time should be spent in dealing with the items reviewed here in order to establish a program which is relevant to client needs and which can be implemented in such a manner that enables a proper evaluation. Sufficient time spent in the planning and establishment phases greatly facilitates implementation and evaluation.

Endnotes

1. Such texts include Orval G. Johnson (Ed.), *Tests and measurements in child development: A handbook* (1976); and Paul McReynolds and Gordon Chelune (Ed.), *Advances in psychological assessment* (Vol. 6, 1984). Both are Jossey-Bass publications. Also see: Newmark, C. S. (Ed.)., *Major psychological assessment instruments,* Rockleigh, NJ: Allyn and Bacon, Longwood Division, 1985.

2. For an excellent discussion of measurement techniques see: Bijou, S. W., Peterson, R. F., Harris, F. R., Allen, K. E., & Johnston, M. W., "Methodology for experimental studies of young children in natural settings," *The Psychological Record,* 1969, *19,* 177–210; and Thomas, E. J. (Ed.), *Behavior modification procedure: A sourcebook,* Chicago: Aldine, 1974.

3. For a detailed description of the various designs that might be used to evaluate social work practice interventions see Herson, M., & Barlow, D. H., *Single case experimental designs* (1976); and Clifford J. Drew and Michael L. Hardman, *Designing and conducting behavioral research* (1986). Both are Pergamon publications.

4. The following computer program packages summarize, graph, and place data in tabular form: *NYBMUL* (Finn, J. D., Buffalo, NY: Computing Center Press, 1969); *SPSS* (Nie, N., Bent, D., & Hull, C. H., New York: McGraw-Hill, 1975); *BMD* (Dixon, W. J. (Ed.), Berkeley: University of California Press, 1970).

REFERENCES

Bandura, A. (1969). *Principles of behavior modification.* New York: Holt, Rinehart and Winston.

Bandura, A. (1977). *Social learning theory.* Englewood Cliffs, NJ: Prentice-Hall.

Berkowitz, B. P., & Graziano, A. N. (1972). Training parents as behavior therapists: A review. *Behavior Research and Therapy, 10,* 297–317.

Bijou, S. W., Peterson, R. F., Harris, F. R., Allen, K. E., & Johnston, M. W. (1969). Methodology for experimental studies of young children in natural settings. *The Psychological Record, 19,* 177–210.

Brown, C. E. (Ed.). (1968). *The multi-problem dilemma.* Metuchen, NJ: The Scarecrow Press.

Carkhuff, R. R. (1969). *Helping and human relations.* New York: Holt, Rinehart and Winston.

Carkhuff, R. R. (1971). Training as a preferred mode of treatment. *Journal of Counseling Psychology, 18,* 123–131.

Carkhuff, R. R., & Berenson, B. G. (1967). *Beyond counseling and therapy.* New York: Holt, Rinehart and Winston.

Corrigan, J. O., Dell, D. M., Lewis, K. N., & Schmidt, L. E. (1980). Counseling as a social influence process: A review. *Journal of Counseling Psychology, 27*(4), 395–441.

Feldman, R. A., Caplinger, T. E., & Wodarski, J. S. (1983). *The St. Louis conundrum: The effective treatment of antisocial youths.* Englewood Cliffs, NJ: Prentice-Hall.

Fischer, J. (1973a). Has mighty casework struck out? *Social Work, 18* (4), 107–110.

Fischer, J. (1973b). Is casework effective? A review. *Social Work, 18* (11), 5–20.

Fischer, J. (1975). Training for effective therapeutic practice. *Psychotherapy, Research and Practice, 12* (1), 118–123.

Garfield, S. L. (1977). Research on the training of professional psychotherapists. In A. Gurman & A. Razin (Eds.), *Effective psychotherapy.* New York: Pergamon.

Geismar, L. L., LaGay, B., Wolock, I., Gerhart, V., & Fink, H. (1972). *Early support of family life.* Metuchen, NJ: Scarecrow Press.

Gottman, J. M., & Lieblum, S. R. (1974). *How to do psychotherapy and how to evaluate it.* New York: Holt, Rinehart and Winston.

Gruver, G. G. (1971). College students and therapeutic agents. *Psychological Bulletin, 76* (2), 111–127.

Handler, E. (1975). Social work and corrections: Comments on an uneasy partnership. *Criminology, 13,* 240–254.

Henderson, R., & Shore, B. K. (1974). Accountability for what and to whom. *Social Work, 19* (4), 287–288.

Kazdin, A. E. (1975). *Behavior modification in applied settings.* Homewood, IL: Dorsey.

Kazdin, A. E. (1977). *The token economy.* New York: Plenum.

Kolevzon, M. (1977). Negative findings revisited: Implications for social work practice and education. *Clinical Social Work Journal, 5,* 210–218.

Lipton, D., Martinson, R., & Wilks, J. (1975). *The effectiveness of correctional treatment: A survey of treatment evaluation studies.* New York: Praeger.

Lundman, R. J. (1976). Will diversion reduce recidivism? *Crime and Delinquency, 22* (4), 428–437.

Lundman, R. J., McFarlane, P. T., & Scarpitti, F. R. (1976). Delinquency prevention: Assessment of reported projects. *Crime and Delinquency, 22* (3), 297–308.

Meyer, H. J., Borgatta, E. F., & Jones, W. C. (1965). *Girls at vocational high: An experiment in social work intervention.* New York: Russell Sage Foundation.

McNaul, J. P. (1972). Relations between researchers and practitioners. In S. Z. Nagi & R. C. Corwin (Eds.), *The social contexts of research.* New York: Wiley.

Mullen, E. J., & Dumpson, J. R. (1972). *Evaluation of social intervention.* San Francisco: Jossey-Bass.

Nelson, R. O., Lipinski, D. P., & Black, J. L. (1975). The effects of expectancy on the reactivity of self-recording. *Behavior Therapy, 6* (3), 337–349.

Reid, J. W., & Shyne, A. W. (1969). *Brief and extended casework.* New York: Columbia University Press.

Rosenblatt, A. (1968). The practitioner's use and evaluation of research. *Social Work, 13* (1), 53–59.

Rosenthal, R. (1966). *Experimenter effects in behavioral research.* New York: Appleton-Century-Crofts.

Rosenthal, R., & Rosnow, R. L. (Eds.). (1969). *Artifact in behavioral research.* New York: Academic Press.

Sarri, R. C., & Selo, E. (1974). Evaluation process and outcome in juvenile correction: Musings on a grim tale. In P. O. Davidson, F. W. Clark, & L. A. Hammerlynck (Eds.), *Evaluation of behavioral programs in community, residential, and school settings.* Champaign, IL: Research Press.

Schinke, S. P., & Gilchrist, L. D. (1984). *Life skills counseling with adolescents.* Baltimore: University Park Press.

Schwartz, W. (1966). Neighborhood centers. In H. S. Maas (Ed.), *Five fields of social service: Reviews of research.* New York: National Association of Social Workers.

Schwartz, W. (1971). Neighborhood centers and group work. In H. S. Maas (Ed.), *Five fields of social service: Reviews of research.* New York: National Association of Social Workers.

Stokes, T. F., & Baer, D. M. (1977). An implicit technology of generalization. *Journal of Applied Behavior Analysis, 12* (2), 349–367.

Suinn, R. M. (1974). Traits for selection of paraprofessionals for behavior modification consultation training. *Community Mental Health Journal, 10* (4), 441–449.

Tharp, R. G., & Wetzel, R. J. (1969). *Behavior modification in the natural environment.* New York: Academic Press.

Truax, C. B., & Carkhuff, R. R. (1967). *Toward effective counseling and psychotherapy: Training and practice.* Chicago: Aldine-Atherton.

Vitalo, R. L. (1975). Guidelines in the functioning of a helping service. *Community Mental Health Journal, 11* (2), 170–178.

Voit, E. (1975). Social work and corrections: Another view. *Criminology, 13,* 255–270.

Weed, P., & Greenwald, S. R. (1973). The mystics of statistics. *Social Work, 18* (2), 113–115.

Wells, R. A., & Miller, D. (1973). Developing relationship skills in social work students. *Social Work Education Reporter, 21* (1), 60–73.

Wodarski, J. S. (1974). A behavioral program for the training of social group workers. *Journal of School Social Work, 1* (3), 38–54.

Wodarski, J. S. (1975). Use of videotapes in social work. *Clinical Social Work Journal, 3* (2), 120–127.

Wodarski, J. S. (1980). Legal requisites for social work practice. *Clinical Social Work Journal, 7*(4), 90–98.

Wodarski, J. S. (1985). An assessment model of practitioner skills: A prototype. *Arete, 10*(2), 1–14.

Wodarski, J. S., & Buckholdt, D. (1975). Behavioral instruction in college classrooms: A review of methodological procedures. In J. M. Johnston (Ed.), *Behavior research and technology in higher education.* Springfield, IL: Charles C Thomas.

Wodarski, J. S., & Feldman, R. A. (1974). Practical aspects of field research. *Clinical Social Work Journal, 2* (3), 182–193.

Wodarski, J. S., Feldman, R. A., & Pedi, S. (1974). Objective measurement of the independent variable: A neglected methodological aspect of community-based behavioral research. *Journal of Abnormal Child Psychology, 2* (3), 239–244.

Wodarski, J. S., Feldman, R. A., & Pedi, S. (1975). Labeling by self and others: The comparison of behavior among antisocial and prosocial children in an open community agency. *Criminal Justice and Behavior, 2* (3), 258–275.

Wodarski, J. S., Feldman, R. A., & Pedi, S. (1976a). The comparison of antisocial and prosocial children on multicriterion measures at summer camp. *Journal of Abnormal Child Psychology, 3* (3), 255–273.

Wodarski, J. S., Feldman, R. A., & Pedi, S. (1976b). The comparison of antisocial and prosocial children on multicriterion measures at summer camp: A three-year study. *Social Service Review, 50* (2), 256–272.

Wodarski, J. S., Hudson, W., & Buckholdt, D. (1976). Issues in evaluative research: Implications for social work. *Journal of Sociology and Social Welfare, 4* (1), 81–113.

Wodarski, J. S., & Pedi, S. (1977). The comparison of antisocial and prosocial children on multicriterion measures at a community center: A three year study. *Social Work, 22,* 290–296.

Wodarski, J. S., & Pedi, S. (1978). The empirical evaluation of the effects of different group treatment strategies against a controlled treatment strategy on behavior exhibited by antisocial children, behavior of the therapist, and two self-ratings measuring antisocial behavior. *Journal of Clinical Psychology, 34* (2), 471–481.

Chapter 3

ESSENTIALS OF ASSESSMENT

The goal of this chapter is to equip the reader with the fundamental tools necessary for accurate assessment, an essential element of effective intervention at all levels of social work practice, whether it be at the individual, group, organizational, or societal level (Achenbach & Edelbrock, 1984; Gingerich, Feldman, & Wodarski, 1976). Rigorous training in assessment is considered to be a sine qua non for qualitative training and social work practice. Insufficient time spent on this process, no matter what empirically based techniques the change agents possess, results in ineffective or irrelevant intervention since an accurate assessment of the child's and/or adolescent's difficulties has not occurred.

A major documented shortcoming of traditional verbal therapies is their reliance on and utilization of assessment systems that fail to offer even minimal utility for the assignment of clients to different treatment procedures. Such nosologies have been evaluated by other writers in terms of their lack of explicitness, precision, reliability, and empirical validity (Eysenck, 1952; Franks, 1969; Harrower, 1950; Hock & Zubin, 1953; Menninger, 1955; Mischel, 1968, 1971, 1972, 1973a, 1973b, 1973c; Robins & Helzer, 1986; Roe, 1949; Rogers, 1951; Rotter, 1954; Scott, 1968; Wachtel, 1973a, 1973b; Zigler & Phillips, 1960, 1961a, 1961b). More serious considerations are raised by 1) the continued reliance upon traditional psychiatric classification systems that fail to predict violent and dangerous behavior on the part of the client (Dix, 1976; Schwitzgebel, 1972); 2) the classic Rosenhan research that illustrates the inability of the traditional classification systems to detect the sane individual from the insane (Bem & Allen, 1974; Crown, 1975; Davis, 1976; Farber, 1975; Mariotto & Paul, 1975; Millon, 1975; Reed & Jackson, 1975; Rosenhan, 1973, 1975a, 1975b; Spitzer, 1975; Weiner, 1975); and, finally, 3) the preliminary research which indicates that the more training professionals have in traditional systems, the less they are able to make accurate assessments of behavior (Crow, 1957; Case & Lingerfelt, 1974; Gingerich et al., 1976).

Positive Aspects of Behavioral Assessment

Behavioral assessment is based on three essential operations: 1) the analysis of target behaviors chosen for modification in terms of observable events; 2) definition of the behaviors in a manner that enables two persons to consistently agree that the selected behavior has occurred; and 3) the systematic collection of data to determine if selected antecedent or consequent events (behaviors) significantly influence the rate of the client's behavior chosen for modification (Baer, Wolf, & Risley, 1968; Bijou, 1970; Bijou, Peterson, Harris, Allen, & Johnston, 1969). Thus, modification of behavior is attempted from 1) events that occur before a client's behavior (antecedents), or 2) events that occur after a client's behavior (consequences). Depending on the client's behavior, the context of therapy, characteristics of the change agent, and so forth, techniques for the modification of behavior are chosen from either or both categories.

The positive aspects of behavioral assessment are its emphases on specification and measurement of goals and objectives for the intervention process. For instance, when working with antisocial children it is possible to specify and operationalize antisocial behaviors in terms of the following actions: hitting others, damaging physical property, running away, climbing out of windows, making loud noises, using aggressive verbal statements, throwing objects such as paper, candy, erasers, and chairs, and so forth. Likewise, positive behaviors to be exhibited by workers in modifying client behaviors can be quantifiable as to the amount of praise, directions, positive attention, positive physical contacts, and so forth, as can such negative behaviors as holding, criticism, threats, negative attention, and time-out. The final operation is the acquisition of data to determine whether the worker's behavior actually played a part in the modification of the client's behaviors. These procedures involve measuring the behaviors of clients and worker according to a quantifiable format, an essential focus in an age of accountability.

Components of Behavioral Assessment

The task of any behavioral assessment process is threefold in nature and can be conceptualized as follows:

1. What are the dimensions of behavior that require change in terms of their frequency of occurrence, their intensity, and their duration?

2. What are the conditions under which the target behaviors are acquired and maintained?

3. What are the most effective procedures that the social worker can utilize in order to help clients acquire target behaviors?

The learning approach to behavioral assessment is similar to the traditional psychiatric diagnosis approach, i.e., the posited need for a close relationship between assessment and treatment. However, a functional analysis of the behavior is made in order to ascertain the explicit environmental variables that control the observed behavior. The focus of such a functional analysis is always observable phenomena in the form of antecedent events, behavioral manifestations and their consequences. The unit of such an analysis is always the interactive relationship between the client's overt behavior and the surrounding environment. All behaviors are considered to be maintained by their antecedents and by the consequences they produce for the client. An accurate appraisal of these effects can provide the social worker with an understanding of their instrumental value. Behaviors that produce positive and reinforcing consequences will tend to be repeated, while those which bring about punishments or fail to produce reinforcements will tend to become extinguished.

Although knowledge of the reinforcement history through which certain problematic behaviors have been acquired will help the clinician understand why some behaviors are more difficult to extinguish than others, this knowledge is purely academic since it is not essential to the development of an appropriate behavior change program for the client. Since data provided by various researchers indicate that the alteration of behavior is not related directly to how the client acquired the behavior, the focus of behavioral intervention is always centered on the control and manipulation of the environment and the contingent outcomes that each behavioral performance produces for the client. Traditionally many theorists and researchers have postulated that the variables involved in the alteration of behavior are analogous to the variables involved in its acquisition. Data have not supported such a view of human behavior, however. The behavioral approach is concerned with the assessment of the individual in the context of his environment; thus, intervention procedures are always tailored to modify the specific environmental forces that are maintaining the problematic behavior, and treatment is always designed to deal with the unique behavioral manifestations presented by each client. Moreover, clients are not assigned to sociological categories, which research shows are not related to treatment nor are a causative factor of behavior. Behavior can be assessed in terms of frequency, duration, and intensity. Certain factors will influence the social worker's choice of the dimension to assess, such as the behavior chosen for alteration, availability of technical equipment, and the context of measurement (Bijou et al., 1969).

Dimensions of Behavior

Frequency refers to the number of times a behavior occurs within a specific interval of time. The frequency dimension can be assessed easily by having clients observe, count, and record the number of times they exhibit specific behaviors. When observations of a particular behavior are made and recorded by more than one individual such as a client and a social worker, a client and his/her peers or a client and his/her parents, a reliability check can be established as a prerequisite for evaluating the success of the modification program. For example, records can be kept to reflect the frequency with which cigarettes are smoked, positive statements are addressed to one's peers, prosocial acts are learned by an autistic child, a child hits another child, incorrect language is used, aggressive statements are expressed, physical approaches toward peers, or job applications are submitted.

If a social worker should decide to use a frequency measure, a fixed interval of time should be selected to observe the behavior. If this does not occur, then an accurate account of the behavior may not be achieved due to the influence of time. If the behaviors are observed under varying time lengths, the frequency should be reduced to a percentage score with controls for the confounding of frequency of the behavior by time.

The *duration* dimension can be assessed by measuring the length of time a behavior is exhibited in terms of seconds, minutes, hours, and so forth. For example, how long does it take a client to finish one cigarette, how much time is spent by a child in positive interactions with his/her parents, what is the duration of prosocial play engaged in by an autistic child, what were the number of minutes a child sat still at the dinner table, and how many days passed without family discord. Although duration can be measured reliably some critical events may not occur for more than a split second but, nevertheless, occur at a high frequency. Thus, the duration dimension is not the most appropriate measure and a frequency count may be more meaningful.

The *intensity* dimension is somewhat more difficult to work with because human assessment of this dimension may often prove inaccurate. For this reason, technical equipment has often been employed to aid in the assessment of intensity. Some investigators have measured the intensity of such behaviors as crying and laughing (Butterfield, 1974; Freund, 1971).

Time Sampling

Since it is virtually impossible to observe a client for any extended period of time in order to secure an accurate description of those behaviors which are under consideration, the time sampling procedure becomes a useful method of data collection. Research has shown that time sampling observations can give an accurate and reliable representation of behavior if they are correctly structured and executed (Wodarski, Feldman, & Pedi, 1975). The type of time sampling procedures that are utilized by the social worker will depend on the type of behaviors chosen for observation, i.e., frequency, duration, and intensity of the targeted behavior; the availability of technical equipment, electrical counters, and videotapes; the cost of securing various types of data, i.e., employment of observers; and the context of the measurement, such as behaviors that occur at inconvenient times and/or where observation is not possible. After the behaviors of clients and worker are operationalized, a nonparticipant observer is usually placed in the treatment context to collect data for the worker in order that he may concentrate on his modification plan. The use of behavioral observers to secure data, however, will not be feasible in most agencies because it is too expensive. It is possible that other workers could serve as observers at selected time periods. The behavioral observations facilitate the worker's ability to operationalize client and worker behaviors and provide the data necessary for the worker implementing the treatment to judge its effectiveness.

The critical question is how to structure observations in order to get an accurate representation of behavior. For example, if a social worker should decide that a frequency measure is the most appropriate measure of a client's behavior, a fixed interval of time should be selected to observe the target behavior. Observations should be structured in a way that would allow the worker to sample the client's behavior during various periods throughout the day and in a variety of situational contexts. If this is not done, an accurate account of the behavior may not be achieved due to the influences of time and situation. If the behaviors are observed under varying time lengths, the frequency could be reduced to a percentage score to control for the confounding of time. When a client is observed in a variety of situations the social worker can assess which environmental circumstances exert their influences to either elicit, maintain, decrease, or increase the incidences of problematic behaviors. In this way a frequency times situation analysis can be made.

Requisites for Measuring Behavior

Behaviors must be defined in terms of observables and in such a manner that two or more people can agree that the behavior has occurred. Such a process establishes the reliability of the behavior (Baer et al., 1968; Bijou, 1970; Bijou et al., 1969). Problems may arise if the behaviors are defined too globally, i.e., a child is defined as hyperactive, retarded, antisocial, autistic, and adolescents are classified as schizophrenic, psychotic, neurotic, and so forth. These categorical classification systems consist of behaviors that are too heterogeneous for an adequate specification of behavior. In these instances the behaviors are not operationalized adequately enough to provide reliable observations which are prerequisite to the execution of an accurate behavior analysis.

The Target of Change

In the initial analysis of the referral situation, the critical question that should be asked by the behavioral social worker is "what behaviors are objectionable and to whom are they objectionable? After these behaviors are isolated the worker needs to gather enough information about the difficulties to isolate who will be the target of intervention.

In many instances the individual mentioned in the referral process may not be the target of intervention. For example, a child may be referred for exhibiting the following behaviors: throwing objects, making loud verbal statements, nagging, and so forth in order to secure the attention of his parents. In such instances the behavioral social worker would want to teach the *parents* to reinforce appropriate behavior and to not provide discriminative stimuli for misbehavior, such as not attending to the child when he is exhibiting prosocial behavior.

Where Assessment Should Take Place

Assessment should occur in the context from which the referral was made. For example, if a child is referred to a child guidance clinic for general antisocial behavior at school the assessment procedure should take place at the school rather than at the clinic. Assessment in the general environment in terms of current discriminative stimuli and reinforcement contingencies that are controlling the behavior enables a worker to secure a clear and more accurate account of the behavior. If a worker is dealing with family discord the assessment should take place where the family happens to quarrel most frequently. Even current simulation exercises to judge discord with peers, family interaction, fear levels of an object, assertiveness, and so forth may be inaccurate if they are different from the context in which the behaviors occur, and other variables may control the client's behavior such as expectations and demand characteristics of the measurement context (Bernstein & Nietzel, 1974; Borkovec, 1972, 1973; Borkovec & Nau, 1972; Borkovec, Stone, O'Brien, & Kaloupek, 1974; Kazdin, 1973; Smith, Diener, & Beaman, 1974; Speltz & Bernstein, 1976; Tasto & Suinn, 1972; Tryon & Tryon, 1974).

Characteristics of Behavior

The social worker in the clinical context can help the client change the following aspects of his behavioral repertoire:

1. Behaviors can be increased in their frequency. For example, parents may need to show their child more affection through verbal praise and physical contact.

2. Behaviors can be decreased in their frequency such as negative self-thoughts, nonattending, and assaultive behavior.

3. Behaviors can be acquired such as development of language skills in autistic children.

4. The form of an already acquired behavior can be altered. For example, it can be connected to other discriminative stimuli, or the duration or intensity can be reduced or increased.

Thus, after the worker decides what behaviors of the client need to be changed, he or she must isolate the discriminative stimuli and consequences which are controlling the behavior, and choose appropriate modification procedures.

Two Critical Questions

Does the client want to change? What will happen if the behavioral change does occur? Substantial empirical literature exists to indicate that a worker will be unable to help a client change his behavior unless the client is motivated to do so (Feldman & Wodarski, 1975; Goldstein, Heller, & Sechrest, 1966; Goldstein & Simonson, 1971; Reid & Epstein, 1972). Thus, a prerequisite to the successful use of behavior modification techniques with clients is their desire to change. This can be assessed by the amount of home reading completed, information provided on events controlling the behavior, and the client's general consistency in applying the techniques.

Once a behavior is changed, what are the implications for the client, others in their environment, and the worker? Can the environment support and maintain the new behavior? That is, can the client and worker program the environment to maintain the change? For example, in work with delinquent children various research reports indicate that substantial change in academic and social behaviors can occur under controlled conditions. However, few studies provide data that indicate that these acquired behaviors can be supported by the client's original environment (McCombs, Filipczak, Friedman, & Wodarski, 1978; Wodarski & Filipczak, 1977).

Incentive Analysis

Once behaviors are chosen for modification an incentive analysis should be undertaken. Three avenues provide information about the client's incentive profile. Information can be developed on the incentives that the client will work for by observing the client, by asking significant others, and by giving the client a reinforcement survey (Cautela, 1972). The next critical step is to isolate those incentives that can be employed and are powerful enough to produce the desired change. Various factors will control the incentive powers of the various items chosen, such as how much of the item the client presently has, how much of the item the client has had in the past, how much others around the client have of the item, can the item be presented every time the behavior occurs, what quantity of the incentive can be employed, are other incentives that maintain the behavior too powerful, can the worker control these other incentives or punishments provided by others for the desired behavior.

Treatment Analysis

Once the target of intervention is chosen the worker has to decide if there are any biological factors that may prohibit the client from achieving the behavioral goals, such as a child who needs glasses before behavior modification techniques can be used to teach him to read. Sociological factors may impede the modification in terms of significant others providing reinforcers for undesirable behaviors. In such instances the worker must decide whether the reinforcers the worker can provide the client outweigh the reinforcers provided by others or he must implement a strategy to change the reinforcing patterns of these significant others.

If the client is being taught to manage his own behavior an analysis of self-control potential must occur, such as is this client motivated to change? will the client read the necessary materials? will the client diligently record his behavior? and will the client consistently implement the techniques? Moreover, an incentive analysis of the worker's reinforcing potential for the client has to take place and the critical question becomes does the worker possess those qualities that are attractive enough to the client in order to use him/herself as a motivator for change. If the worker does not have these characteristics the most appropriate change agent must be isolated.

In the treatment analysis the worker will want to consider with the client how much energy the client will have to engage and how taxing the intervention will be. Such a cost effective analysis is crucial to determining whether therapy should be initiated. The final consideration in the treatment analysis should be whether the monitoring of the treatment intervention can occur to provide essential data on how well the treatment is being implemented and its effects on client behavior in order to alter the treatment plan if no behavioral change is occurring.

Aids in Assessment

Five techniques that can be used as aids in assessment are self-inventories, behavioral interviews, behavioral samples, behavioral diaries, and baselines. The critical aspect of any measure chosen is the reliability of the data provided. Thus, the data provided by any of these sources should be collaborated by others (Goldfried & Sprafkin, 1974).

Self-Inventories

A number of questionnaires are being developed that should facilitate the acquisition of information necessary for the social worker to make an accurate assessment. The availability will increase in the future. For example, inventories that measure the following are available.

Child and Family Assessment.

Pioneering work by Hudson (1982) has provided four relevant scales for work with families. Each scale consists of 25 self-rated statements which clients score on a continuum of 1–5:

1 — Rarely or none of the time
2 — A little of the time
3 — Some of the time
4 — A good part of the time
5 — Most or all of the time

All scales are balanced for an adequate number of positive versus negative items. Norms are available for each instrument. The 25 items cover a broad range of content areas. Inspection of each item can provide foci for treatment.

Index of Family Relations. This index is designed to measure the degree, severity, or magnitude of a problem, as felt or perceived by the client, that pertains to relationships of family members to one another. It can be regarded as a measure of intrafamilial stress and as a measure of the client's family environment (Hudson, Acklin, & Bartosh, 1980).

Child's Attitude Toward Mother. This index is designed to measure the degree, severity, or magnitude of a problem a child has with his/her mother (Giuli & Hudson, 1977).

Child's Attitude Toward Father. This index is designed to measure the degree, severity, or magnitude of a problem a child has with his/her father (Giuli & Hudson, 1977).

Parental Attitude Scale. This index is designed to measure the degree, severity, or magnitude of a problem a parent has in a relationship with his/her child or children, regardless of the age of the child (Hudson, Wung, & Borges, 1980).

Olson and his associates (1982) have also produced scales for the assessment of families. These five scales likewise are characterized by high reliability and ease of administration. They can be used separately or in coordination with data provided by the Hudson scales.

Family Satisfaction. This scale consists of fourteen items rated on a continuum of 1–5 and assesses family cohesion and family adaptability. Items are rated:

1—Dissatisfied
2—Somewhat dissatisfied
3—Generally satisfied
4—Very satisfied
5—Extremely satisfied

Parent-Adolescent Communication. Two inventories have been developed; one for parents and the other for adolescents. They both consist of 20 items and rated on a continuum of 1–5. The items assess the openness of family communication and pinpoint existing problems. The focus is on the freedom or free-flowing exchange of information, both factual and emotional, as well as on the sense of lack of constraint and degree of understanding as satisfaction experienced in interactions. The second focus, problems in family communications, centers on the negative aspects of communication, hesitancy to share, negative styles of interaction, and selectivity and caution in what is shared.

F–COPES. This is a 29-item scale in which the items are rated on a 1–5 continuum and center on family coping strategies, family resources, and social and community resources. F–COPES measures the following aspects of family interaction: confidence in problem solving, reframing family problems, passive appraisal, seeking spiritual support, and acquiring support from extended family, friends, neighbors and community resources.

Family Strengths. This scale consists of 12 items rated on a 1–5 continuum and focuses on family pride and family accord. Entries fall into the following categories:

Pride: family attributes relating to respect, trust, and loyalty with the family
Positive values and beliefs: optimism and shared values
Accord: attributes relating to a family's sense of mastering a skill.

Quality of Life. Two inventories, an adolescent form (25 items) and a parent form (40 items), are available. The adolescent form rates satisfaction on a 1–5 continuum for the following areas: family life, friends, extended family, health, home, education, leisure, religion, mass media, financial well-being, and neighborhood and community. The parent form rates satisfaction on a 1–5 continuum for the following areas: marriage and family life, friends, extended family, health, home, education, time, religion, employment, mass media, financial well-being, and neighborhood and community.

Two additional scales can be used to assess children and families: the Family Integration Scale, developed by Hans Sebald; and the Childhood Level of Living Scale, developed by Norman Polansky.

Family Integration Scale. This 8-item scale, rated on a four-point continuum, is designed to measure family integration (Johnson, 1976). Family integration is described as the frequency with which family members spend time interacting with each other, i.e., helping with school work, discussions of difficult areas, engaging in hobbies, going places as a family, and completing a task together.

Childhood Level of Living Scale. This 99-item scale is designed to measure the quality of the child's living environment. The scale has two parts: part A deals with physical care, including issues of food, clothing, quality of shelter, safety and health care; part B deals with emotional-cognitive care, including provision of growth experiences and emotional support for the child, i.e., encouraging competence, instilling a sense of discipline, and encouraging normal development. This instrument has been used primarily for initial and ongoing assessment in work with child neglect cases (Polansky, Chalmers, Buttenwieser, & Williams, 1978).

Individual Assessment.

Walter Hudson (1982) has made a significant contribution to individual assessment with three outstanding inventories. They are the Generalized Contentment Scale, Index of Self-Esteem, and Index of Peer Relations.

Generalized Contentment Scale. This 25-item scale, rated on a 1–5 continuum, is designed to measure the degree, severity, or magnitude of nonpsychotic depression.

Index of Self-Esteem. This 25-item scale, rated on a 1–5 continuum, is designed to measure the degree, severity, or magnitude of a client's problem with self-esteem, i.e., how he/she perceives him/herself.

Index of Peer Relations. This 25-item scale, rated on a 1–5 continuum, is designed to measure the degree, severity, or magnitude of a client's problem in relationships with peers. It can be used as a global measure of peer relationship problems, or the therapist can specify the peer reference group (i.e., work associates, friends, classmates).

Two inventories that may be used to provide collaborative data are How I Perceive Myself, by Eui-Do-Rim, and the Self-Appraisal Scale, by Judith Greenburg (Johnson, 1976).

How I Perceive Myself. This 10-item scale is designed to measure self-concept with respect to what the children think of themselves and what they think their classmates think of them. This measure may be used with children in kindergarten to the third grade.

Self-Appraisal Scale. This 24-item scale, rated on a 3-point continuum, is designed to measure personal and academic self-concepts. This measure may be used with male and female children age 9–13.

Olson and his associates (1982) have developed an instrument which provides data on adolescent stresses and strains.

A-File. This inventory consists of 50 items designed to record normative and nonnormative life events and changes adolescents perceive their families have experienced during the past 12 months. The 50 items center on role or status transitions, sexuality, family losses, responsibilities and strains, school strains, and substance use and legal conflicts (Olson et al., 1982).

Four scales, Rotter Internal-External Locus of Control, Manifest Alienation, Manifest Anxiety, and Progress Evaluation, offer comprehensive information about adult problems in daily living.

Rotter Internal-External Locus of Control. This is a 29-item forced-choice scale designed to measure the perception of the amount of control persons have over their environment. It measures the extent to which they attribute responsibility for the occurrences of favorable and unfavorable outcomes to internal causes as compared to forces in the environment.

Rotter (1971) posits that, "People who are confident that they can control themselves and their destinies tend to be surer of themselves." He hypothesizes that people with an internal locus of control orientation are able to cope more effectively with their environments than people with an external locus of control orientation. Individuals scoring high on external locus of control would be more prone to depressive answers on the Hudson Generalized Contentment Scale.

Manifest Alienation. This 20-item measure, rated on a 3-point continuum, is designed to determine the existence of an alienation syndrome in an individual. Alienation syndrome consists of feelings of pessimism, cynicism, distrust, apathy and emotional distance (Gould, 1969).

Manifest Anxiety Scale. This is a 28-item true/false scale designed to measure an individual's degree of internal anxiety by assessing overt symptoms of anxiety (Taylor, 1953).

Progress Evaluation Scales. These scales are designed to measure the impact of mental health programs on children, adolescents, adults, and developmentally disabled individuals in these age groups. The 5-point scales measure family interaction, occupational functioning, ability to get along with others, feelings and mood, use of free time, problems, and attitude toward self. Separate forms are available for adults (age 18 and up), adolescents (age 13–18), children (kindergarten to age 12), and developmentally disabled individuals. The form may be completed by the client, the therapist, or a significant other. The scales can be used to assess client entry status, establish treatment goals, and measure outcome in terms of personal, social, vocational, and community adjustment. A baseline can be obtained and the scales can then be used to provide ongoing feedback to client and therapist (Ihilevich & Gleser, 1982).

Behavior Interviews

The clinical interview can provide a suitable setting to observe the client's reaction to certain stimuli. The client's reaction, i.e., how the client presents himself physically and verbally, handles stress, and so on, gives the social worker a cue as to how the client approaches various life situations and provides the opportunity to gather information about reinforcement preferences, the possible antecedents and consequences that control the behaviors chosen for modification, how motivated the client is to change, and finally, who would be the best mediators of change (Holland, 1970; Kanfer & Grimm, 1977; Thomas, 1974; Wahler & Cormier, 1970; Wolpe, 1970, 1973).

Behavior Samples

No information can substitute for the actual observation of the client in the environment in which the problematic behavior occurs. The process gives the worker an accurate picture of the discriminative stimuli and consequences that are operating in such an environment. For example, observing a child on the playground provides the worker with firsthand knowledge of his social interactional skills, how many discriminative stimuli for such behaviors (such as approaching behaviors, eye contact, touching, and smiling) are provided by other children, who provides them, and what consequences are provided after the child exhibits an interactional behavior, at what frequency, and by whom. Videotapes provide another means by which the worker can observe the client's behaviors. If the worker is dealing with a couple, he/she may ask them to videotape interactions in the home or videotape their behavior during a simulation task in his/her office. In the past, adequate behavior sampling systems have not been available; however, recently various adequate systems have been developed.

Behavioral Diary

In many instances the worker will not be able to observe the client. In these instances clients and/or significant others can keep a diary containing certain information on the antecedents and consequences which control the behavior that can prove to be a valuable asset in the modification of the behavior. In many instances the worker will have to help the client structure the process (how to observe, when to observe, how to record, and so forth) for securing the necessary data on antecedents and consequences that control the behavior.

Baselines: A Prerequisite

A prerequisite for adequate behavior analysis is to secure a baseline prior to implementation of treatment. The best type of baseline measure is secured by trained behavioral observers. Usually these observers have been taught to establish reliability on behavioral categories through an extensive training procedure. If observations on behaviors cannot be secured by trained observers, there are other less desirable data sources, such as baselines taken by the client him/herself or by significant others in his/her environment. These baselines are less reliable but many times their use is necessitated by various organizational or other environmental constraints. Certain of these constraints may involve lack of money for trained observers or the investigation of behavior that occurs at a time when it is not readily observable by others. When baseline data are not secured by a trained observer, the data should be obtained from two or more independent sources in order to check on consistency.

There are various considerations that should be addressed before a social worker decides on the exact procedures for securing a baseline. The first consideration involves where the baseline should be taken. A context should be chosen in which the individual's behavior occurs at a high frequency. If the behavior occurs in more than one context, baselines may be secured for the various contexts. Such a procedure enables the assessment of a broader range of contexts where the behavior occurs, provides for the determination of whether or not behavioral changes in one context are analogous to those in another, and provides a more accurate measure of behavior. Additional considerations pertain to where the behavior occurs. If the behavior is readily accessible to observation, this will not be a problem. If it is inaccessible, such as one that occurs late at night or in contexts where observation is not possible, the investigator will have to use reports by the client, or others who are present when the behavior occurs, to secure the data. An important consideration is who can best secure the relevant data. As previously mentioned, it is preferable to have a trained observer record data. In any case, an individual who is consistent and reliable should be chosen.

Contracts

After an adequate assessment is executed, contracts should be carried out between the worker and clients for the following reasons. Research indicates that contracts included as a major aspect of the therapeutic process act as powerful tools in that they provide the motivation and structure necessary for the initiation and facilitation of client change and legally protect the worker in terms of malpractice suits (Feldman & Wodarski, 1975; Goldstein et al., 1966; Goldstein & Simonson, 1971; Martin, 1974, 1975; Reid & Epstein, 1972; Wodarski, 1976).

Private Agencies

Contracts involving clients who come to private agencies of their own volition involve fewer legal requisites for the social worker than do contracts wherein participation is involuntary and occurs in agencies supported largely by public funds (Friedman, 1975; Stepleton, 1975). Contracts executed in a private agency should include the following aspects which would be specified as clearly and concretely as possible to protect the worker and the client:

1. *Client and therapist duties.* Included here should be the roles, expectations, and obligations of each participant.

2. *Purpose of the interaction.* The goals should be clearly defined.

3. *Target problems and areas of difficulty to be worked on.* For example, preparing for an employment interview, discussing ways to alleviate stress, developing anger control, improving one's physical appearance; and learning new study skills.

4. *Various goals and objectives that might be accomplished.* Increase self-acceptance, decrease negative self-thoughts, improve anxiety management through the use of systematic desensitization or covert conditioning, and so forth.

5. *Administrative procedures or constraints.* For example, payment of fees, contract renegotiation procedures, provision of data by client, and confidentiality.

6. *Techniques that will be used.* Client centered therapy, behavior modification, group techniques, and so forth.

7. *Duration of the contract.* Such as number of sessions planned to accomplish specific goals, involvement of others, and length of the sessions (Seabury, 1976).

These contracts should specify clearly the nature of the treatment in terms of the probable outcomes; that is, how effective are the treatment approaches according to the empirical evidence that exists, what risks and benefits are involved in participating in the treatment in terms of the percentage of individuals whose behavior deteriorates as compared to those who improve during the course of treatment, and other reasonably forseeable consequences of the treatment. In all instances these contracts should be written as explicitly as possible for the protection of the worker and the client.

Public Agencies

Contracts structured between public agencies and involuntary clients are more complicated than those of private agencies (Friedman, 1975; Martin, 1974). Out of a series of court cases involving conditions in state institutions for the mentally retarded, the mentally distressed, correctional offenders, and so forth was established the doctrine of the *right to treatment* (Asher, 1974; Ennis & Siegel, 1973; Schaar, 1976; Schwitzgebel, 1971; Spece, 1972). This legal precedent establishes the client's right to a treatment plan that is clearly related to his return to his community. No longer can an institution provide only custodial care to its clients. Furthermore, transfer of a client to another institution with a treatment program that does not provide a reasonable opportunity for him to be returned to the community is no longer permissible.

Institutional treatment procedures may not be described in vague terms. As in contracts of private agencies, the goals for the client must be stated in such a manner that it can be easily determined whether or not they can be attained. How the treatment program will help the client attain these goals must also be delineated. For example, if a treatment program involves a job that is routinely performed at an institution the task must be justified in terms of its relationship to treatment objectives and the client must receive appropriate remuneration according to the minimum wage standards set by the Office of Labor (Schaar, 1975).

No Behavioral Change: Problems to Look For

Behavioral Equation

Problems may arise in the following areas: the behavior is non-specifically defined; the behavior is defined in a manner too global to enable specification of the discriminative stimuli and consequences which control its occurrence or to allow for its measurement to determine if the frequency, duration or intensity of the behavior has changed; the worker may not have isolated and changed or eliminated all of the discriminative stimuli that control the behavior; in some instances new discriminative stimuli may now control the behavior; the worker and the client may not have isolated and eliminated all of the consequences that control the behavior.

Reinforcement Analysis

The contingency contract may not be specified in such a manner that the client and others understand what is involved in the effort to modify the behavior (DeRisi & Butz, 1975). The type of reinforcer chosen for the client may not be appropriate for the individual. That is, the reinforcer is weak compared to other reinforcers that are currently maintaining the behavior. Three critical questions center on how appropriate the incentives are: How much of the reinforcer has the client had in the past, how much does the client currently possess, and how much of the reinforcer do others around him possess. The power of the reinforcer is inversely related to the answer to all three of these questions. The reinforcer may be appropriate but the amount is not proportional to the effort involved in changing the behavior. Likewise, the amount or the size of the reinforcer is appropriate but the reinforcer is not provided at a high enough frequency or the schedule of reinforcement is too erratic to override the cost involved in the client's changing the behavior. The appropriate reinforcers and delivery conditions are sufficient, but the worker has not isolated those significant others in the client's environment who are providing the reinforcement that maintains the behavior and who may in fact be punishing behaviors that are being reinforced. The significant others chosen to participate in the modification plan may be inconsistently applying the agreed upon plan of behavioral change or may not be attractive enough to facilitate the behavioral changes. Another major maintenance factor centers on how many individuals in the client's environment model the behavior and are subsequently reinforced.

Summary

In this chapter we have reviewed the essentials of behavioral assessment. The emphasis has been on the worker's securing the most concrete information possible on the events that precede and occur after the behavior chosen for alteration. In the coming years behavioral assessment will focus on complex reinforcement contingencies, multiple discriminative stimuli, complex reinforcement matrices occurring between client and significant others, and so forth. Thus, the knowledge base will become increasingly complex but only then will we be able to reflect and cope with the intricacies of assessment in the natural environment.

REFERENCES

Achenbach, T. M., & Edelbrock, C. S. (1984). Psychopathology of childhood. *Annual Review of Psychology, 35,* 227–256.

Asher, J. (1974). Supreme court agrees to hear landmark right-to-treatment case. *APA Monitor, 5*(1), 4.

Baer, D. M., Wolf, M. M., & Risley, T. R. (1968). Some current dimensions of applied behavior analysis. *Journal of Applied Behavior Analysis, 1,* 91–97.

Bem, D. J., & Allen, A. (1974). On predicting some of the people of the time: The search for cross-situational consistencies in behavior. *Psychological Review, 81*(6), 506–520.

Bernstein, D. A., & Nietzel, M. T. (1974). Behavioral avoidance tests: The effects of demand characteristics and repeated measures of two types of subjects. *Behavior Therapy, 5*(2), 183–192.

Bijou, S. W. (1970). What psychology has to offer education now. *Journal of Applied Behavior Analysis, 3,* 65–71.

Bijou, S. W., Peterson, R. F., Harris, F. R., Allen, K. E., & Johnston, M. W. (1969). Methodology for experimental studies of young children in natural settings. *The Psychological Record, 19,* 177–210.

Borkovec, T. D. (1972). Effects of expectancy on the outcome of systematic desensitization and implosive treatments for analogue anxiety. *Behavior Therapy, 3*(1), 29–40.

Borkovec, T. D. (1973). The role of expectancy and physiological feedback in fear research: A review with special references to subject characteristics. *Behavior Therapy, 4*(4), 491–505.

Borkovec, T. D., & Nau, S. D. (1972). Credibility of analogue therapy rationales. *Journal of Behavior Therapy and Experimental Psychiatry, 3*(4), 257–260.

Borkovec, T. D., Stone, N. M., O'Brien, G. T., & Kaloupek, D. G. (1974). Evaluation of clinically relevant target behavior for analogue outcome research. *Behavior Therapy, 5*(4), 503–513.

Butterfield, W. H. (1974). Instrumentation in behavior therapy. In E. J. Thomas (Ed.), *Behavior modification procedure: A source book.* Chicago: Aldine.

Case, L. P., & Lingerfelt, N. B. (1974). Name-calling: The labeling process in the social work interview. *Social Service Review, 48,* 75–86.

Cautela, J. R. (1972). Reinforcement survey schedule: Evaluation and current applications. *Psychological Reports, 30,* 683–690.

Crow, W. J. (1957). The effect of training upon accuracy and variability in interpersonal perception. *Journal of Abnormal and Social Psychology, 55,* 355–359.

Crown, S. (1975). On being sane in insane places: A comment from England. *Journal of Abnormal Psychology, 84*(5), 453–455.

Davis, D. A. (1976). On being detectably sane in insane places: Base rates and psychodiagnosis. *Journal of Abnormal Psychology, 85*(4), 416–422.

DeRisi, W. J., & Butz, G. (1975). *Writing behavioral contracts.* Champaign, IL: Research Press.

Dix, G. E. (1976). "Civil" commitment of the mentally ill and the need for data on the prediction of dangerousness. *American Behavioral Scientist, 19,* 318–334.

Ennis, B., & Siegel, L. (1973). *The rights of mental patients.* New York: Avon Books.

Eysenck, H. (1952). *The scientific study of personality.* London: Routledge Kegan Paul.

Farber, I. E. (1975). Sane and insane: Constructions and misconstructions. *Journal of Abnormal Psychology, 84*(6), 589–620.

Feldman, R. A., & Wodarski, J. S. (1975). *Contemporary approaches to group treatment.* San Francisco: Jossey-Bass.

Franks, C. M. (Ed.). (1969). *Behavior therapy: Appraisal and status.* New York: McGraw-Hill.

Freund, K. A. (1971). Note on the use of the phallometric method of measuring mild sexual arousal in the male. *Behavior Therapy, 22,* 223–228.

Friedman, P. R. (1975). Legal regulations of applied behavior analysis in mental institutions and prisons. *Arizona Law Review, 17,* 39–104.

Gingerich, W. J., Feldman, R. A., & Wodarski, J. S. (1976). Accuracy in assessment: Does training help? *Social Work, 21*(1), 40–48.

Giuli, C. A., & Hudson, W. W. (1977). Assessing parent-child relationship disorders in clinical practice: The child's point of view. *Journal of Social Service Research, 1*(1), 77–92.

Goldfried, M. R., & Sprafkin, J. N. (1974). *Behavioral personality assessment.* Morristown, NJ: General Learning Press.

Goldstein, A. P., Heller, K., & Sechrest, L. B. (1966). *Psychotherapy and the psychology of behavior change.* New York: Wiley.

Goldstein, A. P., & Simonson, N. R. (1971). Social psychological approaches to psychotherapy research. In A. Bergin & S. Garfield (Eds.), *Handbook of psychotherapy and behavior change: An empirical analysis.* New York: Wiley.

Gould, L. (1969). Conformity and marginality: Two faces of alienation. *Journal of Social Issues, 25*(2), 39–63.

Harrower, M. (Ed.). (1950). *Diagnostic psychological testing.* Springfield, IL: Charles C Thomas.

Hock, P., & Zubin, J. (Eds.). (1953). *Current problems in psychiatric diagnosis.* New York: Grune & Stratton.

Holland, C. J. (1970). An interview guide for behavioral counseling with parents. *Behavior Therapy, 1*(1), 70–79.

Hudson, W. W. (1982). *The clinical measurement package.* Homewood, IL: Dorsey Press.

Hudson, W. W., Acklin, J. D., & Bartosh, J. C. (1980). Assessing discord in family relationships. *Social Work Research and Abstracts, 16*(3), 21–29.

Hudson, W. W., Wung, B., & Borges, M. (1980). Parent-child relationship disorders: The parent's point of view. *Journal of Social Service Research, 3*(3), 283–294.

Ihilevich, D., & Gleser, G. G. (1982). *Evaluating mental health programs: The progress evaluation scales.* MA: Lexington Books.

Johnson, O. G. (1976). *Tests and measurements in child development: Handbook II.* San Francisco: Jossey-Bass.

Kanfer, F. H., & Grimm, L. G. (1977). Behavior analysis: Selecting target behavior in the interview. *Behavior Modification, 1*(1), 7–28.

Kazdin, A. E. (1973). The effect of suggestion and pretesting on avoidance reduction in fearful subjects. *Journal of Behavioral Therapy and Experimental Psychiatry, 4*(3), 213–221.

Mariotto, M. J., & Paul, G. L. (1975). Persons versus situations in the real-life functioning of chronically institutionalized mental patients. *Journal of Abnormal Psychology, 84*(5), 483–493.

Martin, R. (1974). *Behavior modification: Human rights and legal responsibilities.* Champaign, IL: Research Press.

Martin, R. (1975). *Legal challenges to behavior modification.* Champaign, IL: Research Press.

McCombs, D., Filipczak, J., Friedman, R., & Wodarski, J. S. (1978). Long-term follow-up of behavior modification with high risk adolescents. *Criminal Justice and Behavior, 5,* 21–34.

Menninger, K. (1955). The practice of psychiatry. *Digest of Neurology and Psychiatry, 23,* 101.

Millon, T. (1975). Reflections on Rosenhan's "On being sane in insane places". *Journal of Abnormal Psychology, 84*(5), 456–461.

Mischel, W. (1968). *Personality and assessment.* New York: Wiley.

Mischel, W. (1971). *Introduction to personality.* New York: Holt, Rinehart, and Winston.

Mischel, W. (1972). Direct versus indirect personality assessment: Evidence and implications. *Journal of Consulting and Clinical Psychology, 38* 319–324.

Mischel, W. (1973a). Facing the issues. *Journal of Abnormal Psychology, 82*(3), 541–542.

Mischel, W. (1973b). On the empirical dilemmas of psychodynamic approaches: Issues and alternatives. *Journal of Abnormal Psychology, 82*(2), 335–344.

Mischel, W. (1973c). Toward a cognitive social learning reconceptualization of personality. *Psychological Review, 80,* 252–283.

Olson, D. H., McCubbin, H. I., Barnes, H., Larsen, A., Muxen, M., & Wilson, M. (1982). *Family inventories: Inventories used in a national survey of families across the family life cycle.* St. Paul: University of Minnesota, Family Social Science.

Polansky, N. A., Chalmers, M. A., Buttenwieser, E., & Williams, D. (1978). Assessing adequacy of child caring: An urban scale. *Child Welfare, 57*(7), 439–449.

Reed, P. L., & Jackson, D. N. (1975). Clinical judgment of psychopathology: A model for inferential accuracy. *Journal of Abnormal Psychology, 84*(5), 475–482.

Reid, W. J., & Epstein, L. (1972). *Task-centered casework.* New York: Columbia University Press.

Robins, L. N., & Helzer, J. E. (1986). Diagnosis and clinical assessment: The current state of psychiatric diagnosis. *Annual Review of Psychology, 37,* 409–432.

Roe, A. (1949). Integration of personality theory and clinical practice. *Journal of Abnormal and Social Psychology, 44,* 36–41.

Rogers, C. (1951). *Client centered therapy.* Boston: Houghton Mifflin.

Rosenhan, D. L. (1973). On being sane in insane places. *Science, 79,* 250–258.

Rosenhan, D. L. (1975a). The contextual nature of psychiatric diagnosis. *Journal of Abnormal Psychology, 84*(5), 462–474.

Rosenhan, D. L. (1975b). Letters to the editor. *Science, 81,* 365–369.

Rotter, J. B. (1954). *Social learning and clinical psychology.* Englewood Cliffs, NJ: Prentice-Hall.

Rotter, J. B. (1971). External control and internal control. *Psychology Today,* June, 37–59.

Schaar, K. (1975). Minimum wage regs pose problems. *APA Monitor, 6*(8), 11.

Schaar, K. (1976). Community care ordered for D.C. mental patients. *APA Monitor, 7*(1), 13.

Schwitzgebel, R. K. (1971). *Development and legal regulations of coercive behavior modification techniques* (NIMH Monograph No. 73-9015). Washington, DC: U.S. Government Printing Office.

Schwitzbegel, R. K. (1972). Limitations on the coercive treatment of offenders. *Criminal Law Bulletin, 8,* 267–320.

Scott, W. (1968). Research definitions of mental health and mental illness. *Psychological Bulletin, 74,* 1–45.

Seabury, B. A. (1976). The contract: Uses, abuses and limitations. *Social Work, 21,* 16–21.

Smith, R. E., Diener, E., & Beaman, A. L. (1974). Demand characteristics and the behavioral avoidance measure of fear in behavior therapy analogue research. *Behavior Therapy, 5*(2), 172–182.

Spece, R. G., Jr. (1972). Note, conditioning and other technologies used to "treat"? "rehabilitate"? "demolish"? prisoners and mental patients. *Southern California Law Review, 45,* 616–682.

Speltz, M. L., & Bernstein, D. A. (1976). Sex differences in fearfulness: Verbal report, overt avoidance and demand characteristics. *Journal of Experimental Psychiatry and Behavior Therapy, 7*(2), 117–122.

Spitzer, R. L. (1975). On pseudoscience in science, logic in remission, and psychiatric diagnosis: A critique of Rosenhan's "On being sane in insane places". *Journal of Abnormal Psychology, 84*(5), 442–452.

Stepleton, J. V. (1975). Legal issues confronting behavior modification. *Behavioral Engineering, 2,* 35–43.

Tasto, D. L., & Suinn, L. M. (1972). Fear survey schedule changes on total and factor scores due to nontreatment effects. *Behavior Therapy, 3*(2), 275–278.

Taylor, J. A. (1953). A personality scale of manifest anxiety. *Journal of Abnormal and Social Psychology, 48*(2), 285–290.

Thomas, E. J. (Ed.). (1974). *Behavior modification procedure: A source book.* Chicago: Aldine.

Tryon, W. W., & Tryon, G. S. (1974). Desensitization and demand characteristics. *Behavior Therapy, 5*(2), 297–298.

Wachtel, P. L. (1973a). On fact, hunch and stereotype: A reply to Mischel. *Journal of Abnormal Psychology, 82*(3), 537–540.

Wachtel, P. L. (1973b). Psychodynamics, behavior therapy, and the implacable experimenter: An inquiry into the consistency of personality. *Journal of Abnormal Psychology, 82*(2), 324–334.

Wahler, R. G., & Cormier, W. H. (1970). The ecological interview: A first step in outpatient child behavior therapy. *Journal of Experimental Psychiatry and Behavior Therapy, 1,* 279–289.

Weiner, B. (1975). On being sane in insane places: A process (attributional) analysis and critique. *Journal of Abnormal Psychology, 84*(5), 433–441.

Wodarski, J. S. (1976, June). *Recent supreme court legal decisions: Implications for social work practice.* Paper presented at the 103rd Annual Forum, National Conference on Social Welfare, Washington, D.C.

Wodarski, J. S., & Filipczak, J. (1977, May). *Long-term follow-up of behavior modification with high-risk adolescens: Cohort two.* Paper presented at the Johns Hopkins University Symposium on Alternative Educational Programs for Disruptive Secondary School Students, Baltimore, Maryland.

Wodarski, J. S., Feldman, R. A., & Pedi, S. J. (1975). Effects of different observational systems and time sequences upon nonparticipant observer's behavioral ratings. *Journal of Behavior Therapy and Experimental Psychiatry, 6*(4), 275–278.

Wolpe, J. (1970). Transcript of initial interview in a case of depression. *Journal of Experimental Psychiatry and Behavior Therapy, 1*(1), 71–78.

Wolpe, J. (1973). *The practice of behavior therapy.* New York: Pergamon.

Zigler, E., & Phillips, L. (1960). Social effectiveness and symptomatic behaviors. *Journal of Abnormal and Social Psychology, 61,* 231–238.

Zigler, E., & Phillips, L. (1961a). Case history data and psychiatric diagnosis. *Journal of Consulting Psychology, 25,* 458.

Zigler, E., & Phillips, L. (1961b). Psychiatric diagnosis: A critique. *Journal of Abnormal and Social Psychology, 62,* 237–246.

Chapter 4

VIEWING SOCIAL WORK CLIENTELE
FROM VARIOUS THEORETICAL PERSPECTIVES
A HISTORICAL OVERVIEW

Essential to social work practice are the various theories employed in assigning causation to the child's and adolescent's behavior (Brieland, 1977; Minahan, 1981; Wodarski, 1983). It is the purpose of this chapter to illustrate how practitioners can be influenced by their theoretical conceptualizations of their clients: (1) how they will predict and explain a client's behavior; (2) how much change they believe can take place in the client; and (3) the selection of the types of methods, techniques, and interventions they will use in working with the client. Two major considerations related to theoretical conceptualizations are addressed. First, what is the extent to which all of these theories are valid in (1) their causal explanations and predictions of behavior, (2) the amount of change they hypothesize can take place in the client, and (3) the methods, techniques, and interventions they propose to change a client's behavior? Second, what evaluative research is available to show whether the theories have different success rates with clients?

Seven theoretical conceptualizations of human behavior employed by social workers in practice are presented from a historical perspective, thus establishing the background for the subsequent integration of theoretical frameworks and the rationale for the consideration of other variables in the explanation and causation of human behavior. Second, through a case illustration that applies these theoretical conceptualizations to an adolescent, it is shown how the social worker's behaviors may be influenced in different directions according to a theoretical perspective. In the third section of this chapter the state of the art in theory-directed practice is discussed. The last section addresses itself to the question of theory validity and theory evaluation and comparison.

77

Theoretical Conceptualizations of Human Behavior

Psychosocial Theory

The first of the seven theoretical conceptualizations to be considered is one developed by Florence Hollis in her text, *Social Casework: A Psychosocial Therapy* (1972). This approach, with different small variations, is espoused by Helen Perlman and Gordon Hamilton as well as by most practicing social workers. Hollis and other theorists tend to view a client's behavior as a result of the forces inside the individual (called stresses), the forces of the environment (called presses), and the interactions that take place between these forces when they meet (Hamilton, 1951; Hollis, 1972, 1977; Hollis & Woods, 1981; Perlman, 1977).

The individual is conceptualized primarily in Freudian terms. The forces inside the individual are the intrapsychic parts of the personality, consisting of the id, ego, and superego. The individual from birth on is motivated by a set of drives that are derived from libidinal and aggressive instincts he/she inherited at birth. He/she goes through an orderly developmental sequence according to the Freudian scheme (Hollis, 1972, 1977). Usually the individual's general personality characteristics are formed by the time he/she reaches 5 years of age. Early experiences of childhood are considered very important because they later influence the individual's perception of the environment. The environmental forces that influence behavior consist of concrete realities such as food, clothing, and shelter and the social-environmental characteristics, such as the values, norms, and beliefs, of the social group of which the individual is a member (Hollis, 1972, 1977; Hollis & Woods, 1981).

In this theoretical framework the individual has control over shaping his/her destiny and is viewed as having the capacity to do something about his/her problems (Hollis, 1972, 1977). Treatment consists of the social worker's modifying environmental presses and/or increasing the client's capacity to deal with outer presses and inner stresses. Crucial to understanding how much a client can change is knowledge of the capacity of that individual's ego to deal with his/her problems. The ego, with its certain adaptive qualities, "is said to be the executive of the personality because it controls the gateways to action, selects the features of the environment to which the individual will respond, and decides what instincts will be satisfied and in what manner" (Hall & Lindzey, 1978, pp. 37–38).

Depending on what the evaluation of the ego's capacity is, either one or both of two treatment procedures will be selected. If the social worker evaluates the ego's functioning as severely or temporarily impaired, he/she can use a set of treatment techniques called the Supportive Treatment Method, i.e., techniques ranging from reflection of feelings to setting realistic limits on behavior (Community Service Society of New York, 1964). If the trouble lies in the person's expressing a stereotyped way of dealing with his/her environment that is dysfunctional, and if the social worker evaluated the client's ego as having the capacity to tolerate undergoing self-scrutiny and the ability to learn new behaviors, then the techniques of the Modifying Treatment Method can be called into action. This method usually is used with persons whose ego is evaluated as being healthy (Community Service Society of New York, 1964). The aim of the modifying method is to confront the client with the most appropriate strategies for use in alleviating presses or stresses.

Ecological Theory

A theoretical framework similar to the psychosocial approach is that developed by William E. Gordon and set forth in his paper entitled "Basic Constructs for an Integrative and Generative Conception of Social Work" (1969). According to this theory, behavior is the result of a transaction that occurs when a person and an environment come together at what is called an interface. At this interface there must be an exchange of activity between the person and the environment in order for both to grow and develop. However, this activity must occur on both sides in order for growth to take place (Bartlett, 1970; Gordon, 1969), and problems arise when activity occurs only in one. The amount of change that can occur in an individual varies with the amount of activity the individual can bring to the interface and the amount of activity the environment can contribute to the transaction.

Coping behaviors are activity-producing attempts by the individual to interact with his/her environment. These coping behaviors interact with the qualities of the impinging environment that produce activity (Gordon, 1969). Social work treatment is geared toward assuring that an exchange of activity takes place between the individual and the environment. It can accomplish this by interventions aimed at changing the coping behaviors of the individual and/or changing the qualities of the impinging environment to enable matching of person and environment (Gordon,

1969). Carel B. Germain and Alex Gitterman (1980) have specified and elaborated individual intervention foci for the ecological model: changes in self-image; ways of looking at the world; the processing of information derived from cognition, perception, and patterns of relating to others; and uses of environmental resources and goals. Qualities of the impinging environment that may be the focus of intervention consist of opportunity structures of society, organizations designed to meet adaptive needs, primary and secondary support networks, and an unsuitable physical environment.

Sociobehavioral Theory

A different view of the individual is presented by sociobehavioral theorists. Until recently these theorists did not postulate an internal view of behavior. Behavior had been defined as the observable responses of human activity (Thomas, 1968). All behavior, be it simple, complex, or maladaptive (such as neurotic behavior) was learned by the same set of rules (Bruck, 1968). No distinction was made between normal and neurotic behavior.

All behavior occurred because it had been reinforced. The individual was viewed as having inherent biological tendencies at birth, and became what he/she was at any moment in time because of a previous history of reinforcements and punishments of these tendencies. If the history of reinforcement and punishment had been different he/she would have become another type of individual (Bruck, 1968; Werner, 1965). Historically, complex behavior occurs for the sociobehavioralist according to the concept of shaping. "The growth and development of the child is seen as the product of a specific shaping procedure by which the child's immediate environment reinforces their existing behavior and gradually shifts the conditions of reinforcement toward complex forms of behavior as they grow older" (Bruck, 1968).

Traditionally, the goal of treatment has been the alteration of behavior by the application of the same principles that governed the learning of the behavior (Thomas, 1967). The focus was to unlearn behavior that may have become self-reinforcing. These theorists placed tremendous value on social reinforcements, such as verbal reinforcements, as change agents to be used by the therapist in a clinical interview. The amount of change that could occur in the client was believed to be unlimited; change depended on the ability of the therapist to manipulate stimulus-response patterns of the maladaptive behavior (Bruck, 1968). However, these traditional postulates have changed radically in the last two decades; now as much emphasis is placed on cognitive variables as on external variables (Goldstein, 1981; Wodarski & Bagarozzi, 1979). Moreover, social learning theory posits that reinforcement is no longer a necessary condition for learning to occur (Wodarski, 1983).

Existentialism

John J. Stretch, in his article, "Existentialism: A Proposed Philosophical Orientation for Social Work" (1967), offered the field an interesting way of looking at the individual. He saw the individual as seeking answers to give meaning to his/her life. The individual has the power to create and change the world but cannot answer basic questions such as "What is the meaning of existence?" and "What is life all about?" The inability to answer these complex questions causes anxiety (Binswanger, 1963; May, 1969; Straus, 1966; Stretch, 1967).

It is believed that the concept of the individual has lost meaning in our world. A person is no longer considered an individual but rather a part of a large social unit. Because one can only find the meaning of existence in being an individual, inability to define oneself in such a manner causes anxiety (Stretch, 1967). The individual cannot know what the future holds; life must be taken instance by instance. However, an individual must make decisions in life and is held responsible for these decisions; inability to make a decision results in anxiety. Stretch views the individual as being constantly in a state of crisis as a result of living in an unpredictable world. As soon as one crisis is solved, another takes its place.

According to this viewpoint social work should be devoted to helping individuals solve crises. Moreover, it should be devoted to helping people interact with others because this, according to the social existentialist, is the only way the individual can find meaning. Individual fulfillment will come only after one answers the basic questions of life. An individual's ability to reduce anxiety hinges on answering these questions. If we accept this point of view of the individual then we also concede that it is not possible to move away from a crisis-filled life. This framework was fashionable in the 1960's and 1970's, however, in the 1980's its influence has decreased substantially.

Functional Theory

Ruth Elizabeth Smalley, in her book *Theory for Social Work Practice* (1967), presented what has been called the functional school approach to human behavior, which dominates the philosophy of the School of Social Work at the University of Pennsylvania. According to her theory, individuals have an inner force that motivates them to grow. This growth is an orderly process with some internal mechanism causing them to organize their experiences while they grow (Smalley, 1967). Individuals have reason and purpose in life, and they have the capability to make choices and to engage in decision making. The environment an individual lives in has a profound effect on his/her development; even the first environment inside the mother's womb affects the personality.

The individual goes through developmental stages, and the relationships he/she experiences with others in these stages are crucial to self-realization. The individual constantly seeks to develop his/her potential; the self starts developing from conception and continues developing until death. Smalley defines the self as the concept an individual has of him/herself. An important part of the self is the *will* — the organizing and controlling force within the individual that drives him/her to realize his/her potential. Smalley points out "that the will will resist help out of fear of disorganization, change, or subjection to the will of another. It is only as the will can yield to the self's own push toward more life, toward realization that help can be accepted and used. And this is possible only through the kind of relationship which frees the self to know and claim itself" (1967, p. 26).

The social worker's function is viewed as one of helping individuals to use the casework relationship to free their will (Smalley, 1967). The will's creative and organizing force can then be used to help individuals develop their potential and grow into self-realization. In this approach the social worker and the client engage in the process of forming a relationship through which the client sets goals to meet his/her needs that are appropriate to the purpose that has brought the client and the social worker together. Goals set by the client are considered appropriate when they go along with the defined purposes of the agency. The client then uses his/her free will to accomplish these goals. Client change depends on the degree to which client purpose and agency purpose come together and the extent to which the individual's will can be freed (Smalley, 1967).

Sociological Theory

This theoretical conceptualization might be called social work's socio-logical view of the individual. It is found in bits and pieces in different articles appearing in the literature. William G. Hill, in his article "The Family as a Treatment Unit: Differential Techniques and Procedures" (1968), saw the client as part of a larger interrelated whole unit called the family. The problems of a particular individual in the family were viewed as part of the dysfunction of the family whereas all other approaches presented thus far have viewed problems as individual dysfunctional matters. Because an individual's problems stem from faulty interactions within the family, all members are causing the problem; therefore, all members of the family are clients and the family is treated as a whole. Such systems' postulates form the basis of the practice of major treatment models of family therapy. The goals of treatment are to help family members to define their roles in order to develop clearer communica-tion patterns among themselves, and to develop the concept that every-one in the family is an individual related to various social systems (Hill, 1968). This model emphasizes that the underlying structure and organi-zation of the family must change to prevent the recurrence of the same destructive patterns. The therapist must work with the family to find new, more attractive roles for all members of the family. The role of the therapist is collaborative and the parents are respected as the source of control in the family (Johnson, 1986; Schwartzman, 1985).

William P. Lentz, in an article entitled "Delinquency as a Stable Role" (1966), showed how the sociological concept of role can be viewed to explain a person's behavior. Roles are learned behaviors, and the roles individuals learn are determined by how others act toward them and the self-concepts they hold. For example, the delinquent assumes the role of a delinquent because others cast him/her in this role. How stable, or resistant to change, the delinquent role becomes depends on how many people cast the individual in this role and to what extent this casting causes him/her to incorporate into the self-concept the idea that he/she is delinquent. The rewards provided for such behaviors are likewise important. Lentz brings out the fact that there are many institutions within the social system of which the delinquent is a part that contribute to stabilization of the delinquent role. Institutions such as the police, juvenile courts, and social welfare agencies all reinforce the role in various ways (Feldman, Caplinger, & Wodarski, 1983; Lentz, 1966). If we accept Lentz's view, then the amount of change that can be expected to take place in working with a delinquent is limited. In order to help such individuals change, the social system of which they are a part must be changed so that its institutions will not reinforce the delinquent role (Lentz, 1966). Unless social workers can change the social system, their influence in modifying a delinquent's behavior is minimal.

Herbert S. Strean, in an article entitled "Role Theory, Role Models, and Casework: Review of the Literature and Practice Applications" (1967), used the concept of role to explain what the objectives of individual treatment of delinquents might be. He viewed the delinquent as someone who has been inadequately socialized. The role of the social worker would then be to teach delinquents appropriate roles that would aim them in their socialization.

Another explanation of human behavior was offered by Lawrence Shulman in his article, "A Game-Model Theory of Interpersonal Strategies" (1968). Game-model theorists view human behavior as an interaction composed of the roles individuals take in a situation and the rules that govern the interaction. The rules are usually implicitly or explicitly stated and they help individuals to know how to act toward other persons and what to expect from them in return. A game in game-model theory is defined as "a complex pattern of human interaction governed by a set of rules in which the players (participants) actively assume certain roles for the purpose of achieving a hidden pay-off" (Shulman, 1968). The concept of hidden payoffs is crucial to the significance of game-model theory. Many interactions are governed by the rules and roles engaged in by the participants. What distinguishes a game-model theory interaction from other types of interactions is the concept of the hidden payoff for the individual involved in that interaction (Kelley & Thibaut, 1978).

The extent to which the social worker can get the client to reduce game behaviors depends on his/her ability in treatment to reject the client's game role and the rules that go along with playing his/her game that would lead to receiving a hidden payoff. For example, in "playing it dumb" the client insists that he/she is inadequate to perform some task that is a part of the solution to his/her problem. The payoff occurs if the social worker accepts this statement and performs the task for the client. The social worker has thus rewarded the client for playing dumb. It is the social worker's responsibility to provide an opportunity for the client to learn an appropriate role with its set of rules (Shulman, 1968).

Another sociological approach posits that clients' difficulties are caused by the social structures of society—the institutions, such as schools, welfare organizations, and hospitals; the employment opportunity structures of the society; and the norms of cultures. This approach contends that clients have no deficiencies and that structural changes in society would alleviate client problems. It emphasizes the importance of macro-level variables such as social-psychological, sociological, economic and political variables on clients (Mathis, 1975; Weinert, 1982).

Structural Theory

Task-centered casework is a theoretical system of short-term intervention that emerged in 1972 with the publication of *Task Centered Casework* by Reid and Epstein. Two subsequent works (Reid, 1978; Reid & Epstein, 1977) have further elucidated the relevant aspects of the task-centered approach. Task-centered casework is unique in development because researchers and practitioners have worked together to specify its constructs and have tested an intervention variable.

In 1975, Reid took a major step in placing task-centered casework on firm empirical grounds by operationalizing the variable of task performance in a 5-step plan called a Task Implementation Sequence (TIS). TIS is a progressive treatment sequence including "enhancing commitment, planning task implementation, analyzing obstacles, modeling, rehearsal, guided practice, and summarizing," with the goal being to elicit specific client behaviors (Reid, 1975). The introduction of "operational tasks" was part of the beginning effort to specify the model's constructs and thereby place the paradigm on firmer scientific grounds by specifying the unit of attention—the task—in more measurable terms.

The client's difficulties are perceived as fitting one of the seven target typologies Reid and Epstein discussed; that is, difficulty in role performance (Reid & Epstein, 1972). Reid and Epstein state that clients with perceived problems in role performance are aware of a gap between the way they execute their roles and the way they would like to do so.

Conceptually defined, "task-centered treatment is a short-term model of social work practice designed to alleviate specific problems of individuals and families" (Reid & Epstein, 1972). The operational definition can be stated in a step-by-step progression; the client's problems are explored, a target problem is identified, a task is formulated, time limits are structured to attain casework goals, work on the task is carried out, and termination is effected. The conceptual system of viewing the individual is basically behavioral. The key to the success of task-centered casework may be the structural elements of the model, its emphasis on short-term service, and the specification of goals to be achieved by the client in concrete steps.

Theoretical Influences on Social Work Practice

All of the preceding theoretical conceptualizations may be employed in an effort to explain, predict, and change behavior. Treatment is therefore dependent on the social worker's perspective and will vary according to that perspective. In this section a case history of an adolescent is presented. It is followed by a section that compares the different theoretical conceptualizations with regard to their explanation of the boy's behavior, their expectations as to how much behavior change will take place, and their recommendations of interventions that could be used to change his behavior. The case history illustrates how the various theoretical approaches influence the social worker's perception of a client and his/her ensuing treatment of that client.

Case History

Eddy became known to the agency through his mother, who has been on public assistance for 12 years. Eddy's father, Mr. S., left their home 4 years ago. Since that time Eddy has presented many behavioral problems, which center around school. His inability to achieve up to his potential, his acting out toward school officials, and his handwriting difficulties are the most pressing problems. Eddy also has trouble relating to his peers. He desires and needs recognition from them, but does not know how to gain this recognition. His overaggressive behavior alienates his peers rather than helping him to gain friendship and recognition.

Eddy's problems began to occur when he was in the fifth grade, shortly before his father left home. He is now in the seventh grade and is still presenting problems to the school officials and to his family. Eddy is still doing poorly in his schoolwork. His achievement and his grades are poor, although, according to several tests, his IQ measures from 120 to 132. His poor school achievement may be due to the fact that, when he was in the sixth grade, he was told by a school principal that he was very intelligent and should not have any problems with schoolwork. It is the social worker's opinion that this may be a contributing factor in his lack of motivation concerning school achievement; that is, he perceives that he should not have to try in order to get by. Eddy continues to act out in an aggressive manner toward school officials, especially female teachers. Eddy, to a limited degree, has been able to perceive the problems he is experiencing, but still does not have a clear picture of how his poor achievement will affect his future and how his overaggressive behavior will only alienate those from whom he seeks recognition.

Eddy's problems are affecting his relationship with his mother. She knows that he should be achieving better in school and because he has not shown this achievement, she has become frustrated and has expressed a certain amount of hostility toward him. Eddy's mother realizes that he has the problems described above and she perceives that these problems are caused by some psychological disturbance. Mrs. S. has talked with school officials concerning Eddy's behavior and has tried to motivate him by showing interest in his schoolwork and by physically punishing him for his bad grades. She encourages his father to visit him more often because this seems to improve Eddy's behavior.

Eddy spends the major portion of his free time reading and engaging in activities of a varied nature that he likes. He does not like to do homework or to work around the house, which his mother requires. He likes physical sports but does not excel in any of them. He likes to watch television and to talk with different people. Occasionally he will go fishing with one of the boys in the neighborhood or with his father.

Eddy's eating habits are not good, but this is probably because his family is on welfare and the mother is not able to provide nutritionally balanced meals at all times. Also, he uses his lunch money for other purposes; he saves it for school activities or other things he wants to buy. Eddy has trouble sleeping and has many dreams and nightmares. When Eddy was first brought to the attention of the agency he exhibited passive behavior; he has since become progressively more aggressive. None of the social workers up to the present time have been able to keep Eddy interested in any one activity for any length of time. For the last 2 years caseworkers have been working with Eddy in trying to help him in the problem areas mentioned above.

The family includes six members: Mrs. S. (age 30), her four children— Eddy (13), Mike (8), Melody (6), and Steve (4)—and her mother Mrs. C. (50). The family's interaction as a whole is satisfactory for the crowded conditions under which they live. There do not seem to be many conflicts within the home. However, the family members do not always work well as a unit and the family ties do not appear very strong. All of the family members' attitudes toward Eddy are good. He seems to get along well with everyone in the family. Mrs. S. and Mrs. C. both want the best for Eddy and want to help him as much as possible, but they cannot perceive the problem at all times.

Eddy relates well to his brothers and sister; he also seems to enjoy playing with them. He sometimes plays the father role toward them, which they easily accept. Eddy has at times expressed hostility toward his mother. He wishes that she would manage the family's money better, would not discipline him, and would not make him do chores around the house.

Theoretical Conceptualizations of the Case

Hollis' Approach (The Person in His/Her Situation)

Causes

1. Unconscious hostility he has toward his mother for his father's absence (due to the divorce), which he may be displacing toward the authority figures at school, especially female teachers.

2. Inadequate ego control of aggressive behaviors.

3. Ego's inability to perceive how his school behavior now will affect his future.

4. Lack of adequate identification figure.

Change. A moderate amount of change can probably take place because his ego has the capacity to develop more fully. Change will also depend on the extent to which his environment can be modified and a substitute male model can be provided for him.

Interventions (Could Use Techniques Under Supportive Method)

1. Giving information as to why he needs to do the best he can at school now.

2. Ventilation of feeling toward mother and father.

3. Setting realistic limits on acting-out behaviors.

4. Utilization of habitual patterns of behavior. Because he attacks authority figures, try to get him to attack his books instead.

5. Modification of stereotyped pattern of always blaming someone else.

Gordon's Ecological Person-Environment Transaction Focus

Causes

1. Eddy does not have the right coping behaviors.

2. The wrong type of transaction of activity is taking place between Eddy and his environment for both of them to grow and develop.

Change. The amount of change depends on changing Eddy's coping behaviors and on the qualities of the impinging environment.

Interventions

1. Change Eddy's aggressive coping behaviors by developing more appropriate behaviors for his school environment.

2. Change qualities of the impinging environment; provide him with an adequate diet; get teacher to reinforce him only for socially desirable school behaviors.

Sociobehavioral Theory

Cause. Eddy's maladaptive behaviors of aggressiveness, poor handwriting, and unproductive schoolwork have been learned because they have been positively reinforced.

Change. Change depends on the social worker's ability to manipulate Eddy's stimulus-response patterns and to find and use reinforcers that have the potential to change Eddy's behavior.

Interventions

1. Reinforce socially acceptable behaviors in the area of school activities and peer relations.

2. Negatively reinforce or extinguish unacceptable behaviors such as fighting, peer handwriting, and aggressive acting out toward female teachers.

Stretch's Existentialism

This approach is not directly applicable to this adolescent's behavior, but it might fit into the scheme of things as follows.

Causes.

1. Eddy is trying to answer the questions of what life is all about.

2. Eddy is trying to answer the question of what the meaning of his existence is.

3. Eddy is trying to establish his individuality.

Change. Change depends on getting Eddy involved in social interaction so he can find meaning in his life.

Interventions

1. Helping Eddy through the crises that he faces, such as his perceptions of rejection by his peers, teachers, and his own family.

2. Help involve him in more social interactions of a positive nature so he can find meaning in his life.

Smalley's "Functionalism" Theory

Causes

1. Eddy's will is resisting subjugation to adults' wills such as his mother's and those of school officials.

2. Eddy's will has not been freed to help him realize his self-potential.

Change. Change depends on Eddy's will being freed to help in the controlling and organizing of his growth toward self-realization, and on his ability to set goals within the context of agency services.

Intervention. The use of the casework relationship to help Eddy free his will.

Sociological Approach (Hill's "Family as a Unit" Concept)

Cause. Eddy's behavior is a result of his family's not fulfilling its functions.

Change. Change depends on the family changing.

Interventions. Treating the family to develop (1) clearer communication among themselves, (2) more clearly defined roles, and (3) an individual concept of each family member.

Sociological Approach (Lentz's and Strean's Role Concept)

Causes

1. Eddy has learned a deviant role because of the way others have acted toward him in his social system, which has led to his viewing himself as a delinquent.

2. Eddy has been inadequately socialized to what his respective role should be.

Change. Change depends on his ability to learn another role and the social worker's ability to teach it.

Intervention. Social worker teaches Eddy's appropriate role through interaction with him.

Sociological Approach (Shulman's Game Theory)

Causes

1. Eddy's game behaviors are due to the payoffs he receives when he engages in aggressive and inadequate school behaviors.

2. The payoffs he receives from engaging in these games could be: (a) the attention he receives from them; (b) indirect expression of hostility; or (c) anxiety-reducing behavior.

Change. Change depends on Eddy not receiving payoffs for these particular games from significant persons in his environment, such as his peers, school officials, family members, and the social worker's skill in helping to accomplish this.

Interventions

1. Modification of environment so a reduction can take place in the number of hidden payoffs Eddy receives from playing the game.

2. Provision of an opportunity to learn new role behaviors.

Sociological Approach (Structural)

Cause. Social structures of society are not providing Eddy with opportunities to develop his potential.

Change. Change depends on changing the social structure of the society, i.e., institutions, norms, and so forth.

Intervention. Social worker changes society's structures to be more responsive to Eddy's needs.

Task-Centered System

Causes. Basically the same as sociobehavioral theory; also, an inability to execute the requisites of adolescent role developmental tasks.

Change. Change depends on the caseworker's ability to shape behaviors that will help Eddy acquire the requisite behaviors for adequate role performances.

Intervention. Approach mastering life span developmental tasks through contracting, structure, analyzing obstacles, modeling, rehearsal, and guided practice.

Theory-Directed Practice: The State of the Art

There are very few works in the literature in which theories are presented as complete logical systems, i.e., where their relationship to practice and empirical evidence to support their postulates are elaborated. One finds bits and pieces of a particular theory throughout the whole range of social work literature. Many writers focus solely on one specific concept derived from a larger theory and never relate its significance to the larger theory; thus, explication of comprehensive theories and derivations of subsequent treatment approaches has not occurred in a logical, consistent manner.

Research suggests that treatment programs have failed because they have focused only on one aspect of a client's difficulties. Therefore, requisite information needed to alter a client's behavior is apparently not available through the theoretical frameworks discussed. Data indicate that the complexity of human behavior demands more comprehensive theories of behavioral causation with treatment paradigms specified in accordance with the theory (Wodarski, 1981b; Wodarski, in press; Wodarski & Ammons, 1981; Wodarski & Harris, in press; Wodarski & Lenhart, 1984). Moreover, gender and ethnic-minority variables in the causation of human behavior are often not considered (White, 1984).

Historically, writers have tried to unite psychoanalytic concepts with sociological concepts—for example, as in the concept of role. Usually these theorists fall back on the psychoanalytic explanation of behavior and use sociological concepts only to reinforce these explanations. Likewise, theorists do not generally define their terms clearly; "libidinal drives" is one such term. The ill-defined term is then used to derive other terms before its function has been clarified in the theoretical scheme of things. Sociobehavioral theory is a step in the right direction in that its theorists have made an attempt to clearly define the terms used in their theoretical scheme and have shown how these terms can be applied to working with people. An example of both attempts is the concept of reinforcement. A concept cannot be applied by practitioners unless it can be specified in terms of the operations involved.

All theories seem to fall short of being able to predict how much change can take place in a client. For example, functional theory states that the social worker uses the caseworker-client relationship to free a client's will so he/she can develop. However, the theory offers no criteria as to what the optimal time is for freeing the client's will. What happens if his/her will is freed at an early age as compared to later in life? At what time must his/her will be freed for the self to adequately develop?

Most theories also fall short of having empirical referents for their concepts. For instance, how does one measure the concept of will in functional theory? What are its properties that can be manipulated in a relationship? In Gordon's ecological theory, how can one measure the amount of activity provided by the person and the amount provided by the environment when they meet at their interface for a transaction?

The critical question is, which of these theories can help improve social work practice? There is an urgent need to evaluate through research the effectiveness of various theoretical conceptualizations with certain clients. We need to set up criteria to determine when to use a particular theory or what type of combination of theories helps certain clients the most (Wodarski, Buckholdt, & Hudson, 1976). We need more accurate definitions of the many terms used in practice to enable social workers to communicate more clearly among themselves. Why a client is behaving in a certain way and why the social worker should exhibit certain behaviors in helping him/her change instead of exhibiting another set of behaviors should be cogently described by the theory (Wodarski, 1981b).

Theory Evaluation and Comparison

Let us now consider briefly the question: What is the extent to which all of these theories are valid in (1) their causal explanations and predictions of behavior; (2) the amount of change they hypothesize can take place in the client; and (3) the methods, techniques, and interventions they propose to change a client's behavior?

Social work's concern with this question until recently has been minimal. Kadushin (1967) addressed himself to this question by drawing up a list of postulates derived from human behavior theory, and stating that we can look at the effects of adoption of children from different theoretical conceptualizations and come up with different predictions as to the effect the adoption will have on the child's personality. For example, from the psychoanalytic viewpoint the adoptive experience is seen as a traumatic experience that occurs early in a child's life. Thus, because early childhood experiences play such an important part in a child's personality development, the child who is adopted will always be damaged to some extent in his/her personality functioning. Kadushin and others have carried out follow-up studies of children who have been adopted and have found that in 80–85% of cases the children's personality functioning was as good as that of children who were not adopted (Kadushin, 1967). These findings, Kadushin stated, are contradictory to the expected outcomes from the psychoanalytic perspective.

Kadushin chose to explain the successful personality development of the children according to sociobehavioral theory. He postulated that if the children had stayed in the original home they probably would have learned many maladaptive behaviors. He went on to emphasize that adoptions may provide new learning experiences for the children: "moving into the adoptive home meant moving into an environment that was set up to condition the child to a change in behavior. Previously learned, now inappropriate behaviors were unrewarded or were actively discouraged; new, more appropriate, more adaptive behaviors were rewarded and actively encouraged" (Kadushin, 1967). Even though the findings of Kadushin's research may present methodological questions, this research is the first of its kind to specify different predictions for human behavior derived from different theoretical frameworks. More research that tests various human behavior propositions deduced from theory is needed. Moreover, evaluation research to test different aspects of human behavior theories is imperative.

There also are a limited number of studies in social work that have attempted to assess the outcome of social work practice. Thomas (1968) commented that "the results of evaluative studies of casework and other traditional forms of interpersonal helping have been consistently disappointing." These studies question the effectiveness and efficiency of the traditional psychoanalytic models social work has used in trying to help clients. Briar (1967) stated that "research has shown that the model of clinical casework dominant for many years is suitable for no more than a fraction of the clients who come to us." He feels that in a traditional social work agency, such as a family service agency, this model is only applicable to about 25% of the cases served.

Following the theoretical and empirical perspectives of Bergin (1963, 1966, 1967a, 1967b, 1971, 1975) and Eysenck (1952, 1961, 1965, 1966), who initially reviewed the studies that attempted to evaluate the effectiveness of traditional forms of verbal psychotherapy in the fields of psychology and psychiatry, Fischer (1973) courageously tackled for the profession of social work the critical issue of social casework's effectiveness. Not surprisingly, Fischer arrived at conclusions similar to those discussed by Bergin and Eysenck concerning the lack of effectiveness of psychotherapy.

An article by Reid and Hanrahan (1982) that provided positive evidence of interventions used by social workers failed to provide any testing of human behavior theory postulates.

Accumulated research studies conducted thus far indicate that sociobehavioral techniques have strong potential for producing therapeutic changes in people (Wodarski, 1981a, 1981b; Wodarski & Bagarozzi, 1979). However, sociobehavioralists use a variety of techniques when working with people. Because many of their techniques could not be classified as behavioralistic, the success rates they cite cannot be attributed to the sociobehavioral method. Even with the substantial research evidence that exists to suggest that learning techniques have merit in helping people change certain types of problematic behaviors that they exhibit (Bruck, 1968), theoretical conceptualizations of human behavior causation developed from a sociobehavioral perspective still do not enable sufficient prediction of behavior.

Summary

The implications of a social worker's viewing the individual from different theoretical perspectives have been revealed. It is the responsibility of each practitioner to evaluate through the research available in our field and others the validity and reliability of the various assumptions made about the individual in these various theoretical conceptualizations and to choose treatment procedures accordingly. It is only when practitioners address these issues that social work practice can hope to achieve the goal of helping clients to the fullest possible extent to live productive lives. In all aspects of practice practitioners need to reexamine many of the assumptions held about clients who exhibit problematic behaviors and the interventions used in working with them.

Because there are no comprehensive theories available on which social workers can base their practice technologies, we must use instead the data from various studies that indicate the critical variables that should be analyzed in order to facilitate the intervention process.

REFERENCES

Bartlett, H. M. (1970). *The common base of social work practice.* New York: National Association of Social Workers.

Bergin, A. E. (1963). The effects of psychotherapy: Negative results revisited. *Journal of Counseling Psychology, 10,* 224–250.

Bergin, A. E. (1966). Some implications of psychotherapy research for therapeutic practice. *Journal of Abnormal Psychology, 71,* 235–246.

Bergin, A. E. (1967a). An empirical analysis of therapeutic issues. In D. Arbuckle (Ed.), *Counseling and psychotherapy: An overview.* New York: McGraw-Hill.

Bergin, A. E. (1967b). Further comments on psychotherapy research and therapeutic practice. *International Journal of Psychiatry, 3,* 317–323.

Bergin, A. E. (1971). The evaluation of therapeutic outcomes. In A. E. Bergin & S. L. Garfield (Eds.), *Handbook of psychotherapy and behavior change: An empirical analysis.* New York: Wiley.

Bergin, A. E. (1975). When shrinks hurt: Psychotherapy can be dangerous. *Psychology Today, 9,* 96–104.

Binswanger, L. (1963). *Being-in-the-world: Selected papers of Ludwig Binswanger.* New York: Basic.

Briar, S. (1967). The current crisis in social casework. In *Social work practice: Selected papers, 9th annual forum National Conference on Social Welfare, Dallas, Texas.* New York: Columbia University Press.

Brieland, D. (1977). Historical overview: Special issues on conceptual frameworks for social work practice. *Social Work, 22* (5), 341–346.

Bruck, M. (1968). Behavior modification theory and practice: A critical review. *Social Work, 13* (2), 43–55.

Community Service Society of New York. (1964). *Method and process in social casework.* New York: Family Service Association of America.

Eysenck, H. J. (1952). The effects of psychotherapy: An evaluation. *Journal of Consulting Psychology, 16,* 319–324.

Eysenck, H. J. (1961). The effects of psychotherapy. In H. J. Eysenck (Ed.), *Handbook of abnormal psychology.* New York: Basic.

Eysenck, H. J. (1965). The effects of psychotherapy. *International Journal of Psychiatry, 1,* 97–187.

Eysenck, H. J. (1966). *The effects of psychotherapy.* New York: International Science Press.

Feldman, R. A., Caplinger, T. E., & Wodarski, J. S. (1983). *The St. Louis conundrum: The effective treatment of antisocial youths.* Englewood Cliffs, NJ: Prentice-Hall.

Fischer, J. (1973). Is casework effective? A review. *Social Work, 18* (1), 5–20.

Germain, C. B., & Gitterman, A. (1980). *The life model of social work practice.* New York: Columbia University Press.

Goldstein, H. (1981). *Social learning and change: A cognitive approach to human services.* Columbia: University of South Carolina Press.

Gordon, W. E. (1969). Basic constructs for an integrative and generative conception of social work. In G. Hearn (Ed.), *The general systems approach: Contributions toward an holistic conception of social work.* New York: Council on Social Work Education.

Hall, C. S., & Lindzey, G. (1978). *Theories of personality* (3rd ed.). New York: Wiley.

Hamilton, G. (1951). *Theory and practice of social casework* (2nd ed). New York: Columbia University Press.

Hill, W. G. (1968). The family as a treatment unit: Differential techniques and procedures. *Social Work, 11* (2), 62–68.

Hollis, R. (1972). *Social casework: A psychosocial therapy* (2nd ed.). New York: Random House.

Hollis, R. (1977). Social casework: The psychosocial approach. In J. B. Turner et al. (Eds.), *Encyclopedia of social work: 17th edition, Vol. 1.* Washington, DC: National Association of Social Workers.

Hollis, F., & Woods, M. E. (1981). *Casework: A psychosocial therapy* (3rd ed.). New York: Random House.

Johnson, H. C. (1986). Emerging concerns in family therapy. *Social Work, 31*(4), 299–306.

Kadushin, A. (1967). Reversibility of trauma: A follow-up study of children adopted when older. *Social Work, 12* (4), 33–42.

Kelley, H. H., & Thibaut, J. W. (1978). *Interpersonal relations: A theory of interdependence.* New York: Wiley.

Lentz, W. P. (1966). Delinquency as a stable role. *Social Work, 11* (4), 66–70.

Mathis, T. P. (1975). Educating for black social development: The politics of social organization. *Journal of Education for Social Work, 11*(1). 105–112.

May, R. (Ed.). (1969). *Existential psychology* (2nd ed.). New York: Random House.

Minahan, A. (1981). Introduction to special issue. *Social Work, 26* (1), 5–6.

Perlman, H. H. (1977). Social casework: The problem-solving approach. In J. B. Turner et al. (Eds.), *Encyclopedia of social work: 17th issue, Vol. 2.* Washington, DC: National Association of Social Workers.

Reid, W. J. (1975). A test of a task-centered approach. *Social Work, 20,* 3–9.

Reid, W. J. (1978). *Task-centered system.* New York: Columbia University Press.

Reid, W. J., & Epstein, L. (1972). *Task-centered casework.* New York: Columbia University Press.

Reid, W. J., & Epstein, L. (Eds.). (1977). *The task-centered practice.* New York: Columbia University Press.

Reid, W. J., & Hanrahan, P. (1982). Recent evaluations of social work: Grounds for optimism. *Social Work, 27* (4), 328–340.

Schwartzman, J. (Ed.). (1985). *Families and other systems.* New York: Guilford Press.

Shulman, L. (1968). A game-model theory of interpersonal strategies. *Social Work, 13* (3), 16–22.

Smalley, R. E. (1967). *Theory for social work practice.* New York: Columbia University Press.

Straus, E. W. (1966). *Phenomenological psychology: The selected papers of Erwin W. Straus.* New York: Basic.

Strean, H. S. (1967). Role theory, role models, and casework: Review of the literature and practice application. *Social Work, 12* (2), 77–88.

Stretch, J. J. (1967). Existentialism: A proposed philosophical orientation for social work. *Social Work, 12* (2), 97–102.

Thomas, E. J. (Ed.). (1967). *Behavioral science for social workers.* New York: Free Press.

Thomas, E. J. (1968). Selected sociobehavior techniques and principles: An approach to interpersonal helping. *Social Work, 13* (1), 12–26.

Weinert, B. A. (1982). A dialogue for change: Policy politics and advocacy. *Administration in Social Work, 6*(2/3), 125–137.

Werner, H. D. (1965). *A rational approach to social casework.* New York: Association Press.

White, B. W. (Ed.). (1984). *Color in a white society: Selected papers from the NASW conference Color in a white society, Los Angeles, 1982.* Silver Spring, MD: National Association of Social Workers.

Wodarski, J. S. (1981a). *Role of research in clinical practice.* Austin, TX: PRO-ED.

Wodarski, J. S. (1981b). Treatment of parents who abuse their children: A literature review and implications for professionals. *Child Abuse and Neglect: The International Journal, 5* (3), 351–360.

Wodarski, J. S. (1983). The conceptualization of clinical practice through the social learning paradigm. *Social Work, 28* (2), 154–160.

Wodarski, J. S. (in press). Violent children: A practice paradigm. *Social Work in Education.*

Wodarski, J. S., & Ammons, P. W. (1981). Comprehensive treatment of runaway children and their parents. *Family Therapy, 8* (3), 229–240.

Wodarski, J. S., & Bagarozzi, D. (1979). A review of the empirical status of traditional modes of interpersonal helping: Implications for social work practice. *Clinical Social Work Journal, 7* (4), 231–255.

Wodarski, J. S., Buckholdt, D., & Hudson, W. (1976). Issues in evaluative research: Implications for social work practice. *Journal of Sociology and Social Welfare, 4* (1), 81–113.

Wodarski, J. S., & Harris, P. (in press). Adolescent suicide: A review of influences and the means for prevention. *Social Work.*

Wodarski, J. S., & Lenhart, S. D. (1984). Alcohol education for adolescents. *Social Work in Education, 6* (2), 69–92.

Chapter 5

LIFE SPAN DEVELOPMENT PERSPECTIVE

A recent innovation in the development of human behavior theory has been the life span development perspective. This approach is different from other human behavior theories that do not provide such a longitudinal perspective. The theorists emphasize that development occurs throughout an individual's life and that changes in the course of aging reflect biological, social, psychological, physical, and historical events, as well as the individual's activities as his/her own agent of change. Lately, this view is being shared by a significant number of practitioners (Baltes & Brim, 1979; Brim & Kagan, 1980; Newman & Newman, 1979; Riley, 1979). It is important for the change agent (i.e., counselor, social worker) to be familiar not only with the life span perspective, but also with the implications that each developmental stage has for the client and the change agent and for subsequent practitioner interventions.

Intervention efforts have been shown to be effective at every level of development (Baltes & Brim, 1979). In contrast to more traditional viewpoints that suggest that development begins with birth and is completed by young adulthood, at which time the individual is seen as unmalleable and difficult to treat because of "unresolved childhood conflicts" (Davison & Neale, 1982), the life span approach posits that behavior and personality remain flexible throughout life and major changes can occur at any time. This viewpoint suggests that many individuals have untapped reserves and potentials that are frequently not recognized by change agents operating from more traditional models (Featherman, 1981).

This chapter elucidates the relevance of the life span developmental approach to practice. Each developmental period is also discussed in terms of implications for change agents as they work with children and adolescents in each stage, and appropriate interventions are reviewed.

99

Pregnancy and Prenatal Development

Fetal development occurs in a psychosocial context. Genetic factors link the fetus to family ancestry, as well as providing individuality that manifests itself in various competencies and, at times, abnormalities. During the 9-month fetal development period the fetus undergoes rapid differentiation of body organs, integration of survival functions, regulation of body temperature and breathing, maturation of digestion, and development of sensory receptors. Five phases of birth occur: early signs of labor, onset of labor, a transition period when the mother's cervix is not yet fully dilated, birth, and the postpartum period. Influences on fetal growth and functioning include the mother's age at the time of pregnancy, drugs consumed by the mother during pregnancy, delivery, chronic environmental stress during pregnancy, availability of adequate nutrition for the mother, and the mother's attitude toward pregnancy, including her knowledge about birth and her cultural background (Istvan, 1986).

Implications for the Social Worker

The primary task for the social worker when treating a pregnant woman is either to provide the expectant mother with education regarding prenatal development and birth or to ensure that the expectant mother has and is using resources to provide this function. As a result of policies enacted during the Reagan administration, services that in the past were government subsidized may be seriously curtailed, leaving the social worker in human services agencies carrying a primary responsibility. Caseworkers should be aware of, and be able to provide the expectant mother with, information regarding proper nutrition, the effects of commonly used prescription and street drugs and alcohol on the developing fetus, the effect of anesthetics used in the birth process, and the influence of the mother's emotional state on the fetus.

The last point deserves further elaboration. Newman and Newman (1979) reported that, when an expectant mother experiences chronic emotional stress, the stress is frequently accompanied by hormonal changes, specifically changes in the mother's blood levels of epinephrine and norepinephrine. These fluctuations may affect the fetus by increasing the heart rate, constricting blood vessels, and increasing the mother's uterine contractions, all of which may increase the vulnerability of the fetus. In addition, many obstetricians report that women with more stable personalities and positive orientations to pregnancy react more calmly and positively to the stresses of labor than do women who have been under chronic stress and/or who are inadequately prepared for the birth experience during pregnancy (Klein, Potter, & Dyk, 1950; Zemlick & Watson, 1953). Therefore, it is important that the social worker not only assist the expectant mother in preparing for the birth experience, but also provide support to the expectant mother to aid her in either reducing or effectively coping with stresses that occur during the prenatal period.

Newman and Newman (1979) reported that the most common stress factor for expectant mothers is inadequate financial resources. This is especially true for single parents, and the social worker, where possible, must be available to assist the client in obtaining relief (Wodarski, 1982).

Frequently, the expectant father may have problems accepting his wife's preoccupation with her pregnancy and adjusting to his new role as an expectant father. This may increase the expectant mother's stress level, and marital counseling may be indicated to assist both spouses in their struggle to adjust to their new roles.

Finally, it should be noted that two age groups may require special knowledge and attention. When the expectant mother is older than 35, the possibility of birth defects is increased, especially in the case of Down's syndrome (Newman & Newman, 1979). The social worker should be able to assist the expectant mother in obtaining appropriate medical care and tests to determine whether this is a problem. The client may need supportive counseling during this period. An expectant mother under the age of 21 also requires special consideration. Planned Parenthood statistics indicate that 21% of all births in the United States occur among women between the ages of 12 and 21. The young pregnant woman will need counseling to assist her in deciding whether to abort, to have and keep the baby, or to have the baby and relinquish it to foster care or adoption. It may also be necessary to provide services to other people who are involved with the pregnant minor (expectant father, family) and to work with the school system to coordinate realistic educational services for her (Newman & Newman, 1979).

Sarvis and Rodman (1974) indicate that available evidence suggests that women do not tend to experience negative emotional reactions to abortions. However, this alternative may not be available to some clients because, at the present time, no state is obliged to pay for abortions with public funds, and many clients may not have financial resources available to be able to consider this alternative.

In summary, the social worker will have three main functions during the prenatal development and pregnancy stage: to provide the expectant mother with education, to provide counseling services to the expectant mother and her family, and to provide interventions that reduce stress, such as relaxation training (Wodarski & Bagarozzi, 1979). The educational services will include assisting the mother in obtaining public services when needed.

Infancy (Birth to 2 Years)

The newborn infant is engaged in the rapid development of motor skills, social relationships, and conceptual skills. The infant is not entirely helpless because he/she can perceive the environment and evoke responses from the caregivers; however, the parents are obviously viewed as holding primary responsibility for the infant.

The psychosocial crisis that occurs during infancy is "trust versus mistrust." The process that is central to attaining a successful resolution of this crisis is mutuality with the caregiver, i.e., developing social attachments to other human beings. In other words, the infant should gradually be able to develop trust for the caregiver as he/she begins to view the adult as a separate and permanent person. The caregiver should be perceived by the infant as a source of security who will encourage further exploration and facilitate meeting the child's biological needs. If the infant does not experience such interactions, he/she begins to develop mistrust.

During infancy, the ability to perceive primitive causality and object permanence (Piaget, 1970) is developed. The infant learns that if he/she cries when hungry, he/she will be fed. The infant also gradually realizes that an object exists even when it is not in his/her sight. Around the age of 7 months it is normal for the infant to develop stranger anxiety. Exposure to a variety of people gradually modifies this response. The typical infant also develops separation anxiety around the age of 9 months. Repeated exposures to brief separations from the primary caregiver may modify the intensity of the child's anxiety (Newman & Newman, 1979).

During the developmental stage of infancy, it is important that the parents be able to facilitate emotional and cognitive development by providing consistency and warmth for the infant. The environment should be structured so that it stimulates the infant's sensory, motor, and social exploration of his/her surroundings and meets his/her biological needs. The infant learns to trust adults or mistrust according to care given by the caregivers.

Implications for the Social Worker

In providing services to the infant, the social worker's primary treatment efforts will be directed toward the parents to enable them to provide a stimulating environment for the child to grow in terms of cognitive and social competencies. Parental effectiveness courses, one major means of attaining these objectives, should focus on helping parents develop better communication and consistent child management skills, two variables research has shown are necessary conditions for successful child rearing (Hoffman, 1977). The exception to this occurs if an infant is being abused, in which case the social worker will have to work with Protective Services to guarantee that the infant does not sustain further injuries. As soon as the infant is placed in a safe environment, however, the social worker should continue to meet with the parents to assist them in developing adequate parenting skills. It is important that the infant return to the home environment as soon as possible, especially if he/she has been placed in an institutional setting. Skeels (1966) reported that infants who are separated from a consistent caregiver for long periods of time tend to have retarded motor development, delayed language development, and cold emotional responses. Moreover, these children often develop inadequate self-images.

The primary goal of the social worker is to assist the parents in providing the infant with an environment conducive to the successful resolution of the crisis of trust versus mistrust. Yarrow (1964) posited that the critical period of attachment and trust occurs between the ages of 6 months and 2 years and that the primary mechanism is the development by the infant of a social smile that is rewarded by the primary caregiver. Newman and Newman (1979) addressed the issue of day care and stated that, if an infant receives consistent care at a day care center and consistent care from the parents at home, a successful bond of trust will develop.

If the infant must be separated from the primary caregivers because of uncontrollable environmental factors (such as hospitalization of the infant or parent), the social worker should encourage arrangements for the infant to continue to have some contact with the primary caregiver. The social worker should be familiar with various community agencies and hospitals so that he/she can aid the family in maintaining consistent contact.

Under normal circumstances, the role of the social worker is that of educator and support/treatment provider. The parents may need education regarding the needs of the infant and/or support while adjusting to the demands of parenthood. Counseling may be done individually or with both parents to provide these services. Group counseling with parents has been especially effective because it allows new parents to gain support from each other (Turner, 1976; Wodarski, 1982).

At times, the social worker may treat an adult client who did not achieve a positive resolution of the trust versus mistrust crisis in infancy. He/she should be alert to this possibility when obtaining the psychosocial history. Typically, the client may have a history of relationship difficulties resulting from his/her inability to trust (Newman & Newman, 1979). The social worker should attempt to establish a trusting relationship with the client and work with the client in assisting him/her to function more effectively in social and family relationships (Turner, 1976).

Toddlerhood (2 to 4 Years)

Toddlerhood is described as a time when the child is engaged in the developmental tasks of learning self-control, language development, fantasy and play, elaboration of locomotion, goal setting, exploration of the environment, and development of a separate identity. During this period the child faces the psychosocial crisis of "autonomy versus shame and doubt." The central process for development in the growing toddler is imitation. The child masters such tasks as toilet training, independence, and socialization of anger primarily through imitation. Language remains primarily concrete, and thought and language become integrated. The toddler frequently has an imaginary friend whom he/she may use in efforts to distinguish right from wrong.

The toddler usually passes through a time period when his/her primary word is "no," which is a child's means of attempting to control and order the environment. The establishment of autonomy requires tremendous effort by the child as well as extreme patience and supportiveness by the parents. The child begins to develop feelings of self-confidence and independence. Parents should not be overprotective, so as to facilitate the child's development of independence and confidence.

Implications for the Social Worker

As in the previous stages of psychosocial development, the social worker's primary interventions are most likely to occur in working with the parents. If a toddler develops symptoms such as temper tantrums, phobias, and so forth, this is usually an indication that he/she is not receiving adequate parenting at home.

It is especially important that the parents provide the toddler with appropriate and consistent limits as the child begins to learn to control him/herself. There are three primary forms of discipline that parents use. The first is labeled power assertive and is carried by use of physical punishment and threats. The second, psychological, may be characterized by love withdrawal and guilt, which emphasizes the toddler's dependency on the parents. Third, inductions, which emphasize the conceptual nature of the conflict, point out the consequences of the behavior and parental expectations, and offer suggestions for alternate behavior (Patterson, 1981). Inductions also encourage the child to empathize with the other person involved. Hoffman (1963) stated that power assertion techniques tend to encourage weak moral development and induction techniques lead to advanced moral development. Thus, the social worker should assist the parents in learning to discipline the toddler with induction techniques.

During this stage of development, the toddler learns primarily by imitation. If parents model aggressive and uncontrolled behavior at home, the toddler will imitate this behavior (Wodarski, in press). In such cases the social worker's interventions would again be geared toward the parents in an effort to promote their ability to exhibit appropriate socialization behaviors (Bandura, 1977).

Because the toddler is still in the early stages of language development, he/she concretely interprets verbal messages such as "God will punish you" and "big boys don't cry"; that is, such statements are accepted at face value. Development of sex role, morality, and competence are especially vulnerable to such labels (Newman & Newman, 1979), so the parents should be made aware of this and encouraged to use direct communication rather than all-encompassing statements. Parent effectiveness training groups are especially useful in teaching these skills.

In some cases, the social worker may also wish to intervene directly with the child. Play therapy seems to be the most effective treatment method. The social worker should allow the child to create imaginary situations in which problems can be expressed and resolved (Singer, 1975; Turner, 1976).

Finally, parents frequently need to place children in day care settings because of career aspirations or financial pressures that require both parents to work. The ideal day care service should provide continuity in personnel and employment of both male and female aides, and should be similar in environment to the child's home and neighborhood. The policies should enhance the toddler's feelings of community and autonomy. The social worker will be most helpful to the parents if he/she is familiar with neighborhood day care centers, including knowledge about how individual centers are run as well as costs.

The social worker may at times be required to work with adults who did not successfully complete this stage of development. Problems will manifest themselves by low self-esteem in the client, difficulty in controlling aggressive impulses, and lack of moral development. Here, the social worker's job is to focus on assisting the client in developing realistic goals and learning appropriate skills to reduce the problem areas as defined by the client and the social worker (Jackel, 1976).

Early School Age (5 to 7 Years)

During the early school age the child engages in sex-role identification, which includes the understanding of gender labels, sex-role standards, sex-role preference and identification with the same-sex parent. Early moral development continues and the child enters the stage of concrete operations (Newman & Newman, 1979; Piaget, 1970). The psychosocial crisis that the child must deal with is "initiative versus guilt." The central process by which this occurs is identification. Initiative results when the child responds actively to his/her environment and is eager to investigate it. It is necessary for the child to develop a strong sense of autonomy so that he/she will be motivated to explore the environment. The child also must have confidence in his/her ability to control him/herself. If adults severely limit investigation and experimentation, the child develops an overwhelming sense of guilt.

Implications for the Social Worker

The child's sex-role identification is of primary importance during this stage. Many factors influence this process, but the social worker should be especially aware of three of these. First, if the child is born into a family that was hoping for a child of the opposite sex, the family may present obstacles that keep the child from developing an appropriate sex-role identification. Second, it is important for the child to have a same-sex role model with which to identify. Thus, if the same-sex parent is absent from the home, the family should be encouraged to provide an alternate same-sex role model (a relative or close friend of the family who can spend time with the child). The third factor relates to our rapidly changing cultural norms regarding appropriate sex-role behavior. The social worker needs to be cognizant that sex roles are changing and that a variety of roles and behaviors are appropriate for all children.

During this stage the child is continuing to develop moral standards through a gradual internalization of parental values and standards. Numerous researchers report that females experience more guilt than males during this developmental stage, and it has been suggested that this results from the unclear messages that society presents to females regarding their roles and appropriate behaviors (Eagly & Crowley, 1986; Rebelsky, Allinsmith, & Grinder, 1964; Sears, Maccoby, & Levin, 1957). Thus, it may be useful for the social worker to assist the family and the child in clarifying appropriate behaviors. Parental discipline should continue as during the toddler stage; that is, parents and social workers should help the child interpret the undesired behavior, generate alternative actions, explain the reason behind discipline if any is given, and stimulate empathy for the victim of the behavior.

During this stage, the child has his/her first experience with structured education. Early successful experiences are essential if the child is to develop into a well-functioning adult (Newman & Newman, 1979). The child becomes a part of a larger system, so that the social worker may frequently be dealing not only with the child's family, but also with the school and other related institutions. The child is exposed not only to family influences, but also for the first time to influences from school officials, teachers, and peers. Separation may be traumatic for the child and the parents. This is the first time someone else influences the socialization process. Moreover, the peer group becomes an important socialization force, i.e., it begins to set limits for acceptable behavior, thus reducing again the parental importance. During this time, the child is rapidly developing a sense of self-esteem and self-images of "Who am I" and "Who would I like to be?" Coopersmith (1967) listed seven characteristics of children who have high self-esteem: maternal certainty of child-rearing; minimal daily family conflict; closeness with siblings; closeness with peers; parental warmth; consistent firm discipline; and involvement in family decisions. Inconsistency, harsh discipline, minimal parental attention and continuous moving are factors that contribute to low self-esteem. The social worker should be aware of these factors and plan multiple interventions that will include the child, the child's family, and the school.

A common problem during this stage is the development of school phobia. Rosenburg (1965) posited that phobias are expressions of low self-esteem, high anxiety, interpersonal awkwardness, isolation, and expectations of failure. The school-phobic child should be made to attend school. It will be helpful in such cases to provide the child with encouragement and support from the social worker, the child's family, and the school (Lassers, Nordon, & Bladholm, 1976).

If a child has unsuccessful school experiences, the likelihood that he/she will eventually drop out of school is greatly increased (Newman & Newman, 1979). Moreover, school dropout is highly correlated with subsequent delinquent activities (Feldman, Caplinger, & Wodarski, 1983). The child who does not successfully complete this stage will have numerous problem areas as an adult. Besides the obvious problems of low self-esteem and a sense of incompetence, the individual will be faced with very real pressures of needing to earn a living. The social worker's role with such a client will be to assist the adult in obtaining marketable skills through appropriate community institutions and/or agencies while concurrently working with the client to change entrenched feelings of low self-esteem.

Middle School Age (8 to 12 Years)

During the middle school age period, the child is engrossed in learning social cooperation with his/her same-sex peer group. During this period the same-sex peer gains more influence in the child's life. The child is continuously engaged in self-evaluation, which occurs during skill learning both at school and while interacting in team events with peers. The psychosocial crisis during this period is "industry versus inferiority," which is linked to achievement motivtion. The central process of development in this stage is education, and important elements include the impact of grading, individual differences, developing academic and social competencies and adequate work habits, and school failure. This is also the time period when the individual obtains a beginning awareness of sexual differences between males and females and sex education begins.

Implications for the Social Worker

As the child continues to develop, he/she experiences an increased emphasis on intellectual growth, competence, and a growing investment in work. In daily interactions with peers, the child is exposed to differing points of view and intimacy with one or more same-sex peers. Sullivan (1949) posited that this first experience of intimacy outside the family of origin provides the individual with an important learning experience that will influence future heterosexual relationships. The child becomes very sensitive to social norms, expectations, and peer pressure and is preoccupied with self-evaluation in terms of academic, physical, and social tasks. The child is engaged in learning academic, athletic, and artistic skills (Pflaum, 1974). Societal norms encourage the child to continually compare him/herself with peers. Because no one is good at everything, the child may begin to develop low self-esteem. If he/she is vulnerable due to an inadequate resolution of one of the prior psychosocial crises, this period may be extremely difficult.

As noted above, the central process is education. The child must remain motivated to participate in various educational activities in order to set the stage for later learning and a subsequent investment in work behaviors. Smith (1969) reported that achievement motivation is a function of early and continual encouragement by parents, a permissive orientation toward exploration and investigation, and reward and praise for efforts. School officials and teachers also perform significant roles in obedience, academic performance, and social behavior. At times, educators may be negatively influenced by a child's prior records or by the performance of older siblings who completed classes that the child is currently in. The importance of a successful school orientation has already been noted. If the child is experiencing problems in school, it is imperative that the social worker enlist the support of significant teachers and administrators in the treatment of that child (Turner, 1976).

It is also important that the child receive appropriate sex education during this stage. Newman and Newman (1979) cited Planned Parenthood statistics that indicate that 21% of all births in the United States occur among women between the ages of 12 and 21. The responsible social worker should encourage families and schools to provide sex education to help the child clarify and understand questions related to sexual functioning and sexual behavior (Schinke, Blythe, & Gilchrist, 1981; Schinke, Gilchrist, & Blythe, 1980; Wodarski & Lockhart, 1987).

Early Adolescence (13 to 17 Years)

During early adolescence the individual is preoccupied with physical maturation, intellectual maturation, and heightened emotional sensitivity. He/she is now able to perform formal operations (Piaget, 1970), meaning that abstract thinking is possible and the adolescent is capable of conceptualizing changes that may occur in the future. He/she can anticipate consequences of behavior and is especially sensitive to consistent and inconsistent behavior. Membership in a peer group is extremely important, and peer groups are more structured and organized than they were in earlier stages. Group membership is most frequently based on physical attractiveness. The adolescent also begins engaging in heterosexual relationships. Parents and significant adults influence the child's identity and self-esteem less than the all-important peers.

The psychosocial crisis at this stage is "group identity versus alienation." The adolescent receives pressure from his/her parents, peers, and school to identify with a group. A positive resolution of the crisis results in the individual allying with a group that he/she perceives as meeting his/her social needs and providing him/her with a sense of group belonging. A negative resolution results in the adolescent experiencing a sense of isolation and continually feeling uneasy in the presence of peers. The central process operating during this period is peer pressure (Newman & Newman, 1979).

Implications for the Social Worker

During this stage the social worker needs to be concerned with the individual, the family, and the school. Families will frequently seek treatment because of conflicted relationships at home. Gold and Douvan (1969) described the family during this stage as a place where the adolescent continues to meet expectations of parents but gradually begins to assume his/her position as an adult. Baumrind (1975) reported that, in families where parents are unhappy and conflicted, teenagers engage in high levels of rebellious behaviors. Parents who share decision making tend to have children who identify strongly with them. Parents who combine authority with reason and frequent communication tend to have adolescents who are assertive, responsible, and independent. These factors should be considered by the social worker when working with families.

During this stage, the peer group serves as a transitional world for the adolescent. Gordon (1957) posited that participation in extracurricular activities is the most important determination of the adolescent's status with peers. The self-concept of the adolescent is very susceptible to status fluctuations that occur with moves and high school transitions. The social worker should encourage and support the adolescent in becoming involved in extracurricular activities to assist in such transitions.

School officials and teachers should also be aware of the importance of extracurricular activities and of the difficulties that mobile adolescents may have in adjusting to a new school during this stage so that they can provide encouragement and support. Packard (1972) suggested that schools would be wise to develop "Welcome Wagon" groups to orient new students because our society is so highly mobile. This would help decrease the adolescent's feelings of isolation and alienation in a new setting. This is especially important in view of Bachman, Green and Wirtmen's (1971) finding that in order to "save face" adolescents frequently drop out of high school if they are not accepted by their peers.

Most social workers will encounter the problem of alcohol and drug abuse among teenagers. Such abuse becomes a problem when it is used by the adolescent to avoid the hard work that is required during this stage to achieve requisite academic competencies and lasting psychological growth (Newman & Newman, 1979). In this situation, the worker should mobilize family, school, and community resources to abort the drug and alcohol abuse, including Alcoholics Anonymous and Narcotics Anonymous groups for teenagers. Because of the prevalence of this problem, all communities and schools should provide alcohol and drug educational experiences for teenagers (Wodarski & Lenhart, 1984).

When working individually with adolescents, Turner (1976) reported that short-term, goal-oriented, planned treatment is most effective. The relationship between social worker and adolescent should attempt to provide a corrective experience to the client, i.e., that adults *can* be trusted as aides in his/her attempts at gaining self-mastery.

Later Adolescence (18 to 22 Years)

During this psychosocial stage, individuals are primarily engaged in achieving autonomy from parents, with new peer groups having a substantial impact on their identity. Sex-role identity again becomes a major factor. The individual is also exploring his/her morality and begins to perceive society's expectations for him/her. Turiel (1974) described this as a transitional stage where old principles are challenged and new ones have not yet emerged. This is the last stage before the individual has to make critical choices in terms of values, goals, and identity.

The individual also will be considering career alternatives. Frequently, he/she may feel that a choice must be made without much experience. Females may be strongly influenced by marriage and career expectations, and both males and females may make choices that reflect continued identification with parents. As the individual attempts to achieve autonomy, he/she may leave home and may stop communicating with the family of origin for a time (Newman & Newman, 1979).

The psychosocial crisis during this stage is "identity versus role diffusion." The individual questions his/her essential character. Anxiety during this stage may encourage identity foreclosure, in which the individual makes choices based on others' expectations rather than experience the anxiety that accompanies forming his/her own identity (Marcia, 1966). Erikson (1959) posited that some individuals form negative identities that are based on social input (e.g., that one is "delinquent") or based on close identification with a negative role model. Role diffusion results when the individual is unable to integrate various roles or make a commitment to a single view of the self (Newman & Newman, 1979).

The central process of development during this stage is role experimentation. The individual may become involved in summer jobs, various religious and political groups, cohabitation, new peer groups, and so forth. Schenkel and Marcia (1972) reported that males become concerned with occupation and politics, whereas females are more likely to experiment with sexuality and religion. However, these differences may disappear as male and female liberation movements create more flexibility in roles.

World of Work

While youths' efforts to become employed are fraught with pain and frustration, the long-term effects of chronic unemployment on the mental health of these young persons are predictable and devastating. "Considering the magnitude of the problem and its deep psychological implications, the topic of unemployment in general has not received from social science researchers the attention that is deserved" (Sherraden & Adamek, 1983, p. 2). Despite this limitation, however, existing studies do reveal consistent evidence and a fairly clear picture of the mental health aspects of unemployment.

It is critical to note the importance Americans place on employment and financial security. The Gallup organization (1980) conducted a study of adults in 1977 and another in 1980 and reported that the two most important problems facing their families at that time were economic and financial security, and unemployment. Unemployment is not simply an economic problem. It is also a psychological and sociological injury. Coles (1976) discovered that work was the most significant measure of "grown-up" status among working class people.

Work has special meaning to the psychosocial development of young people. It is an opportunity to begin a career, to establish one's own identity, to gain independence, to contribute to family finances, to acquire prestige, and to try out adult roles. There is substantial research, for example, that indicates that for the majority of individuals, work is the single most defining aspect of living in American society. Conversely, unemployment at this age lowers feelings of self-esteem, and long spells of joblessness may precipitate catastrophic psychological problems. In Briar's study (1976) of youths, the impact of unemployment made them feel like they were "going crazy" and "suffocating." Some felt "mad at the whole world," "useless," "fed up," "stranded," and "incompetent and a failure." In addition to being bored, frightened, insecure, depressed and confused, some of them claimed their joblessness caused them to have problems with alcohol, eating and sleeping. Increases in family conflicts were also reported. There are also indications that drug addiction, teenage pregnancy and family violence are related to youth joblessness (Dayton, 1978).

Associated with high unemployment rates are increases in homicides; motor vehicle mortality; residence in a mental hospital; and arrest rates for assault, criminal homicide, auto theft, robbery, rape, prostitution and narcotics (Brenner, 1980).

Despite high unemployment, the desire for jobs among youths in general, and among disadvantaged and minority youths in particular, remains strong (Briar, 1976). However, the job prospects for some youth are so bleak that after exhaustive, unsuccessful job searches, they permanently drop out of the conventional labor force. They become alienated and disenfranchised from traditional social institutions. If not treated early, unemployment can have an irreversible impact on employment aspirations, social attachment and mental health.

The problem of youth unemployment is not simply a sign of the *present* economic times. Social and economic indicators forecast that youth joblessness may be a chronic problem. For example, even if the upturn in the economy continues, youth are competing for jobs with previously employed unemployed, and with women and immigrants who are new to the job market. Furthermore, the high birth rates in the black population will continue to result in an increasing pool of black young people seeking to move into the job market.

Implications for the Social Worker

The social worker should have some knowledge of career alternatives and of the technologies available to help adolescents secure and maintain employment in order to assist the adolescent during this stage (Azrin & Victoria, 1980). The adolescent should be encouraged to engage in various work experiences and to consider both job security and job satisfaction in his/her final choice. Clients may need assistance from institutions, such as vocational rehabilitation, if they have not achieved adequate skills through traditional educational methods. At times, family treatment may be indicated if the individual is experiencing difficulty in becoming autonomous.

Turner (1976) stressed that treatment for the older adolescent having behavioral difficulties should utilize a multisystem approach that includes various community services in the treatment plan. This approach allows the individual to develop the numerous skills and the support systems that are necessary to achieve positive identity.

Conclusion

This chapter has provided the social worker with a concise summary of the developmental psychosocial life stages of children and adolescents as well as the implications of each stage for the human service worker. It should be stressed that at every developmental stage the individual has strengths and competencies. All interventions should be designed to respond to and build on strengths that are already present in the individual.

It is also important to note that many crises facing the individual are as much a function of the environment as of the individual. Responsible social workers must keep abreast of social conditions and lobby for appropriate programs at the community, state, and federal levels to supplement the services they are able to offer as individuals. In our rapidly changing culture, myriad challenges will continue to confront us not only as social workers, but as individuals, and we must meet these challenges responsibly. The life span development approach enables practitioners to anticipate future consequences for children and adolescents if they fail to master requisite competencies at each stage of development and to plan subsequent appropriate interventions in terms of assessing the individual's physical, psychological, and social attributes that will interact with his/her environment to facilitate the accomplishment of requisite developmental tasks in order to be successful in American society.

REFERENCES

Azrin, N. H., & Victoria, A. (1980). *Job club counselor's manual.* Baltimore, MD: University Park Press.

Bachman, J. G., Green, S., & Wirtmen, I. D. (1971). *Youth in transition, Vol. 3: Dropping out—problem or symptom?* Ann Arbor, MI: Institute for Social Research.

Baltes, P. B., & Brim, O. G. (Eds.). (1979). *Life span development and behavior* (2nd ed.). New York: Academic Press.

Bandura, A. (1977). *Social learning theory.* Englewood Cliffs, NJ: Prentice-Hall.

Baumrind, D. (1975). Early socialization and adolescent competence. In S. Dragastin & G. H. Elder (Eds.), *Adolescence in the life cycle: Psychological change and social context.* Washington, DC: Hemisphere Publishing.

Brenner, M. H. (1980). Estimating the social costs of youth employment problems. In *A review of youth employment problems, programs and policies: The youth employment problem* (Vol. 1). Washington, DC: U.S. Government Printing Office.

Briar, K. H. (1976). *The effect of long-term unemployment on workers and their families.* D.S.W. dissertation, The University of California at Berkeley.

Brim, O. G., & Kagan, J. (Eds.). (1980). *Constancy and change in human development.* Cambridge, MA: Harvard University Press.

Coles, R. (1976). Work and self-respect. *Daedalus, 105*(4), 29–38.

Coopersmith, S. (1967). *Antecedents of self-esteem.* San Francisco, CA: Freeman.

Davison, G. C., & Neale, J. M. (1982). *Abnormal psychology.* New York: Wiley.

Dayton, C. W. (1978). The dimensions of youth unemployment. *Journal of Employment Counseling,* March, 3–27.

Eagly, A. H., & Crowley, M. (1986). Gender and helping behavior: A meta-analytic review of the social psychological literature. *Psychological Bulletin, 100*(3), 283–308.

Erikson, E. H. (1959). The problem of ego identity. *Psychological Issues, 1*(1), 101–164.

Featherman, D. L. (1981). *Life span perspective in social science research.* Madison: University of Wisconsin.

Feldman, R. A., Caplinger, T. E., & Wodarski, J. S. (1983). *The St. Louis conundrum: The effective treatment of antisocial youths.* Englewood Cliffs, NJ: Prentice-Hall.

Gallup Organization. (1980). *American families, 1980: A summary of findings.* Princeton, NJ: Gallup Organization.

Gold, M., & Douvan, E. (1969). *Adolescent development: Readings in research and theory.* Boston: Allyn & Bacon.

Gordon, C. W. (1957). *The social system in the high school.* New York: Free Press.

Hoffman, M. L. (1963). Parent discipline and the child's consideration for others. *Child Development, 34,* 573–588.

Hoffman, M. L. (1977). Personality and social development. In M. Rosenzweig & L. Porter (Eds.), *Annual review of psychology.* Palo Alto, CA: Annual Reviews.

Istvan, J. (1986). Stress, anxiety, and birth outcomes: A critical review of the evidence. *Psychological Bulletin, 100*(3), 331–348.

Jackel, M. M. (1976). Clients with character disorders. In F. Turner (Ed)., *Differential diagnosis and treatment in social work.* New York: Free Press.

Klein, H. R., Potter, H. W., & Dyk, R. B. (1950). *Anxiety in pregnancy and childbirth.* New York: Hoeber.

Lassers, E., Nordon, R., & Bladholm, S. (1976). Steps in the return to school of children with school phobia. In F. Turner (Ed.), *Differential diagnosis and treatment in social work.* New York: Free Press.

Marcia, J. E. (1966). Development and maturation of ego identity status. *Journal of Personality and Social Psychology, 3,* 551–558.

Newman, B. M., & Newman, P. R. (1979). *Development through life: A psychosocial approach.* Homewood, IL: Dorsey.

Packard, V. (1972). *A nation of strangers.* New York: McKay.

Patterson, G. R. (1981). *Coercive family processes.* Eugene, OR: Castilla Press.

Pflaum, S. W. (1974). *The development of language and reading in the young child.* Columbus, OH: Merrill.

Piaget, J. (1970). Piaget's theory. In P. H. Mussen (Ed.), *Carmichael's manual of child psychology* (3rd ed.). New York: Wiley.

Rebelsky, R. G., Allinsmith, W. A., & Grinder, R. (1964). Sex differences in children's use of fantasy confession and their relation to temptation. *Child Development, 34,* 955–962.

Riley, M. W. (Ed.). (1979). *Aging from birth to death: Interdisciplinary perspective.* Boulder, CO: Westview Press.

Rosenburg, M. (1965). *Society and the adolescent self-image.* Princeton, NJ: Princeton University Press.

Sarvis, B., & Rodman, H. (1974). *The abortion controversy.* New York: Columbia University Press.

Schenkel, S., & Marcia, J. E. (1972). Attitudes toward premarital intercourse in determining ego-identity status in college women. *Journal of Personality, 3,* 472–482.

Schinke, S. P., Blythe, B. J., & Gilchrist, L. D. (1981). Cognitive-behavioral prevention of adolescent pregnancy. *Journal of Counseling Psychology, 28*(5), 451–454.

Schinke, S. P., Gilchrist, L. D., & Blythe, B. J. (1980). Role of communication in the prevention of teenage pregnancy. *Health and Social Work, 5*(3), 54–59.

Sears, R. R., Maccoby, E. E., & Levin, H. (1957). *Patterns of childbearing.* Evanston, IL: Row & Peterson.

Sherraden, M. W., & Adamek, M. (1983). Unemployment and adolescent mental health. *Practice Applications, 1,* 1–15.

Singer, J. L. (1975). *The inner world of daydreaming.* New York: Harper Colophon.

Skeels, H. M. (1966). Adult status of children with contrasting early life experiences. *Monographs of the Society for Research in Child Development, 31*(3).

Smith, C. P. (1969). The origin and expression of achievement related motives in children. In C. P. Smith (Ed.), *Achievement related motives in children.* New York: Russell Sage Foundation.

Sullivan, H. S. (1949). *The collected works of Harry Stack Sullivan.* New York: Norton.

Turiel, E. (1974). Conflict and change in adolescent moral development. *Child Development, 45*(1), 14–29.

Turner, F. J. (Ed.). (1976). *Differential diagnosis and treatment in social work.* New York: Free Press.

Wodarski, J. S. (1982). Single parents and children: A review for social workers. *Family Therapy, 9*(3), 311–320.

Wodarski, J. S. (in press). Violent children: A practice paradigm. *Social Work in Education.*

Wodarski, J. S., & Bagarozzi, D. (1979). *Behavioral social work.* New York: Human Sciences Press.

Wodarski, J. S., & Lenhart, S. D. (1984). Alcohol education for adolescents. *Social Work in Education, 6*(2), 69–92.

Wodarski, J. S., & Lockhart, L. L. (1987). Teenage parents on welfare: The social crisis of the 80's. *Society,* March/April, 48–52.

Yarrow, L. J. (1964). Separation from parents in early childhood. In M. L. Hoffman & L. W. Hoffman (Eds.), *Review of child development research.* New York: Russell Sage Foundation.

Zemlick, M., & Watson, R. (1953). Maternal attitudes of acceptance and rejection during and after pregnancy. *American Journal of Orthopsychiatry, 23,* 570.

Chapter 6

PROCEDURES FOR THE MAINTENANCE AND GENERALIZATION OF ACHIEVED BEHAVIORAL CHANGE

The incidence of child and youth behavioral difficulties continues to occupy the attention of a number of social workers. Treatment evaluations of therapeutic practices based on traditional techniques are not encouraging. With the exception of programs based on the behavioral approach, little data exist to support practice efforts with children and adolescents (Kazdin, Esveldt-Dawson, French, & Unis, 1987; Lovaas, 1987; Schinke, 1981; Wodarski & Bagarozzi, 1979). Even with the various behavioral programs, however, there remains yet the unresolved problem of the maintenance and generalization of behavioral change once achieved.

Maintenance can be viewed as the length of time elapsed between the termination of therapy and the continuance of the behavior. Generalization refers to the extent the behaviors learned in the clinical context occur at appropriate times, and to socially relevant persons in the socially relevant settings. Thus, if the goal of a treatment program is for a child to develop adequate social and academic behaviors, then once these behaviors are acquired the crucial subsequent issues of maintenance and generalization must be addressed. The literature on maintenance and generalization indicates the processes will not occur by chance, and therefore any sophisticated treatment program must directly address them (Kazdin, 1975, 1977; Koegel & Rincover, 1977; Rychtarik, Foy, Scott, Lokey, & Prue, 1987; Stokes & Baer, 1977).

Few would deny the controversy surrounding the efficacy of the present-day therapeutic services aimed at changing behavior. Many issues pertain to where the services should be provided and by whom, proper duration of services, and appropriate criteria for evaluation.

This chapter elucidates the role of the social worker in the maintenance and generalization of behavioral change. Specific items discussed

119

include training relatives or significant others in the client's environment; training behaviors that have a high probability of being reinforced in natural environments; varying the conditions of training; gradually removing or fading the contingencies; using different schedules of reinforcement; using delayed reinforcement and self control procedures, and so forth where relevant case examples are used to illustrate the procedures. Prior to discussion of these items, the literature on follow-up endeavors of three comprehensively based behaviorally focused treatment programs for delinquents is briefly reviewed. This review provides the rationale for the inclusion of the treatment components to ensure the maintenance and generalization of behavior in any treatment program.

Review of Follow-Up Findings

Programming Interpersonal Curricula for Adolescents (PICA) was the federally-funded and community-based applied research program conducted in a laboratory school. Procedures based on social learning theory were employed to improve basic reading, arithmetic, and interpersonal skills of selected students. These adolescents were designated by their teachers as having major academic and behavior problems in their original schools (Cohen, Filipczak, Slavin, & Boren, 1971).

Although no control group was used in the pilot laboratory study, the students did make large scale and important progress in attendance, reading, and arithmetic skills as compared to data provided by normative samples. In most instances, achievement test gains for PICA students were greater than that of the "normal" junior high students, exceeding 1.0 grade levels per school year.

Other information corroborated the progress noted by the standardized tests. For example, students from the first program year were found to improve their grades in regular school classes (social studies and sciences) by 1.3 grade levels (from "F" to "C−"). One-year follow-up of these same students indicated the number of juvenile charges placed against them decreased to 12 percent of that found in the year before enrollment (from 17 charges to 2 charges).

The second follow-up occurred approximately five years after the students' participation in the original program. The attitudes and performances of 15 of the original 24 adolescents were assessed on a range of self-report measures, incorporting such variables as their employment and educational status, evaluation of program participation, involvement in leisure time and community activities, relationships with friends and family, and anticipated adverse consequences of engaging in delinquent acts. Data resulting from this follow-up study did not demonstrate the long-term merits of a behavioral program with this population (McCombs, Filipczak, Friedman, & Wodarski, 1978).

Preparation Through Responsive Education Programs (PREP), a federally-funded and community-based applied research project similar in operation to PICA with the exception of its being housed in a public school, was based on social learning theory aimed at achieving a number of short-term and long-term goals with pre-delinquent children. Each goal attempted to expand the students' academic and social skills and permitted them to function more appropriately within their original academic environments. As outcome data suggest, there were significant differences between the experimental and control group scores favoring the experimental groups in academic areas such as vocabulary development, reading comprehension, language skills, arithmetic computation, mathematics application, disciplinary referrals, and class grades (Cohen & Filipczak, 1971; Filipczak, Friedman, & Reese, 1977; Filipczak & Wodarski, 1979).

Follow-up occurred approximately four years after the students participated in PREP. The behavior of 40 of the originally randomly assigned 60 adolescents was assessed on variables such as their employment and educational status, evaluation of program participation, involvement in leisure time and community activities, self-esteem, aspirations and expectations, involvement in delinquent activity, relationships with family and friends, and anticipated adverse consequences of engaging in criminal acts. Twenty-one experimental participants and 19 control group participants were located. Statistical tests were performed to assess whether those experimental participants and controls who were not located for the follow-up study were significantly different from follow-up participants on 64 program evaluation variables available for the various social and academic behaviors. The analyses reveal that the children who participated in the follow-up investigation who were exposed to the experimental manipulation are representative of the entire population of antisocial children who participated in the community-based program. Follow-up data comparisons between experimental and control group participants indicate no long-term merits of the behavioral program with this population (Wodarski & Filipczak, 1977).

The third community-based, residential treatment program (CRISIS) involved 53 pre-delinquent children with follow-up data. The immediate efficacy of the behavioral modification techniques was verified in terms of academic and social skills such as room cleaning, attending school, getting to bed on time, increasing problem solving and decision making skills, leading group discussion sessions, participating in staff meetings, preparation of discharge plans, practicing performances likely to be important in natural settings such as social and self-control skills, and so forth. However, follow-up results, including comparisons with a matched control group at three-month and nine-month intervals, indicate failure of the program to maintain desirable social outcomes for dischargees. A number of variables were compared at follow-up: grades, attendance at school, juvenile court contacts for running away, truancy, incorrigibility, criminal acts, placement changes by juvenile courts and children and family service agencies, institutional placements, family placements, and changes in foster care placements (Davidson & Wolfred, 1977).

Thus data from all three follow-up investigations indicate that behavior modification programs can achieve significant behavioral changes in pre-delinquent and delinquent children. However, the maintenance and generalization of appropriate behaviors does not readily occur. The generalization question can be thought of in terms of do behaviors occur in different relevant social environments, in the presence of significant others and at appropriate times. For example, a program that teaches conversational skills such as association and clustering of words, duration of utterances, reducing the number of interruptions, asking clear questions, the ability to make interpretive, reflective and summary statements, and certain voice qualities such as appropriate tone, and nonverbal behavior such as posture, body motion, eye contact, touching, and so forth, would have a true test of generalization when a previously labeled "delinquent" approaches a possible employment interview, a teacher, or law enforcement officer and exhibits the appropriate conversational behaviors.

Possible Avenues to the Maintenance and Generalization of Behavior Social Networks

Social Networks

Peers. Significant influencing agents in providing reinforcement for deviant or prosocial behavior are peers (Feldman & Wodarski, 1975; Kandel, 1981; Lewis & Lewis, 1984; Rose, 1972, 1977; Wahler, 1969; Wodarski, Feldman, & Flax, 1973). Even though this idea is well established, it is very difficult to develop procedures to modify the normative reinforcement structure under which peers operate (Petersen & Hamburg, 1986). It appears, however, that group contingencies may be the most appropriate procedures for modifying the manner in which peers dispense reinforcers to each other.

Group contingencies refer to reinforcements that are presented to all or most group members following the display of certain behaviors by the group or selected members. Such behaviors may be denoted by the group's accomplishment of certain tasks, such as planning job interviews or successfully resolving a problem, or by the accomplishments of specific members, such as more frequent prosocial behavior by one or two selected members. In either case a significant portion of the group's membership receives reinforcement following manifestation of the desired behavior by the entire group or by certain of its members.

Group contingencies modify behaviors most readily by producing the greatest group pressure (1) when all group members have to exhibit given behavior at a certain criterion rate or (2) when one or two group members are required to exhibit a certain rate of prosocial behavior in order for each group member to receive reinforcement. The situation and the behaviors to be modified determine which of these contingencies the worker should structure. The effectiveness with which group contingencies modify behaviors decreases as the proportion of group members who receive reinforcement decreases.

If children have been through a treatment program and have acquired necessary academic and social skills, workers could structure group contingencies that would support such behaviors through peer reinforcement. For example, John is 14 years old and three years behind in math and he exhibits various destructive behaviors such as hitting others, damaging physical property, and making loud noises in class. He goes to a behavioral program such as PREP to increase his mathematic and social skills. After he achieves the desired levels of these behaviors his peers are informed that if he continues to maintain the behaviors at acceptable rates they will periodically gain desired reinforcers. Employment of group contingencies depends on the peers cooperating and the worker offering desirable enough rewards. Reinforcers that could be utilized might include trips, food, a party, utilization of desirable facilities in the community, tickets for special events such as rock concerts and sporting events, social praise, and so forth.

Another example of how peer reinforcement influences behavior is seen in the "buddy system." Here adolescents and a social group worker determine that the group should continue intact and serve as a support system for the members once formal treatment is completed. They therefore build a buddy system into the formal structure of group operations. Under such an arrangement, group members are taught to work in subgroups of two or three as part of the group process and as part of their homework assignments. Buddies may serve as monitors who track each other's social and academic behavior, as models for effective performance and as companions who provide important feedback and reinforcement in the absence of a professional therapist. Such procedures increase the probability that the relevant behaviors will be maintained and generalized to appropriate contexts.

It is important to emphasize that the use of the social network of peers in group treatment assumes the possibility for certain members to obtain reinforcement when members other than themselves are the enactors within the group. Thus, for example, it is possible to structure a group contingency wherein all members will receive reinforcement, such as the opportunity to attend a professional sports event, if just one group member substantially improves his antisocial behavior during a given time period. Such a contingency is extremely potent for the lone enactor since all the group members will direct strong conformity pressures toward him in order to assure their own reinforcements. In contrast, if fewer members are promised reinforcements for progress made by a single member, the corresponding conformity pressures are likely to be much weaker.

For example, let us assume that a social worker has managed to make contact and develop a working relationship with a group of antisocial inner city adolescents who have been causing disturbances within the neighborhood. His/her goal in working with these youngsters may be to help them reduce their aggressive behaviors and to teach them more socially acceptable ways of problem solving and conflict management. In order to accomplish this, the social worker will have to possess valued resources which the group members desire but are unable to obtain without his assistance. These reinforcements may be, for example, the social worker's ability to have the group members gain access to a neighborhood swimming pool from which the youngsters previously have been barred because of their behavior, or the social worker's ability to secure a club room in the local community center for the group to use for meetings. In either case, the continued use of these facilities by all group members may be made contingent upon the enactment of specified prosocial behaviors by one or two of the group members or all group members. The use of group contingencies in such a manner definitely alters the reinforcing patterns exhibited by peers toward each other (Feldman & Wodarski, 1975; Wodarski & Bagarozzi, 1979).

Implementation of group contingencies is easier in institutional settings where the worker can exercise greater control over the reinforcers available to the group, can observe the reinforcing patterns of peers and thus plan corresponding interventions. However, effective use in open settings can occur if powerful enough reinforcers are isolated and used (Wodarski & Bagarozzi, 1979).

Parents. The parents' role in influencing a child may not be negated. Extensive data exist to support the training of parents as significant reinforcement agents in the maintenance process. One simple rationale for training parents in behavioral procedures is the amount of time they spend with their children (Berkowitz & Graziano, 1972; Graziano, 1977; O'Dell, 1974). Moreover, parents can be trained easily to use stimulus control techniques to influence rates of behavior and to provide appropriate consequences for desired behavior. With minimal effort parents can be taught to identify motivators to facilitate the acquisition and maintenance of appropriate behaviors, how to use contingency contracting, how to change their own behavior, and so forth. In all of these instances where the training of parents or significant others is involved, once the behavioral procedures are mastered it is essential that significant others apply them consistently (Wodarski, 1976). Use of parents in maintenance of behavior is illustrated as follows.

Fifteen-year-old Stanley had difficulties completing his home work at night. His studying difficulties were affecting his academic performances at school and as these performances deteriorated his rates of antisocial behavior increased. Stanley's parents facilitated the study process by providing a context for studying, i.e., a physical situation that had a minimal number of stimuli to disrupt the studying process, and provided appropriate reinforcement for adequate durations of studying behaviors. Moreover, his parents also played a significant role in implementing various reinforcement systems developed with school social workers, such as vouchers indicating Stanley's daily and weekly academic and social performances. This facilitated the occurrence of appropriate behaviors at school with parents providing the reinforcement. Ongoing research tends to demonstrate that parents can play a significant role in modifying the following behaviors exhibited by their children: aggressive, delinquent, noncompliant, social, leadership, independence, and so forth (Rinn & Markel, 1977).

Possible difficulties in the use of parents in behavioral programs center around their frequent inability to refrain from attempting to modify their children's behavior while observing them during the baseline period. In such instances, the social worker may arrange to make home visits during which he can model the self-control behaviors for the clients, offer constructive feedback, coach them in the use of specific techniques and supervise their performances through providing guided practice instructions so that they can develop the skills necessary for making accurate behavioral assessments.

If parents find it difficult to locate sources of reinforcement which can later be used to reward their children, the social worker may have to make another series of home visits to help them overcome this difficulty. If another group member is skilled in behavioral observation and assessment, however, he may serve as a buddy who can help other group members identify those satisfying behaviors which frequently are engaged in by their children, such as watching particular television programs, eating certain types of foods and treats and playing certain games. Once these reinforcing behaviors have been identified, their use as incentives can be discussed and evaluated with the other group members at the next session.

Parents' involvement in such a manner facilitates the alteration of behavior. However, the worker must guage the parents' motivation to implement the procedures consistently. Additionally, problems may be avoided if the peer reinforcement patterns correspond to the parents'.

Peers and Parents Combined. Intervention programs should assist adolescents to identify and examine peer pressure and explore ways to make individual, deliberate decisions, especially since peers have significant impact on each other's behaviors. Thus we posit that interventions should be offered through a peer group experience. Peer learning structures should create a learning situation in which the performance of each group member furthers the attainment of overall group goals. This increases individual members' support for group performance, strengthens performance under a variety of similar circumstances, and further enhances the attainment of group goals. Group reward structures capitalize on peer influence and peer reinforcement. These are considered to be some of the most potent variables in the acquisition, alteration, and maintenance of prosocial norms among youths (Buckholdt & Wodarski, 1978). Peer programs that foster the adolescent's sense of self-worth, awareness of one's own feelings, and assertiveness will help adolescents learn to act in their own interest, with a stronger sense of control over their own lives.

The other most significant variable that influences an adolescent's behavior is the family. In particular, parents serve as models (Kandel, 1980). Furthermore, particular types of parenting behavior (lack of positive reinforcement, setting appropriate expectations, communication skills, and problem solving skills) can serve as predictors of adolescent behaviors (Pulkkinen, 1983), and can discriminate between adolescent prosocial and antisocial behavior (Rees & Wilborn, 1983). Therefore, it would appear that teaching problem solving and communication skills would be critical ingredients of an adolescent intervention program.

By introducing interventions with peers and parents, it can be determined which is most effective, either singularly or combined, in helping adolescents. Such interventions will set the groundwork to test a major hypothesis of social control theory; that is, by employing two foci, both individuals and families, behavior is altered more readily than by employing only one.

Training Socially Relevant Behaviors

The choice of behaviors that have a probability of being reinforced is essential. Nothing beats acquiring skills such as vocational, academic and social that can help an individual gain reinforcement in the real world (Kazdin, 1977; Stokes & Baer, 1977). Treatment approaches based on developing understanding, insight, and so forth, may produce negative results because they do not teach the adolescent skills that secure reinforcement for them and thus are not maintained by the natural reinforcement system in which the child operates once he leaves the therapeutic situation.

For example, Jane is 16 years old and has difficulties in meeting and conversing with friends. This has contributed significantly to her development of a negative self-image. Moreover, the lack of attention from appropriate significant others played a significant role in her engaging in delinquent activities of truancy and thefts of students' and adults' possessions. Through the process of assertive training she is taught how to initiate and maintain conversations in terms of giving and receiving compliments and asking questions that elicit future interactions. Such behaviors bring her new rewarding experiences such as making new friends and gaining popularity. These experiences decrease her negative self-image and bring her the attention she desires.

Thus, increasing academic, vocational, and social behaviors that will help the individual secure reinforcers in the future increase the probability of maintenance and generalization of behavior.

However, a crucial question to be asked is what ethical obligations does the worker have if such behaviors are acquired and the client's environment does not provide sufficient reinforcement.

Changing the Conditions of Training

When therapeutic services are provided in only one context, generally the therapist's office, and by only one worker, generalization of behavior is impeded. According to social behavioral theory, various stimuli of the therapeutic context become discriminative stimuli for the behavior. These discriminative stimuli then control the amount of generalization that can take place in the behavior. Thus, therapy provided by only one worker and in only one context substantially narrows the number of discriminative stimuli that control the behavior and thus reduces the maintenance and generalization of achieved desirable behavioral changes (Holmes, 1971; Kazdin, 1977; Waters & McCallum, 1973).

To facilitate the generalization and maintenance of behavior we should utilize multiple workers and/or varied training situations. For example, Jack, age 16, is seen by two different workers, one a male and the other a female. One of his difficulties related to his talking back to his parents, i.e., when they refused his requests, he raised his voice, muttered unintelligible statements, was unable to state problems in an inoffensive manner, and he could not state options and negotiate them in a reciprocal way so that reinforcers for both parties were exchanged. In addition to varying the therapist, therapy sessions were held in some instances at either worker's home. These two processes facilitated the maintenance and generalization of behavior and helped ensure that behaviors acquired were not limited only to a narrow range of discriminative stimuli.

The social worker's role at the close of treatment is to help facilitate transfer and maintenance of relevant behavior to a variety of different stimuli. A variety of techniques can be used toward this end:

1. Repeating practice of newly acquired skills so that they are over-learned, that is, connected to a greater variety of stimuli and thus becoming more resistant to extinction.

2. Holding treatment sessions in a variety of environmental settings, finding different relevant locations where newly acquired behaviors can be practiced, and using a variety of workers to increase the number of discriminative stimuli to which the behaviors are connected.

3. Using role plays which present unpredictable, stressful and novel situations to the adolescents which they may encounter once they leave therapy. For example, role play simulation exercises will be used to help students practice how to refuse drugs in a socially acceptable manner within normal peer contexts. The basic aim is to help adolescents develop more effective ways of dealing with social pressures to consume drugs. Specific situations will be practiced where individuals apply pressure to persuade others to consume excessive amounts of drugs. Students practice reactions to statements like: "One drink won't hurt you," "What kind of friend are you?" or "Just have a little one, I'll make sure you won't have any more" (Foy, Miller, Eisler, & O'Toole, 1976).

4. Helping the adolescent join already existing community groups which will foster the maintenance of new behaviors, e.g., joining "Y" sports programs, Weight Watchers and other such natural groups which provide a social system that reinforces the behavior.

5. Using multiple models who exhibit the desired terminal behavior not only to facilitate the acquisition of the behavior but also to increase the number of discriminative stimuli which control the behavior, thus increasing the potential for the generalization of the behavior to desired contexts.

Once treatment has terminated follow-up interviews, telephone calls and mailed questionnaires should be used by the therapist in order to assess whether changes are being maintained or to determine whether new difficulties have cropped up. Follow-up procedures of this type also serve as additional supports for maintaining behavioral gains. This is especially true if follow-up meetings are held and the adolescent knows that maintenance of behavioral gains will be reinforced by other group members.

Gradually Removing or Fading the Contingencies

Variable Schedules of Reinforcement. As behaviors are being acquired workers will want to reinforce them every time they occur. Once the behaviors reach the appropriate levels we want to reduce the amount of reinforcement that we give children. Here workers will want to use some type of a schedule of variable reinforcement, that is, not reinforcing the behavior every time it occurs.

For example, 15-year-old Mary has difficulties preparing to go to school, i.e., getting dressed, collecting necessary items such as lunch money and her notebook, and fussing about why she has to go to school, why certain clothes are necessary, and so forth. These difficulties usually cause arguments with her parents on an average of three times a week. The school social worker in graphing her performances at school on academic and social tasks, found a direct relationship between the altercations and school performance. Once the behaviors to be changed decreased to appropriate levels following a behavioral change program, the school social worker instructed the parents not to reinforce the child every time appropriate behaviors occurred.

Various procedures are available to thin reinforcement schedules. Parents may choose to gradually and proportionately reduce the days reinforcement can be secured. They can alternate reinforcement of various behaviors and the types of reinforcers used, that is incorporating more and more of the rewards available in the client's natural environment, and so forth. In Mary's case once behaviors achieved desirable levels, reinforcement was provided every other day. The behaviors of getting to school on time and not being negative were not rewarded simultaneously and the parents shifted from material rewards to praise. Many behavioral programs are characterized by an approach where parents are taught behavioral principles. However, the direct application of variable schedules of reinforcement is not adequately covered.

Delayed Reinforcement

Various procedures can be utilized to increase the maintenance of behaviors through the use of delayed reinforcement. Once a behavior is established at the desired level, tokens which initially were provided every time a behavior occurs can be provided instead at the end of the day, every other day, weekly, and so forth. The idea is that longer and longer periods should elapse between when a behavior is exhibited and when a reinforcement is provided for that behavior. This process reduces the behavior's dependence upon reinforcement. Likewise, as behaviors are established at desirable levels, rewards that are available in the environment where the behavior naturally occurs should be incorporated.

By varying the process of reinforcement administration the ability of the person to discriminate when reinforcement will be available for the performance of the behavior decreases, and this increases the performance of desired behavior.

Data indicate that initially all behaviors should be reinforced in the treatment plan. As the client acquires target behaviors fewer behaviors are reinforced. For example, the behavioral change program may call for the alteration of the following behaviors: poor conversational skills, non-participation in setting vocational objectives, failure to follow reasonable requests, inadequate academic performances, disruptive behaviors in school such as hitting others, damaging physical property, running away, making loud noises, using aggressive verbal statements, throwing objects such as paper, candy, erasers, and chairs, and poor job interviewing skills. As the behaviors decrease or increase to the desired levels, the worker may alternate the behaviors chosen to be reinforced. Initially behaviors may be reinforced immediately after they occur. After the desired frequency has been attained the behavior may be reinforced once daily, weekly, and so forth.

Self-Control Procedures

Advancement of this particular area in the field of behavior modification has been substantial (Thoresen & Mahoney, 1974). Self-control techniques help social workers ensure that the treatment plans discussed in office interviews are actually carried out in the client's environment. Furthermore, they may enable a client to design a modification plan without the aid of the therapist when other problems are encountered after therapy (Wodarski, 1975). Clients can be trained to define behaviors, record behaviors, to consequent the behaviors, to utilize stimulus control procedures, and so forth. When such processes are implemented by the client, the number of learning trials and the contexts in which desired behaviors are practiced are increased, thus increasing the probability that the behaviors will be maintained and generalized (Staats, 1975).

For example, a 16-year-old female delinquent referred for treatment by the juvenile court as a result of excessive absences from school, general idleness, and lack of academic skills, desired to reduce her weight since it brought her negative criticism from significant peers. She was taught how to covertly positively reinforce herself by eating only at meals and for refusing requests for additional food at other times. Other self-management procedures also were incorporated into the treatment plan. Since feeling anxious increased her eating, she was also taught progressive relaxation to reduce her general level of tension. During the 16 interviews she began to lose weight and her general level of tension decreased. Concurrently, she started to develop better social relationships with her peers and her academic performance at school improved. A follow-up interview four months after treatment termination indicated the teenager continued to be successful in relaxing herself and continued to lose weight.

Implications for Practice

The reason many behavioral programs show initial positive results and a subsequent lack of generalization and maintenance is likely due to lack of proper attention to procedures for maintenance and generalization in the planning stages of the program.

In summary, it is emphasized that due to the available mechanisms for delivery of services, such as home visits and work within the client's total environment, social workers are well equipped to provide services necessary to ensure the maintenance and generalization of behavior. In addition, with new training they will be able to evaluate how significant others reinforce the client and how these individuals can be trained to maintain certain desirable behaviors exhibited by the client. This will add to the theoretical knowledge necessary to understand how natural reinforcement systems operate to facilitate the maintenance of behavior.

REFERENCES

Berkowitz, B. P., & Graziano, A. M. (1972). Training parents as behavior therapists: A review. *Behavior Research and Therapy, 10,* 297–317.

Buckholdt, D., & Wodarski, J. S. (1978). The effects of different reinforcement systems on cooperative behavior exhibited by children in classroom contexts. *Journal of Research and Development in Education, 12*(1), 50–68.

Cohen, H. L., & Filipczak, J. (1971). *A new learning environment.* San Francisco: Jossey-Bass.

Cohen, H. L., Filipczak, J., Slavin, J., & Boren, J. (1971). *Programming interpersonal curricula for adolescents (PICA), project year three: A laboratory model.* Silver Spring, MD: Educational Facility Press, Institute for Behavioral Research.

Davidson, W. S., & Wolfred, T. R. (1977). Evaluation of a community-based behavior modification program for prevention of delinquency: The failure of success. *Community Mental Health Journal, 13*(4), 296–306.

Feldman, R. A., & Wodarski, J. S. (1975). *Contemporary approaches to group treatment.* San Francisco: Jossey-Bass.

Filipczak, J., Friedman, R. M., & Reese, S. (1977). PREP: Educational programming to prevent juvenile problems. In J. Stumphauzer (Ed.), *Progress in behavior therapy with delinquents.* Springfield, IL: Charles C Thomas.

Filipczak, J., & Wodarski, J. S. (1979). Behavioral intervention in public schools: Implementing and evaluating a model. *Corrective and Social Psychiatry and Journal of Behavioral Technology Methods and Therapy, 25,* 104–116.

Foy, C. W., Miller, P. M., Eisler, R. M., & O'Toole, O. H. (1976). Social skills training to teach alcoholics to refuse drinks effectively. *Journal of Studies on Alcohol, 37*(9), 1340–1345.

Graziano, A. M. (1977). Parents as behavior therapists. In M. Hersen, R. Eisler, & P. Miller (Eds.), *Progress in behavior modification* (Vol. 4). New York: Academic Press.

Holmes, D. S. (1971). Round robin therapy: A technique for implementing the effects of psychotherapy. *Journal of Consulting and Clinical Psychology, 37,* 324–331.

Kandel, D. (1980). Developmental stages in adolescent drug involvement. In D. Lettieri (Ed.), *Theories of drug abuse* [DHHS Publication No. (ADM) 80-967]. Washington, DC: U.S. Government Printing Office.

Kandel, D. (1981). Adolescent marijuana use: Role of parents and peers. *Science, 181,* 1067–1070.

Kazdin, A. E. (1975). *Behavior modification in applied settings.* Homewood, IL: Dorsey Press.

Kazdin, A. E. (1977). *The token economy.* New York: Plenum.

Kazdin, A. E., Esveldt-Dawson, K., French, N. H., & Unis, A. S. (1987). Problem-solving skills training and relationship therapy in the treatment of antisocial child behavior. *Journal of Consulting and Clinical Psychology, 55*(1), 76–85.

Koegel, R. L., & Rincover, A. (1977). Research on the difference between generalization and maintenance in extra-therapy responding. *Journal of Applied Behavior Analysis, 10,* 1–12.

Lewis, C. E., & Lewis, M. (1984). Peer pressure and risk-taking behaviors in children. *American Journal of Public Health, 74*(6), 580–584.

Lovaas, O. I. (1987). Behavioral treatment and normal educational and intellectual functioning in young autistic children. *Journal of Consulting and Clinical Psychology, 55*(1), 3–9.

McCombs, D., Filipczak, J., Friedman, R., & Wodarski, J. S. (1978). Long-term follow-up of behavior modification with high-risk adolescents. *Criminal Justice and Behavior, 5*(1), 21–34.

O'Dell, S. (1974). Training parents in behavior modification: A review. *Psychological Bulletin, 81*, 418–433.

Petersen, A. C., & Hamburg, B. A. (1986). Adolescence: A developmental approach to problems and psychopathology. *Behavior Therapy, 17*(5), 480–499.

Pulkkinen, L. (1983). Youthful smoking and drinking in a longitudinal perspective. *Journal of Youth and Adolescence, 12*, 253–283.

Rees, C. D., & Wilborn, B. L. (1983). Correlates of drug abuse in adolescents: A comparison of families of drug users with families of nondrug users. *Journal of Youth and Adolescence, 12*, 55–63.

Rinn, R. C., & Markle, A. (1977). *Positive parenting.* Cambridge, MA: Research Media, Inc.

Rose, S. D. (1972). *Treating children in groups.* San Francisco: Jossey-Bass.

Rose, S. D. (1977). *Group therapy: A behavioral approach.* Englewood Cliffs, NJ: Prentice-Hall.

Rychtarik, R. G., Foy, D. W., Scott, T., Lokey, L., & Prue, D. M. (1987). Five-six-year follow-up of broad-spectrum behavioral treatment for alcoholism: Effects of training controlled drinking skills. *Journal of Consulting and Clinical Psychology, 55*(1), 106–108.

Schinke, S. P. (Ed.). (1981). *Behavioral methods in social welfare.* Hawthorne, NY: Aldine.

Staats, A. W. (1975). *Social behaviorism.* Homewood, IL: Dorsey Press.

Stokes, T. F., & Baer, D. M. (1977). An implicit technology of generalization. *Journal of Applied Behavior Analysis, 10*, 349–367.

Thoresen, C. E., & Mahoney, M. J. (1974). *Behavioral self-control.* New York: Holt, Rinehart and Winston.

Wahler, R. G. (1969). Selling generality: Some specific and general effects of child behavior therapy. *Journal of Applied Behavior Analysis, 2*, 239–248.

Waters, F. W., & McCallum, R. N. (1973). The basis of behavior therapy: Mentalistic or behavioristic? A reply to E. A. Locke. *Behavior Research and Therapy, 11*, 157–163.

Wodarski, J. S. (1975). The application of cognitive behavior modification techniques to social work practice. *International Social Work, 18*(3), 50–57.

Wodarski, J. S. (1976). Procedural steps in the implementation of behavior modifiction programs in open settings. *Journal of Experimental Psychiatry and Behavior Therapy, 7*(2), 133–136.

Wodarski, J. S., & Bagarozzi, D. (1979). *Behavioral social work.* New York: Human Sciences Press.

Wodarski, J. S., Feldman, R. A., & Flax, N. (1973). Social learning theory in group work practice with antisocial children. *Clinical Social Work Journal, 1*(2), 78–93.

Wodarski, J. S., & Filipczak, J. (1977, May). *Long-term follow-up of behavior modification with high-risk adolescents: Cohort two.* Paper presented at Johns Hopkins University Symposium on Alternative Educational Programs for Disruptive Secondary School Students, Baltimore, Maryland.

Chapter 7

CHILDREN

Traditionally, childhood has been portrayed as a carefree period in the life span, when enjoyable times are had by all. In reality, however, the transition from childhood to adulthood is fraught with psychological, sociological, and physical changes (Elkind, 1984).

Childhood today is not in the same sphere as was growing up in the 1960's or 1970's. In the past, a majority of children had the support system of relatively warm, caring families, stable school environments, and trusting adults. Contrary to this, a significant percentage of today's children are maturing in a state of relative fear. Family breakups either are being experienced personally by the child, or observed in the homes of their contemporaries (Wodarski, 1982). Demographic trends have led to overcrowded schools where an impersonal atmosphere contributes to a sense of alienation (Holinger & Offer, 1981; Packard, 1983; Wenz, 1979). Primary emphasis, however, can be placed on the inability of children to form close interpersonal relationships with adults at home and outside the family structure. The alienation experienced by both children and adolescents has long-term effects on the individual's outlook on both moral and social issues. Alienation itself breeds a lack of trust within the child (Arnold, 1983; Coles, 1983). Society in the 1980's tends to relegate children to children's activities and adults to adult activities in social settings. Felt rejection in the child results in part from this lack of intergenerational interaction (Kaplan, Robbins, & Martin, 1983). Helplessness and hopelessness characterize the environment of many children (Berkovitz, 1981; Miller, 1981; Petzel & Riddle, 1981; Tabachnick, 1981). This societal atmosphere complicates development for children with special needs.

This chapter will center on the children with special needs who are developmentally disabled in terms of mental retardation and autism, abused and neglected, sexually abused, and who exhibit violent behavior.

137

Developmental Disabilities

Nearly four million persons have developmental disabilities—disabilities that occur before a person is 22 and that have long-lasting, serious effects upon that person's life.

According to Public Law 98-527, the Developmental Disabilities Act of 1984:

> The term 'developmental disability' means a severe, chronic disability of a person which—
>
> (A) is attributable to a mental or physical impairment or a combination of mental and physical impairments;
> (B) is manifested before the person attains age twenty-two
> (C) is likely to continue indefinitely
> (D) results in substantial function limitations in three or more of the following areas of major life activity: (i) self-care, (ii) receptive and expressive language, (iii) learning, (iv) mobility, (v) self-direction, (vi) capacity for independent living, and (vii) economic self-sufficiency; and
> (E) reflects the person's need for a combination and sequence of special, interdisciplinary, or generic care, treatment, or other services which are of lifelong or extended duration and are individually planned and coordinated . . .

If a child is born with a disability, or acquires one in childhood or adolescence, early diagnosis and intervention services can lessen the effects of that disability; ongoing, effective management and treatment of a disability may mean the difference between future dependence and independence for a person who is disabled.

To be most effective, such management and treatment often require the coordinated efforts of a range of highly trained professionals from a variety of disciplines—medicine, psychology, physical and occupational therapy, speech therapy, education, vocational training, and the social services, to mention some of the primary elements in this array of services.

The needs of someone with a developmental disability are quite different from those of a person who becomes disabled later in life. The most common developmental disabilities in this country are mental retardation, cerebral palsy, autism, and epilepsy; the child or young adult who is disabled by these or other developmental disabilities will have different experiences—personal, social, educational, and medical—than other children. Adapting to the disability will involve, in many cases, learning to walk, communicate, or carry out daily activities in ways that differ from those of the nondisabled person. Unlike an older person who becomes disabled, the person with a developmental disability will usually have no pre-disability work record, and no access to workmen's compensation, unemployment insurance, or work-related medical insurance.

Because a developmental disability affects all aspects of a person's life throughout that person's life, one of the most important elements of the statutory definition of this form of disability is emphasis on the "person's need for a combination and sequence of special, interdisciplinary, or generic care, treatment, or other services which are of lifelong or of extended duration, and are individually planned and coordinated."

Mental Retardation

Dramatic changes in conceptualizations and treatment approaches have revolutionized the field of mental retardation during the last few decades. Changes have occurred in our understanding of what mental retardation is, of how mental retardation differs from other learning disorders and mental illness, and of its many causes. These changes have resulted from both basic and applied research examining the cognitive and learning processes of mentally retarded and intellectually average children. Not surprisingly, this research has also precipitated the development of sophisticated strategies for assessment and treatment of mentally retarded children and adolescents.

Description and Definition. The most widely cited and influential definition of mental retardation is that presented by the American Association on Mental Deficiency (AAMD) (Grossman, 1983). According to this definition, mental retardation refers to "significantly subaverage general intellectual functioning existing concurrently with deficits in adaptive behavior and manifested during the developmental period" (Grossman, 1983, p. 1). This definition has several components. First, subaverage intellectual functioning involves performance two or more standard deviations below the mean on an individually administered general intelligence test. Within the subaverage range, four levels of retardation are defined—mild, moderate, severe, and profound—corresponding to successive standard deviations below the mean. Second, deficits in adaptive behavior are defined in terms of the degree to which individuals fail to meet age and cultural standards of personal independence and social responsibility. While expectations concerning adaptive behavior vary for different ages and levels of mental retardation, deficits in adaptive behavior are generally reflected in the following areas: sensorimotor development, communication skills, socialization, academic skills, reasoning and judgment, and vocational skills. Although intellectual deficiencies are essential for the diagnosis of a child as mentally retarded, it is adaptive behavior deficits that dictate his or her need for "special" training and the type of training needed. Finally, the developmental period is considered the period between birth and the 18th birthday (Grossman, 1983).

Mentally retarded children are often viewed as comprising two distinct but overlapping populations (Zigler, 1967). Members of one group typically show evidence of central nervous system pathology, often have "associated handicaps and stigmata," usually have IQs in the moderately retarded range or below, and are diagnosed as mentally retarded at birth or in early childhood (Grossman, 1983). In contrast, members of the other group manifest no signs of neurological dysfunction or other readily detectable physical or clinical signs of mental retardation, have IQs in the mildly retarded range, and, often, are members of the lowest socioeconomic groups. Whereas these children frequently share many characteristics with learning disabled children, they have a lower measured intelligence and are often psychosocially disadvantaged.

Autism

Autism is a rare disorder, occurring at a rate of only 2 to 4 per 10,000 people (American Psychiatric Association, 1980). It is a pervasive, severely handicapping condition that begins in the child's earliest months and typically lasts a lifetime. The unmanageable and often bewildering behaviors of the autistic child can create a chaotic family environment; identification and assessment are thus essential not only for the proper care of the child but also for the welfare of the entire family.

Differential Diagnosis. Two major, overlapping diagnostic schema for the identification of autism are in common use at this time: that of the third edition of the *Diagnostic and Statistical Manual of Mental Disorders* (DSM–III; American Psychiatric Association, 1980), and that of the National Society for Children and Adults with Autism (NSAC; 1978).

According to *DSM-III* (American Psychiatric Association, 1980), the essential criteria for the diagnosis of infantile autism are (a) onset of symptoms before 30 months of age; (b) a pervasive lack of response to other people; (c) gross deficits in the development of language; (d) in children who do speak peculiar language, with oddities such as echolalia and reversal of pronouns; and (e) bizarre responses to the environment, such as resistance to change or a fascination with animate or inanimate objects. These symptoms must be found in the absence of indication of thought disorder such as hallucinations or delusions.

The NSAC (National Society for Autistic Children, 1978) definition of autism emphasizes (a) onset before 30 months of age; (b) disturbances in the developmental rate or sequence, such as normal development in some areas and delay in others; (c) abnormal responses to sensory stimuli; (d) disturbances in the development of speech, language, and cognitive skills; and (e) abnormalities in relationships to people, events, and objects.

Schopler and Sloan (1983) indicate that the NSAC definition encompasses a larger group of children than that of *DSM-III*, since the NSAC drafters were attempting not only to clarify the identification of autism, but also to increase the availability of appropriate resources for children with autistic behaviors. Thus, while the narrower DSM-III definition may have more value for some research and for greater precision in communication, the broader NSAC definition may be more useful in providing help for many children whose behavior resembles those of the child with infantile autism.

In distinguishing autism from other disorders with overlapping symptoms, one must be sensitive to several issues. One is that as the autistic child grows older, the intensity of the symptoms may be dampened; thus, greater expertise and a more careful developmental history is needed to recognize the presence of the disorder. DeMyer (1979) notes that the early onset of symptoms in autism is insidious, occurring from late in the first year through the second, tending to grow worse in the preschool years, then improving at about 4 years of age. It must be emphasized the "improvement" is relative, and that a decrease in severity nonetheless leaves these youngsters pervasively handicapped, often mute, self-stimulating, terrified of change, and profoundly withdrawn from others.

Ornitz, Guthrie, and Farley (1977) report that many young autistic children are thought to be mentally retarded or neurologically impaired before they are identified as autistic. These authors indicate that in half the cases they studied, parents were concerned about their child's development by the time he or she was 14 months old, yet the median age for correct diagnosis was 46 months. In light of the importance of early intervention, such delays are unfortunate.

Childhood-onset pervasive development disorder, a condition that might be confused with autism, differs significantly in that the onset of symptoms is after 30 months but before 12 years (American Psychiatric Association, 1980). Although this distinction may sound clear-cut, it is often difficult, when relying on retrospective report, to determine when a child's symptoms began. The diagnostic distinction is probably less important for treatment purposes than for some research.

Infantile autism must also be distinguished from schizophrenia in childhood. In childhood schizophrenia the onset of symptoms is typically later than in autism and over time will come to include clear indication of thought disorder, such as hallucinations and delusions (Eggers, 1978).

The majority of autistic children test in the mentally retarded range on standardized measures of intelligence. According to *DSM-III* (American Psychiatric Association, 1980), 40% of children with infantile autism have IQs below 50 and only 30% have IQs of 70 or better. Hence, one must take care to distinguish mental retardation from infantile autism.

Although some mentally retarded children will exhibit autistic behaviors, including social withdrawal and severe language deficits, it is usually possible to discriminate the retarded youngster from the autistic since mentally retarded children do not typically show the full syndrome of autism. Ando and Yoshimura (1979) note that the autistic child's social withdrawal changes relatively little with time, whereas the retarded child becomes less withdrawn through intervention or the passage of time. Likewise, language in autistic children is likely to be impaired to a greater degree than one would expect on the basis of IQ, whereas there is usually a closer link between IQ and language in retarded children (e.g., Spreat, Roszkowski, Isett, & Alderfer, 1980).

Child Abuse and Neglect

The effects of child abuse and neglect described in the literature produce a diverse and lengthy list: psychological and emotional reactions in terms of fear, anger, mood changes, hysterical seizures, hyperactivity, nightmares, anxiety, guilt, somatic complaints, withdrawal and isolation, and suicidal tendencies; intrapersonal-social effects such as poor self-image and low self-esteem; and school performance such as underachievement, interpersonal difficulties with parents and peers, learning disabilities and behavioral difficulties (Egeland, Sroufe, & Erickson, 1983; Garbarino, 1983; Kinard, 1980a, 1980b; Lamphear, 1985; Martin, 1976; Schinke, Schilling, Kirkham, Gilchrist, Barth, & Blythe, 1986). The predictive factors described generally focus on the personal characteristics of the abuser, the personal characteristics of the victim, the family dynamics, social structure of communities, and economic factors (Belsky, 1980; Rosenberg & Reppucci, 1985).

Initial data indicate the cost to the individual and society due to child maltreatment is substantial in terms of psychological and emotional reactions, inadequate self-image and depression, interpersonal difficulties in terms of parenting and peer relationships, the lack of academic and cognitive skills to participate in the marketplace, and development of subsequent careers in delinquency, violence, criminality, and so forth (Deykin, Alpert, & McNamarra, 1985; Silver, 1969). With the incidence of child maltreatment increasing, it is a requisite that its effects must be delineated, relevant educational services and human services must be incorporated that can be utilized to reduce dependency and increase self-sufficiency, and the intergenerational cycle that characterizes child maltreatment must be broken through the development of empirically based knowledge.

Currently such various approaches as psychopathological, sociological, social-situational, social learning, and family systems are used in the treatment of parents who abuse their children.

The *psychopathological model* of child abuse emphasizes direct services (David, 1979; Grodner, 1977). The services provided may consist of individual, group and lay treatment, volunteer companions, and self-help groups. These services focus on the psychopathology of the parent and provide him/her with the necessary supports for maintaining the family intact. Treatment goals include helping the parent establish trusting, gratifying relationships with the therapist and with other adults, improving the parent's chronically low self-esteem, enabling the parent to derive pleasure from the child and from his or her own accomplishments, and helping the parent to understand the relationship between his or her own painful childhood and current actions and attitudes toward the child (Garbarino & Stocking, 1980; Green, 1978a, 1978b).

The *sociological model's* approach to intervention in child abuse emphasizes the need for wide-ranging changes in social values and structures.

Parke and Collmer (1975) state that prevention of child abuse, according to this model, would require reconceptualization of childhood, of children's rights and of childrearing. Major sources of stress and frustration, which are felt to trigger child abuse episodes, would need to be eliminated (Egeland, Breitenbucher, & Rosenberg, 1980; Koerlin, 1980). Some of the general suggestions offered by proponents of this model include:

1. Providing adequate income through employment and/or guaranteed income maintenance.
2. Comprehensive health care and social services.
3. Decent and adequate housing.
4. Comprehensive educational opportunities geared toward the realization of each person's potential.
5. Cultural and recreational facilities.

Other proposals that are more specific to child abuse involve comprehensive family planning programs, family life education programs, and support services such as day care and homemaker services.

The *social-situational model's* approach to treatment is based upon the assumption that the cause of child abuse lies not in the individual, but in the social situation, which may, in turn, be maintaining abusive patterns (Frodi & Lamb, 1980; Garbarino, 1979; Parke & Collmer, 1975). This model focuses upon the modification of observable behavior in the home environment. It emphasizes that there is a high degree of interdependence between the abusive parent and the child and, therefore, both must be involved in treatment. This model advocates the use of techniques to modify the child's behavior such as reinforcement, time out, and verbal reasoning. Programs for parent education and retraining are suggested as a means of modifying the parent's disciplinary methods.

The *family systems model's* approach to treatment resembles that of the social-situational model in that it too emphasizes changing the family's patterns of interactions and behaviors. However, this model emphasizes that the underlying structure and organization of the family must change to prevent the recurrence of the same destructive patterns (Levitt, 1977). The therapist must work with the family to find new, more attractive roles for all members of the family. The role of the therapist is collaborative and the parents are respected as the source of control in the family.

Finally, the *social learning* approach to treatment involves the identification of behavioral goals, specific techniques for achieving these goals, and the use of social reinforcers to facilitate this process (Crozier & Katz,

1981; Mastria, 1979; Tracy & Clark, 1974). This approach recommends the use of treatment personnel who are of similar socioeconomic and racial background as the abusive parents as it is felt that the parents are more likely to respond positively to these workers.

These approaches are characterized by their focus on only certain elements contributing to child abuse. This singular focus limits the effectiveness of the various treatment regimens. This section on child abuse elaborates an empirical rationale based on behavioral science literature for a comprehensive treatment program consisting of child management, marital enrichment, vocational skills enrichment, and interpersonal enrichment components.

Scope of the Problem of Child Abuse

Assessing the seriousness and complexity of this social problem presents a difficult task. Three basic criteria were suggested by Manis (1974) to determine the seriousness of social problems: the extent of the frequency of the problem, the severity or level of harmfulness of the problem, and the primacy of the problem (its causal impact on other problems).

If we were to apply this set of criteria in analyzing the problem of child abuse, we would begin by looking at the incidence of the problem. Information regarding incidence, however, is confounded by several factors: differences in definitions between states and varied reporting mechanisms; the combining of abuse and neglect in the reporting statutes and statistics of some states; problems in determining whether reports of abuse have been substantiated; and, perhaps most importantly, the unavailability of data on the number of cases of abuse that take place within the private confines of a family and are never reported (Green, 1978a, 1978b).

Webb and Friedman (1976) proposed to employ randomized response techniques with a probability sample drawn from the entire United States in an effort to determine actual incidences of abuse. However, most estimates of the incidence of abuse use only reported cases as their starting point while failing to address the issue of unreported cases. Nagi (1975) arrived at an estimated annual incidence of approximately 260,000 cases while Cohen and Sussman (1975) have estimated 41,104 annual cases of abuse. Nagi based his estimate on the number of cases reported to a sample of county agencies and applied a correction factor for the number of cases typically substantiated. Cohen and Sussman applied the same technique but based their estimates on a sample of data from different states. Helfer and Kempe (1976) indicate that there were approximately 550,000 incidences of suspected child abuse in the United States in 1975. Newberger (1977) combined the estimates of incidence of abuse and neglect and arrived at a figure in excess of one million. These estimates, though widely diverse, illustrate the severity of this social problem.

The second criterion, the severity of the consequences of abuse, is probably a more valid indicator of the seriousness of the problem, even though Cohen and Sussman (1975) suggest that estimates of deaths resulting from child abuse are about as variable as total incidence estimates. Blumberg (1974) estimated that 25% of all fractures diagnosed in children under five result from abuse. Even more frightening is the evidence that child abuse is currently regarded as the leading cause of death in children and as a significant public health problem (Green 1978a, 1978b). Data on the frequency of irreversible but nonfatal physical injuries resulting from abuse are very important for a total evaluation of the seriousness of the problem of abuse but these data are frequently confounded.

The third criterion, the causal impact of the problem on other problems, is difficult to apply in the area of abuse, mainly due to the lack of follow-up studies. The long-term effects of abuse may be determined by the general conditions under which the abused child is raised (Elmer, 1967, 1975; Friedman & Morse, 1974; Martin, 1972; Martin, Beezley, Conway, & Kempe, 1974; Morse, Sahler, & Friedman, 1970; Rolston, 1971). Abused children raised outside of their own homes (Elmer, 1967; Morse et al., 1970), and children raised in homes characterized as stable suffered fewer long-term effects than did those raised in less stable homes (Martin et al., 1974). That the influence of the overall living conditions is greater than the influence of the actual abuse itself is supported further by Rolston (1971) who looked at formerly abused children living in foster care, and Friedman and Morse (1974) and Elmer (1975) who compared abused children with accident victims.

It appears that the behavioral and psychological effects of abuse may be reversible, but unless the environment is improved either through an effective treatment program or removal of the child to a new home, the abused child will likely develop severe mental and physical health problems. Thus the effects of child abuse are not only immediately evident, but unfortunately consequences endure.

Rationale for Comprehensive Treatment Program

It appears that the behavioral and psychological effects of abuse may be reversible, but unless the environment is improved, either through an effective treatment program or removal of the child to a new home, the abused child will likely develop severe mental and physical health problems. Thus the effects of child abuse are not only immediately evident, but unfortunately consequences endure.

Data indicate that parents who abuse their children face multiple social and psychological difficulties. The clearest empirical finding with regard to child abuse seems to be the lack of consistence by the parent or parents in the handling of their children and the consequent lack of effectiveness in managing the child's behavior (Tracy & Clark, 1974; Elmer, 1967; Derdeyn, 1977; Young, 1964). It has also been pointed out that another common feature of relationships between abusive parents and their children is unrealistic expectations by the parents about what constitutes appropriate behavior at each developmental stage, such as when the child can respond to reasonable requests, length of attention span, ability to entertain themselves, and so forth (Green, 1978a, 1978b; Larry, 1970; Pollack & Steele, 1972; Spinetta & Rigler, 1972; Steele, 1970; Steele & Pollack, 1968). These data provide support for the position that abusive parents would stand to benefit from specific training in what to expect from their children, in procedures for teaching social skills and tasks to their children, and the appropriate application of child management procedures.

Another empirical finding of substance has been the high degree of marital strain evident in abusive families (and the interpersonal strain between unmarried adult partners) (Elmer, 1967; Green, 1978b; Johnson & Morse, 1968; Kempe & Helfer, 1972; Lukianowicz, 1971, 1972; Melnick & Hurley, 1969; Milner & Ayoub, 1980; Nurse, 1964; Smith, 1975; Smith, Hanson, & Noble, 1974; Thomson, Paget, Bates, Mesch, & Putnam, 1971; Young, 1964). In view of this finding, a comprehensive treatment approach should include appropriate interventions that teach communication skills, problem solving, conflict resolution, and so forth, to marital or unwed partners.

Recent evidence suggests that many parents who abuse their children are dissatisfied with their vocational occupations and their interpersonal relationships with others, i.e., have poor self-concepts, feelings of worthlessness, and so forth (Elmer, 1977; Galdston, 1971; Gelles, 1973; Gil,

1975; Green, 1978a, 1978b; Holter & Friedman, 1969; Lystad, 1975; Milner & Wimberley, 1981).

It has been suggested that the reason why treatment programs have not produced significant results in treating parents who abuse their children is that they focus on only one of the factors that operate to produce child abuse, i.e., lack of child management skills, marital dissatisfaction, or vocational or interpersonal skills dissatisfaction (Gaines, Sangrund, Green, & Power, 1978; Gil, 1975; Grodner, 1977; Kempe & Helfer, 1972; Selig, 1976; Tracy & Clark, 1974). It is logical that a treatment approach to abuse must view the problem as multi-determined and services should be structured in such a manner. Previous research conducted by the author and a number of others suggests that treatment programs which focus on a variety of difficulties would be beneficial in reducing abuse (Belsky, 1980; Cain & Klerman, 1979; Wodarski, 1981). Thus the comprehensive treatment program should consist of the following:

1. Child management program
2. Marital enrichment program
3. Vocational skills enrichment program
4. Interpersonal skills enrichment program

Programs to accomplish the acquisition of requisite skills in each area are chosen from the technology of applied behavioral analysis. Recent reviews of parent training programs (Berkowitz & Graziano, 1972; Graziano, 1977; O'Dell, 1974), marital enrichment (Jacobson & Martin, 1976; Bagarozzi & Wodarski, 1977, 1978), and interpersonal skills training (Lange & Jakubowski, 1976; Rich & Schroeder, 1976; Schinke & Rose, 1976) have shown that their effectiveness is substantial as compared to other treatment programs. Data supporting vocational enrichment programs from the behavioral perspective is accumulating (Azrin, 1978; Azrin, Flores, & Kaplan, 1975; Jones & Azrin, 1973; Kelly, Laughlin, Claiborne, & Patterson, 1979).

Child Sexual Abuse

The problem of child sexual abuse has captured the attention of the public, the media, and professionals who work with families and children. As a result of this new awareness, social workers and members of other helping professions are being turned to for answers regarding causation and effective treatment techniques for use in working with child sexual abuse victims and their families.

Though estimates of the incidence of child sexual abuse vary widely, data indicate a prevalent problem. Estimates range from 100,000 to 500,000 youths who are sexually molested each year (Gagnon, 1965; Green, 1979; National Center on Child Abuse and Neglect, 1976; Sarafino, 1979), although it has been pointed out that statistics fail to reveal the problem's magnitude as child abuse often goes unreported (Cohen, 1983; Green, 1979; Taubman, 1984). Researchers report variously 25% (Weber, 1977), 28% (Gagnon, 1965), and 38% (Russell, 1983) of women in their studies were sexually abused before age 18. Females are reported as victims of child sexual abuse much more often than males (Conte, 1984; Weber, 1977; Zefran, Riley, Anderson, Curtis, Jackson, Kelly, McGury, & Suriano, 1982); however, other authors point out that male victims are vastly underreported (Conte, 1984; DeFrancis, 1969; Nasjleti, 1980).

Perpetrators

The overwhelming majority of child sexual perpetrators are men (Adams-Tucker, 1981; Anderson & Shafer, 1979; Berliner & Stevens, 1982; Finkelhor, 1979; Zefran et al., 1982). The perpetrators are known to the child in the majority of the cases (Adams-Tucker, 1981; Conte, 1984; Conte & Berliner, 1981; Zefran et al., 1982), and a majority of these are members of the child's family (Adams-Tucker, 1981; Conte, 1984; Husain & Chapel, 1983).

Certain authors describe a person who sexually abuses children as a dependent, immature, inadequate individual, having an early life history of conflict, disruption, abandonment, abuse and exploitation (Berliner & Stevens, 1982; Cohen, 1983; Groth, Hobson, & Gary, 1982; Swanson, 1968). Groth (1979) sees offenders as often coming from homes characterized by physical and sexual abuse. Panton (1979) found common themes in the MMPI profiles of child sex offenders, such as feelings of insecurity, inadequacy in interpersonal relationships, dependency, and family histories of social isolation and family discord. In describing other characteristics of child sexual abuse, data vary widely. Poor impulse control (Cavallin, 1966; Zefran et al., 1982), maternal deprivation (Cavallin, 1966; Cormier, Kennedy, & Sangowicz, 1962), and paternal deprivation (Weiner, 1962) are cited frequently by authors in descriptions of men committing child sexual abuse.

Whether or not individuals who sexually abuse children are satisfying sexual needs is debated. Sgroi (1982a) sees them as "me first" individuals who satisfy many "nonsexual needs" through sexual activity with children, while Conte (1984) sees difficulty with this description because all sexual involvement includes expression of nonsexual needs. Frude (1982) also sees unfulfilled sexual needs of perpetrators as an important factor in sexual abuse. He, as well as Tormes (1977), sees parents who were victims as children as more likely to become abusers. In summary then, a typical profile of a perpetrator is familiarity with the child, lack of self-esteem, and poor impulse control.

Predictive Factors

Family Characteristics. Child sexual abuse victims have been found to have several commonalities and these are viewed as possible predictors of the abuse. Believed to be relevant are family dynamics, demographic characteristics, and characteristics of the victim. The importance attributed to each varies widely according to investigators of the phenomenon.

Families of victims of child sexual abuse are often described as dysfunctional or pathological (Knudson, 1981; Sgroi, 1982a; Zefran et al., 1982). Though certain common themes arise from these descriptions, the specifics often differ. Sgroi (1982a) viewed families exhibiting sexual abuse as analogous to "character disordered" individuals. Various authors have described these families as being characterized by **paternal dominance** (Sgroi, 1982a; Zefran et al., 1982), **social and sexual estrangement between the father and mother** (Conte, 1984; Gruber & Jones, 1983; Knudson, 1981; Koch, 1980; Taubman, 1984), **social isolation** (Cohen, 1983; Sgroi, 1982a; Zefran et al., 1982), **assignment of adult roles to children** particularly the "mothering" role to the oldest daughter (Cohen, 1983; Conte, 1984; Giarretto, 1982a, 1982b; Sgroi, 1982a; Taubman, 1984; Zefran et al., 1982), **poor communication** (Sgroi, 1982a; Zefran et al., 1982), **emotional and social stress** (Cohen, 1983; Taubman, 1984), and **poor family sexual and physical boundaries** (Finkelhor, 1979). Sgroi (1982a) attributes to these families abuse of power, fear of authority, denial, lack of empathy, emotional deprivation, and magical expectations.

Though many of these accounts specifically refer to familial child sexual abuse, Sgroi (1982a) identifies the following avenues through which families may contribute to the event even in extrafamilial abuse:

poor supervision, poor choice of surrogate caretakers or babysitters, inappropriate sleeping arrangements, and blurred role boundaries.

Victim Characteristics. Descriptions of the demographic factors and personal traits of the victim differ among studies and authors. Adams-Tucker (1981), in her look at the sociodemographic backgrounds of 28 sexually abused children, described the following victim prototype: a white female, nine years old, from a working class family, headed by both parents or the mother only.

Finkelhor (1980a, 1980b) listed social variables he found to be associated with increased risk of child sexual abuse: living in a family with a stepfather, having lived at certain times without the mother, a lack of closeness to the mother, the mother having never completed high school, having a sexually punitive mother, receiving no physical affection from the father, the family having an income of less than 10,000 per year, and having few close friends. He also reports as risk factors having grown up on a farm and coming from a family experiencing marital strife.

In a demographic study of more than 4,000 families seen by the Child Sexual Abuse Treatment Program in Santa Clara County, California, Giarretto (1976) found families to be representative of a cross-section of the county the program serves. Families leaned toward the professional, semi-professional, and skilled blue collar workers, had a median educational level of 12.6 years, and 76.8% were white, 17.5% Mexican American, 3% oriental, and 1.7% black.

The age of the victim at the time of the incident is most often reported as 12 or under (Burgess & Holmstrom, 1974; Burton, 1968; Finkelhor, 1979; Knudson, 1981; Rentoul & Smith, 1973). Chandler (1982) points out this data challenges the assertion by some authors that the victims are sexually mature and develop secondary sex characteristics early (Gentry, 1978), and thus may "encourage" the adult (Gagnon, 1965). Other personal characteristics of the child seen as risk factors of sexual abuse are an unusually attractive and charming personality (Gentry, 1978), an unusually strong need for attention (Tormes, 1977), and mimicking seductive behavior (Gagnon, 1965; Tormes, 1977).

Assessments of the relationship of child sexual abuse to economic factors are diverse. Results of some studies indicate children from low income families are at higher risk (Gagnon, 1965; Julian, Mohr, & Lapp, 1980; Riemer, 1940; Weinberg, 1955). Julian et al. (1980), in a study of 665 substantiated incest cases in 34 states, found that while the median income for a U.S. household of four during the duration of the study was

$18,723, the median income for the incestuous families was between 9,000 and 10,999. Others report families of child sexual abuse victims represent all social, economic, and educational strata (Knudson, 1981; Rosenfeld, 1979; Vander & Neff, 1982).

Certain researchers have found child sexual abuse tends to occur in unbroken homes (Justice & Justice, 1979; Machotka et al., 1967; Meiselman, 1978; Specktor, 1979). However, Adams-Tucker (1981) found only a little over one-quarter of her sample of victims to be living with both parents absent, and were more likely to have a stepfather or stepmother. Gruber and Jones (1983) also found living with a step or foster father to be a risk factor in the sexual victimization of children. Koch (1980) sees a weakening of the taboo against child sexual abuse in stepfamilies because the members are not blood relatives. Perlmutter, Engsl and Sagar (1982) propose that the loosened sexual boundaries in these families is the result of a lack of proximity to the child during the years of growth and development and the failure to develop ties with the child during the time family relationships were being formed. Thus, in summary the available data indicate that victims generally are between the ages of 9–12, live for a period of time with one parent, and come from low income families.

Effects on Victim

The effects of child sexual abuse described in the literature produce a diverse and lengthy list. Most are related to females, but some seem equally applicable to males. As seen in the following presentation of sequelae, a majority of the problems relate to specific times in the victim's life, while others are observed throughout the lifetime. Berliner and Stevens (1982) point out that certain child victims may exhibit symptoms related to the abuse while it is occurring, some at disclosure, and others may have a delayed response. If the abuse is not disclosed, the effects may continue into or arise in adulthood. Perhaps the most obvious problems described are physical consequences, such as venereal disease or bodily injury (Berliner & Stevens, 1982). Psychological or emotional reactions are extensive. Victims of child sexual abuse describe feeling rejected, used, trapped, confused, humiliated, betrayed, and disgraced (Forward & Buck, 1978; James, 1977; Justice & Justice, 1979; Weber, 1977).

Psychological Effects. Other reported victim reactions include fear (Berliner & Stevens, 1982; Knittle & Tuana, 1980; Zefran et al., 1982), anger (Boatman, Borkan, & Schetky, 1981; Knittle & Tuana, 1980; Lubell & Soong, 1982; Sturkie, 1983; Zefran et al., 1982), **phobias and mood changes** (Sgroi, 1982a), **hysterical seizures** (Goodwin, Simms, & Bergman, 1979; Gross, 1979), **hyperactivity** (Sgroi, 1982a), **nightmares** (Berliner & Stevens, 1982; Sgroi, 1982a), **anxiety** (Adams-Tucker, 1981; Geiser, 1981; Knittle & Tuana, 1980; Sgroi, 1982a; Zefran et al., 1982), **guilt** (Berliner & Stevens, 1982; Boatman et al., 1981; Cohen, 1983; Knittle & Tuana, 1980; Sturkie, 1983; Zefran et al., 1982), **somatic complaints** (Adams-Tucker, 1981; Geiser, 1981; Sgroi, 1982a), **withdrawal and isolation** (Adams-Tucker, 1981; Berliner & Stevens, 1982; Cohen, 1983; Geiser, 1981; Knittle & Tuana, 1980; Lubell & Soong, 1982; Sgroi, 1982a; Taubman, 1984; Zefran et al., 1982), **self-mutilation** (Adams-Tucker, 1981; DeYoung, 1982; Knittle & Tuana, 1980), and **suicidal tendencies** (Adams-Tucker, 1981; Knittle & Tuana, 1980; Sgroi, 1982a; Taubman, 1984; Zefran et al., 1982).

Interpersonal-Social Effects. Victims reportedly experience **role confusion** (Giaretto, 1982a, 1982b; Sgroi, 1982a), **poor self-image and low self-esteem** (Boatman et al., 1981; Finkelhor, 1980a, 1980b; Geiser, 1981; Sgroi, 1982a; Taubman, 1984), **developmental lags** (Adams-Tucker, 1981; Berliner & Stevens, 1982; Knittle & Tuana, 1980; Sgroi, 1982a; Sturkie, 1983), and **learning disabilities** (Adams-Tucker, 1981; Geiser, 1981). The developmental and learning deficits might be directly related to truancy and other school problems described (Brooks, 1982; Giaretto, 1982b; Sgroi, 1982a; Taubman, 1984).

This conglomeration of problems along with difficulty in interpersonal relationships (Boatman et al., 1981; Sgroi, 1982a; Taubman, 1984) may contribute to behaviors frequently noted to develop as victims move into adolescence and adulthood.

Social behavioral problems include **delinquency** (Justice & Justice, 1979; Specktor, 1979), **running away** (Adams-Tucker, 1981), **substance abuse** (Geiser, 1981; Giarretto, 1982b; Taubman, 1984; Zefran et al., 1982), and **promiscuity and prostitution** (Giarretto, 1982b; Taubman, 1984; Zefran et al., 1982). **Sexual dysfunction** (Bess & Janssen, 1982; Boatman et al., 1981; Giarretto, 1982b; Sgroi, 1982a), and **difficulty functioning in marriage and parenting roles** (Justice & Justice, 1979; Specktor, 1979) commonly are reported among adults who were victims of child sexual abuse.

It should be noted that there are those who contend child sexual abuse has little or no ill effects for some children (Berliner & Stevens, 1982), little or no lasting effects for any children (Gagnon, 1965), or that sex between adults and children can have a positive effect (Time Magazine, 1980).

Certain authors see the human service network's responses and procedures of the intervention system as a possible source of trauma and further victimization of the child (Conte, 1984; Giarretto, 1982b). Others see this trauma as the major cause of problems for the victims in many cases (Benward & Densen-Gerber, 1975; Schultz, 1973).

Violent Children

For the last several decades there has been growing concern over the trend toward more violent crimes among our youth. Not only is the total number of youths involved in violent crimes increasing, but the number of youths involved in violent crimes at an earlier age (10 and under) seems to be on the increase. "In 1978, for example, the Uniform Crime Reports indicated that nearly two million youths under 18 years of age were charged with an offense" (U.S. Department of Justice, 1979, p. 193). Of these, 58,593 were exceptionally serious offenses such as murder or non-negligent manslaughter, forcible rape, robbery and aggravated assault. "More than 700,000 of the charged youths were under 15 years of age. Even more alarmingly, 79,007 were 10 years old or under."

Between 1969 and 1978 there was a marked upward trend in arrests of under-18 males for most offense categories. Arrests of such youths increased by 10.1% during this period. In general, the rate for violent crime rose by 40.6%. The figure cited for 1974 represented a total of 1,683,000 youths, while the one for 1978 represented 2,279,000 youths. Even though the relative proportion of youths in American society may vary over the years, it is obvious that delinquency rates for the youth population remain high (Baker & Rubel, 1980; Blyth, Thiel, Bush, & Simmons, 1978; Rubel, 1980).

In 1983, almost 1,000 juveniles were arrested for murder, 3,000 for rape, and over 19,000 for aggravated assault. We know these arrest statistics vastly underestimate the number of offenses committed. This research also demonstrates that among the small group of juvenile offenders who commit these types of crimes, a substantial proportion continue to commit crimes as adults (Hamparian, Davis, Jacobson, & McGraw, 1985).

In an attempt to combat the problem, researchers have diligently attacked every theoretical focus, from social to neurological, related to the problem of antisocial behavior of youths. The most frustrating aspect of this dilemma is the overwhelming combination of background factors posited to contribute to the problem (i.e., unemployment, peer association, stress, low SES, marital problems, physical problems, type of neighborhood). Researchers often feel that in focusing on a single aspect of the problem, validity, accuracy, and real-life applicability is lost (Feldman, Caplinger, & Wodarski, 1983; Gibbons, 1986).

The provision of social work services to potentially violent children has been a major focus of practice. Different theories, e.g., psychoanalytic, behavioral and so forth, have been posited to account for violent behavior. Additionally, a variety of treatment modalities have been proposed, such as intensive individual, group, residential treatment and family therapy (Curry, 1985).

Practice trends indicate that social workers historically have had a substantial interest in violent children. In light of the recent questioning of the efficacy of services, the juvenile rights movement and so forth, however, it is necessary to conceptualize the provision of social work services to children from a rational and empirical perspective.

The concept of violent behavior is ambiguous. It is necessary, therefore, to specify first those acts that would be of greatest concern to us as social workers. Violent behavior involves the intent to do physical harm to other individuals, i.e., rape, murder and physical assault. Violence among children is a major concern since recent research indicates that violent children comprise one of the most troublesome groups in terms of service provision. Moreover, if not helped, this group of relatively few chronic offenders are responsible for a disproportionate number of crimes.

Age of Onset and Frequency of Violent Behavior

Substantial data indicate that when adolescents are plotted by reference age and previous arrest history, the earlier the age of first arrests, the greater the probability of future violence. For example, when the first arrest age was from 8–10 years, the mean number of violent offenses in an entire career was .25. Likewise, the incidence for ages 11–13 was .24; for ages 14–16, .22; for ages 17–19, .11; for ages 20–22, .04; and for ages 23–25, .03. Furthermore, 20% of those classified as recidivists by 18 years of age were involved in violent crime as adults (Guttridge, Mednick, & Van Dusen, 1983).

Violent offenders tend to commit more crimes than do other offenders. Moreover, it becomes more likely that an adolescent will be violent as he/she commits more offenses. About 10% of the men credited with 18 or more offenses have committed at least one violent act (Guttridge et al., 1983). Furthermore, while other index offense types (robbery) either decrease or are unaffected by age, only violence shows an increase with age. Wolfgang, Figlio and Sellin (1972) showed an increase of 21% in violent crimes committed from age 10 and under to age 17.

There is evidence of the development of a criminal career over time which could ultimately lead to the commission of a violent crime. Thus there is a substantial link between juvenile crime and adult crime. Data suggest that the violent offender is a chronic adult criminal or recidivist who started his career at an early age, possibly as early as eight years of age, who engages in a high number of crimes, and commits a wide variety of crimes. A small proportion of violent chronic offenders account for a large proportion of all arrests (Farrington & Tarling, 1985).

Critical Variables in the Development of Violent Behavior

Child Management. The most significant variable in the development of violent behavior appears to be the lack of appropriate parenting. For example, in a study by Wilson (1980), it was found that parental laxness (lack of monitoring or discipline) was significantly correlated with delinquency. The data show that families classified as lax were likely to have a delinquency rate over seven times that of the families classified as strict. Likewise, Patterson and Stouthamer-Loeber (1984) found significant correlations between the measures of parent monitoring and discipline and a variety of delinquent behaviors. Loeber (1982) posited that it is the homes where the parental management skills are chronically disrupted or deficient in terms of overmonitoring and lack of monitoring wherein chronically violent youth more often are found.

A significant study by McCord (1979), which is both prospective and retrospective, presents evidence for the significant contribution of the effects of parental aggression, lack of supervision, conflict and lack of maternal affection on criminal behavior. Furthermore, the study suggests that these effects contributed more to the criminal behavior of adults than did aggressive behavior exhibited as youths.

Additional data indicate that violent children usually come from violent families. The theory is that violent children have observed parents solve conflict by violent means and have learned these as a way of solving their own conflicts. Violence is thus modeled as a problem solving strategy. Violent children also start out historically with non-compliant behavior, i.e., they do not respond to reasonable requests by parents. They subsequently get reinforced for such coercive behaviors and learn coercive means of solving problems (Kazdin, 1985). When the child starts school, coercive behaviors accelerate toward parents, and at school, toward prosocial peers and adults.

Cognitive, Social and Academic Skills: Contributing Factors. Due to coercive behavior, violent children do not learn empathic behaviors and adequate cognitive strategies for dealing with anger when provoked. Likewise, they do not learn the means for dealing with stress in an adequate prosocial manner. Thus, once they leave protected homes, violent children are not prepared adequately to deal with stress.

Dishion, Loeber, Stouthamer-Loeber, and Patterson (1984) found that certain academic skills deficits, i.e., verbal intelligence, reading achievement, homework completion and mother's rating of school competence, correlate most significantly with violence in adolescents.

Violent patterns have been related significantly to school rejection of children in school by adults and prosocial peers (Kaplan & Robbins, 1983) Patterson (1982) has postulated that a process exists whereby the lack of social or academic skills increases the chances of failure for the child in school and with peers and family and thus exacerbates his alienation from those prosocial relationships.

In addition to the evidence of the detrimental effect of an academic skills deficit, a study by Thornberry, Moore and Christenson (1985) showed a positive association between drop-out during high school and later criminality. Family rejection compounded the adoption of deviant responses in a study by Patterson and Dishion (1985). Moreover, it was also associated positively with long-term criminality.

Self-Esteem and Peer Relations. The literature indicates that violent individuals have poor self-concepts and difficult peer relationships in terms of integration with prosocial peer groups. Difficulties at school and the experience of rejection and abuse by their parents tend to reduce the feelings of self-esteem among these youth. Complicating the matter is the fact that violent individuals are usually physically unattractive thus leading to their poor self-esteem and rejection by peers (Agnew, 1984; Hanson, Henggeler, Haefele, & Rodick, 1984).

Violent individuals usually are not in the mainstream of prosocial peer culture. Thus they do not form attachments to regular prosocial institutions of society. They usually are part of a small group of peers who reinforce each other for their violent behaviors.

In Hirschi's control theory (1969), youth who lack adequate attachments to school and parents are "free" to engage in delinquent behavior. In terms of motivation for participation in delinquent behavior, delinquent peers were found to support participation in delinquent acts through positive reinforcement (Patterson & Dishion, 1985).

Hanson et al. (1984) found that parent reports of strong participation in a delinquent peer group most consistently predicted serious and repeated arrests among adolescent males. Indeed, association with delinquent peers was found to be most prevalent among those youths classified as official delinquents (Grove & Crutchfield, 1982). Analyses strongly suggest that membership in the delinquent peer group is a strong predictor of subsequent increases in violent behavior (Elliott, Ageton, & Canter, 1979; Patterson & Dishion, 1985).

Alcohol seems to be a variable that is critical later in the process of the development of violent behavior. Violent adolescents cannot process cognitively nor can they manage stress. Alcohol therefore reduces any inhibitions that they may have and subsequently facilitates aggressive responses (Collins, 1981). The critical variable of weapon availability increases the potential for violent behavior. Usually, if a weapon is available, violent children finally will utilize the weapon as a means of reducing stress or of resolving a conflict situation. Violent children are at great risk in communities where weapons are readily available (Wolfgang & Weiner, 1982).

Developmental Process

Of primary importance are the first signs in the development of violent behavior. Accumulated evidence has shown that "antisocial" behavior can be grouped into two basic patterns, the *stealer* and the *aggressor,* in large part due to the type of parental supervision exercised (Hewitt & Jenkins, 1946; Loeber & Schmaling, 1985; Patterson, 1982). Stealers come from homes exhibiting a lack of monitoring and discipline, while aggressors come from homes where parenting may be characterized by more aversive interaction. However, the antisocial activity a child engages in is also to a large degree impacted by their age. A younger child who hits his playmate over the head with a toy may go on to fight with his fists at an older age, and having gained entry into a gang, may be introduced to stealing. We posit that these behaviors fall on a continuum, which left unattended, will increase in frequency, types of contexts where the behavior is exhibited, variety, and severity.

In a study by Robins and Ratcliff (1979), it was found that early aggression, theft and lying were associated with later delinquency. For example, 39% of the children who had been involved in three or more categories of antisocial behavior became delinquent, compared to only 6% of the children with a single kind of antisocial behavior. Shapland (1978) measured 48 types of behavior and their frequency in a self-reported delinquency study of adolescents aged 11-14. Trivial offenses were committed at all ages; however, the more serious acts were committed at the later ages. The number of the types of crimes committed increased with age, and the boys who committed the largest number of offenses also committed a more varied range of offenses.

The type of violent behavior a child displays is a product of the parental management techniques exercised or not exercised, the age of the child, and his involvement in antisocial behaviors. The higher the rate at which the child participates in antisocial behaviors, the greater the potential for entrance into a violent career. Thus, there is evidence of a quantitative development of violent behavior. Certain researchers present data which suggest that potentially violent youths are clearly overtly antisocial at preschool age (Loeber & Schmaling, 1985).

Juvenile Crime to Adult Crime. Substantial data suggest that the exhibition of antisocial and delinquent behavior is a sound basis for predicting future problems. In his study of violent criminals in London, McClintock (as cited by Hood & Sparks, 1970) found that violent recidivists had previous convictions for nonviolent crimes. Violent offenders, more than other offenders, tend to commit more crimes. If the child commits many offenses, it becomes more probable that an individual will be violent (Guttridge et al., 1983). Furthermore, there may be a tendency for these offenders' crimes to grow more serious as they get older (Farrington & Tarling, 1985).

Moreover, the data indicate that juvenile delinquent activities are often followed by adult crime. Farrington (1983) shows a close relationship between juvenile and adult convictions. In addition, the more chronic offenders not only amassed the greatest proportion of crimes, they were also identified as the youths first convicted at the earliest ages (10-12).

Profile of Violent Youth

Having established a category of children who appear to be most at risk for entrance into an environment conducive to committing a violent act, the next logical step is to attempt to identify the children out of that category voted most likely to succeed.

In a study by Loeber and Schmaling (1985) that compared fighters, stealers and versatile youth, i.e., children who fight *and* steal, the versatile youth scored the highest in almost all delinquent acts. Furthermore, the versatile youths were shown to have a higher rate of association with delinquent peer groups and also to be more negative, hyperactive and disobedient. The versatile youth came from homes with the poorest parental management techniques and were the most disturbed on measures of family processes, specifically lack of monitoring, inconsistent rule application, supervision, reasoning, communication, and mother rejection.

A recent study by Patterson (1982) summarizes the similarities and differences between fighters and stealers. Similarities include noncompliance, arrested socialization (maximizes immediate gains at someone else's expense, lack of impulse control), reduced responsiveness to social stimuli (less responsive to ordinary social reinforcers and to threats and scolding, attentional deficits), and lastly, skills deficits (academic achievement, work, peer relations). Differences include solely the kinds of parenting practices. Stealers come from homes exhibiting a lack of monitoring and discipline, while aggressors come from homes where parenting may be characterized by more aversive interaction.

Thus, a profile of the violent youth shows this youngster typically to have a low IQ and assaultive tendencies such as instigating fights and defying authority, and to exhibit cruelty and malicious mischief. He is depressed and frustrated. He feels inadequate, lacks internal inhibitions, and expects immediate gratification. He more often than not comes from a poor neighborhood where he is a witness to violent acts, and he is subjected usually to certain forms of parental abuse (not necessarily physical abuse) (Brown, 1984). He experiences rejection and aggressive behavior being modeled in the home, which is most likely headed by a single parent (Lefkowitz, Eron, Walder, & Huesmann, 1977).

Summary

The establishment, implementation, and evaluation of social work treatment programs for children with special needs is an interrelated and difficult process. It should be emphasized that considerable time should be spent in dealing with the items reviewed here in order to establish programs which are relevant to children's needs and which can be implemented in such a manner that enables a proper evaluation. Sufficient time spent in the planning and establishment phases greatly facilitates implementation and evaluation and ensures provision of requisite services to children with special needs.

REFERENCES

Adams-Tucker, C. (1981). A socioclinical overview of 28 sex-abused children. *Child Abuse and Neglect, 5,* 361–367.

Agnew, R. (1984). Appearance and delinquency. *Criminology, 22*(3), 421–440.

American Psychiatric Association. (1980). *Diagnostic and statistical manual of mental disorders* (3rd ed.). Washington, DC: APA.

Anderson, L. M., & Shafer, G. (1979). The character-disordered family: A community treatment model for family sexual abuse. *American Journal of Orthopsychiatry, 49*(3), 436–445.

Ando, H., & Yoshimura, I. (1979). Effects of age on communication skill levels and prevalence of maladaptive behaviors in autistic and mentally retarded children. *Journal of Autism and Developmental Disorders, 9,* 83–93.

Arnold, L. E. (1983). Unprevented alienation: Case illustration and group discussion. In L. Arnold (Ed.), *Preventing adolescent alienation.* Lexington, MA: D.C. Heath.

Azrin, N. H. (1978, November). *A learning approach to job finding.* Paper presented at Association for Advancement of Behavior Therapy, Chicago.

Azrin, N. H., Flores, H., & Kaplan, S. J. (1975). Job-finding club: A group assisted program for obtaining employment. *Behavior Research and Therapy, 13,* 17–27.

Bagarozzi, D. A., & Wodarski, J. S. (1977). A social exchange typology of conjugal relationships and conflict development: Some implications for clinical practice, assessment, and future research. *Journal of Marriage and Family, 39,* 53–60.

Bagarozzi, D. A., & Wodarski, J. S. (1978). Behavioral treatment of marital discord. *Clinical Social Work Journal, 6*(2), 135–154.

Baker, K., & Rubel, R. (Eds.). (1980). *Violence and crimes in the schools.* Lexington, MA: Lexington Books.

Belsky, J. (1980). Child maltreatment: An ecological integration. *American Psychologist, 64*(4), 320–335.

Benward, J., & Densen-Gerber, J. (1975). Incest as a causative factor in antisocial behavior: An exploratory study. *Contemporary Drug Problems, 4*(3), 323–340.

Berkovitz, I. H. (1981). Feelings of powerlessness and the role of violent actions in adolescents. In Feinstein, Looney, Schwartzberg, & Sorosky (Eds.), *Adolescent psychiatry: Developmental and clinical studies* (Vol. 9). Chicago: University of Chicago Press.

Berkowitz, B. P., & Graziano, A. M. (1972). Training parents as behavior therapists: A review. *Behavior Research and Therapy, 10,* 297–317.

Berliner, R., & Stevens, D. (1982). Clinical issues in child sexual abuse. *Journal of Social Work and Human Sexuality, 1,* 93–108.

Bess, B. E., & Janssen, T. (1982). Incest: A pilot study. *Hillside Journal of Clinical Psychiatry, 4*(1), 39–52.

Blumberg, M. L. (1974). Psychopathology of the abusing parent. *American Journal of Psychotherapy, 28,* 21–29.

Blyth, D. A., Thiel, K. S., Bush, D., & Simmons, R. G. (1978). Another look at school crime: Student as victim. Boys Town, NE: Center for the Study of Youth Development. (mimeograph)

Boatman, B., Borkan, E. L., & Schetky, D. H. (1981). Treatment of child victims of incest. *The American Journal of Family Therapy, 9*(4), 43–51.

Brooks, B. (1982). Familial influences in father-daughter incest. *Journal of Psychiatric Treatment and Evaluation, 4,* 117–124.

Brown, S. (1984). Social class, child maltreatment, and delinquent behavior. *Criminology, 22*(2), 259–278.

Burgess, A. W., & Holmstrom, L. L. (1974). *Rape: Victims and crisis.* Bowie, MD: Robert J. Brady.

Burton, L. (1968). *Vulnerable children.* London: Routledge and Kegal Paul.

Cain, L. P., & Klerman, L. V. (1979). What do social workers read about child abuse? *Child Welfare, 58*(1), 13–46.

Cavallin, H. (1966). Incestuous fathers: A clinical report. *American Journal of Psychiatry, 122*(10), 1132–1138.

Chandler, S. M. (1982). Knowns and unknowns in sexual abuse of children. *Journal of Social Work and Human Sexuality, 1,* 51–68.

Cohen, S. J., & Sussman, A. (1975). The incidence of child abuse in the United States. *Child Welfare, 54,* 432–444.

Cohen, T. (1983). The incestuous family revisited. *Social Casework, 64*(3), 154–161.

Coles, R. (1983). Alienated youth and humility for the professions. In L. Arnold (Ed.), *Preventing adolescent alienation.* Lexington, MA: D.C. Heath.

Collins, J. J. (1981). *Alcohol use and criminal behavior: An executive summary.* Washington, DC: U.S. Department of Justice.

Conte, J. R. (1984). Progress in treating the sexual abuse of children. *Social Work, 29*(3), 258–263.

Conte, J. R., & Berliner, L. (1981). Sexual abuse of children: Implications for practice. *Social Casework, 62*(10), 601–606.

Cormier, B., Kennedy, M., & Sangowicz, J. (1962). Psychodynamics of father-daughter incest. *Canadian Psychiatric Association Journal, 7,* 207–217.

Crozier, J., & Katz, R. C. (1981). Social learning treatment of child abuse. *Journal of Behavior Therapy & Experimental Psychiatry, 65*(1), 17–67.

Curry, J. F. (1985). Aggressive or delinquent adolescents: Family therapy interventions. *Practice Applications, 3* (1).

David, J. R. (1979). Child advocacy: An opportunity. *Military Medicine, 144*(2), 121–123.

DeFrancis, V. (1969). *Protecting the child victim of sex crimes committed by adults: Final report.* Denver, CO: The American Humane Association.

DeMyer, M. K. (1979). *Parents and children in autism.* New York: Wiley.

Derdeyn, A. P. (1977). Child abuse and neglect: The rights of parents and the needs of their children. *American Journal of Orthopsychiatry, 43,* 377–387.

Deykin, E. Y., Alpert, J. J., & McNamarra, J. J. (1985). A pilot study of the effect of exposure to child abuse or neglect on adolescent suicidal behavior. *American Journal of Psychiatry, 142,* 1299–1303.

DeYoung, M. (1982). Self-injurious behavior in incest victims: A research note. *Child Welfare, 61*(8), 577–584.

Dishion, T. J., Loeber, R., Stouthamer-Loeber, M., & Patterson, G. R. (1984). Skills deficits and male adolescent delinquency. *Journal of Abnormal Child Psychology, 12,* 37–54.

Egeland, B. R., Breitenbucher, M., & Rosenberg, D. (1980). Prospective study of the significance of life stress in the etiology of child abuse. *Journal of Consulting and Clinical Psychology, 63*(6), 121–126.

Egeland, B. R., Sroufe, A., & Erickson, M. (1983). The developmental consequences of different patterns of maltreatment. *Child Abuse & Neglect, 7,* 459–469.

Eggers, C. (1978). Course and prognosis of childhood schizophrenia. *Journal of Autism and Childhood Schizophrenia, 8,* 21–36.

Elliott, D. S., Ageton, S. S., & Canter, R. J. (1979). An integrated theoretical perspective on delinquent behavior. *Journal of Research in Crime and Delinquency, 16,* 3–22.

Elmer, E. (1967). *Children in jeopardy.* Pittsburgh, PA: University of Pittsburgh Press.

Elmer, E. (1975). Personal communication.

Elmer, E. (1977). *Fragile families, troubled children.* Pittsburgh: University of Pittsburgh Press.

Farrington, D. P. (1983). Offending from 10 to 25 years of age. In K. Van Dusen & S. Mednick (Eds.), *Prospective studies of crime and delinquency.* Boston: Kluwer.

Farrington, D. P., & Tarling, R. (Eds.). (1985). *Prediction in criminology.* Albany: State University of New York Press.

Feldman, R. A., Caplinger, T. E., & Wodarski, J. S. (1983). *The St. Louis conundrum: The effective treatment of antisocial youths.* Englewood Cliffs, NJ: Prentice-Hall.

Finkelhor, D. (1979). *Sexually victimized children.* New York: Free Press.

Finkelhor, D. (1980a). Risk factors in the sexual victimization of children. *Child Abuse and Neglect, 4,* 265–273.

Finkelhor, D. (1980b). Sexual socialization in America: High risk for sexual abuse. In J. Samson (Ed.), *Childhood and sexuality: Proceedings of the International Symposium.* Montreal: Editions Etudes Viventes.

Forward, S., & Buck, C. (1978). *Betrayal of innocence: Incest and its devastation.* New York: Penguin Books.

Friedman, S. B., & Morse, C. W. (1974). Child abuse: A five-year follow-up of early case findings in the emergency department. *Pediatrics, 54,* 404–410.

Frodi, A. M., & Lamb, M. E. (1980). Child abusers' responses to infant smiles and cries. *Child Development, 51*(1), 238–241.

Frude, N. (1982). The sexual nature of sexual abuse: A review of the literature. *Child Abuse and Neglect, 6*(2), 211–233.

Gagnon, J. H. (1965). Female child victims of sex offenses. *Social Problems, 13*(2), 176–192.

Gaines, R., Sangrund, A., Green, A. H., & Power, E. (1978). Etiological factors in child maltreatment: A multivariate study of abusing, neglecting, and normal mothers. *Journal of Abnormal Psychology, 87,* 531–540.

Galdston, R. (1971). Violence begins at home: The parent center project for the study and prevention of child abuse. *Journal of the American Academy of Child Psychiatry, 10*(2), 336–350.

Garbarino, J. (1979). The human ecology of child maltreatment: A conceptual model for research. *Journal of Marriage and the Family, 61*(1), 12–39.

Garbarino, J. (1983). What we know about child maltreatment. *Children and Youth Services Review, 5,* 3–6.

Garbarino, J., & Stocking, S. H. (1980). *Protecting children from abuse and neglect: Developing and maintaining effective support systems for families.* San Francisco: Jossey-Bass.

Geiser, R. L. (1981). Incest and psychological violence. *International Journal of Family Psychiatry, 2*(3/4), 291–300.

Gelles, R. (1973). Child abuse and psychopathology: A sociological critique and reformulation. *American Journal of Orthopsychiatry, 43,* 611–621.

Gentry, C. E. (1978). Incestuous abuse of children: The need for an objective view. *Child Welfare, 62*(6), 355–364.

Giarretto, H. (1976). Humanistic treatment of father-daughter incest. In R. Holfer & C. Kemp (Ed.), *Child abuse and neglect: The family and the community.* Cambridge, MA: Ballinger.

Giarretto, H. (1982a). A comprehensive child sexual abuse treatment program. *Child Abuse and Neglect, 6,* 263–278.

Giarretto, H. (1982b). *Integrated treatment of child sexual abuse: A treatment and training manual.* Palo Alto, CA: Science and Behavior Books, Inc.

Gibbons, D. C. (1986). Juvenile delinquency: Can social science find a cure? *Crime and Delinquency, 32*(2), 186–204.

Gil, D. G. (1975). Unraveling child abuse. *American Journal of Orthopsychiatry, 45,* 346–356.

Goodwin, J., Simms, M., & Bergman, P. (1979). Hysterical seizures: A sequel to incest. *American Journal of Orthopsychiatry, 49*(4), 698–703.

Graziano, A. M. (1977). Parents as behavior therapists. In M. Hersen, R. Eisler & P. Miller (Eds.), *Progress in behavior modification* (Vol. 4). New York: Academic Press.

Green, A. J. (1978a). Child abuse. In B. Wolman, J. Egan, & A. Ross (Eds.), *Handbook of treatment of mental disorders in childhood and adolescence.* Englewood Cliffs, NJ: Prentice-Hall.

Green, A. J. (1978b). Psychopathology of abused children. *American Journal of Psychiatry, 17*(1), 92–103.

Green, F. C. (1979). Introduction: Child sexual abuse: The physician's responsibility. *Pediatric Annals, 8,* 286–288.

Grodner, B. (1977) A family systems approach to treatment of child abuse: Etiology and intervention. In *Child abuse and neglect: Issues on intervention and implementation* (Vol. II). Symposium presented at 2nd Annual Conference on Child Abuse and Neglect.

Gross, M. (1979). Incestuous rape. *American Journal of Orthopsychiatry, 49*(4), 704–708.

Grossman, H. J. (Ed.). (1983). *Classification in mental retardation.* Washington, DC: American Association on Mental Deficiency.

Groth, A. N. (1979). Sexual trauma in the life histories of rapists and child molesters. *Victimology: An International Journal, 4*(1), 10–16.

Groth, A. N., Hobson, W. F., & Gary, L. S. (1982). The child molester: Clinical observations. *Journal of Social Work and Human Sexuality, 1,* 129–144.

Grove, & Crutchfield, (1982). The family and juvenile delinquency. *The Sociological Quarterly, 23.*

Gruber, K. J., & Jones, R. J. (1983). Identifying determinants of risk of sexual victimization of youth: A multivariate approach. *Child Abuse and Neglect, 7,* 17–24.

Guttridge, P., Mednick, S. A., & Van Dusen, K. T. (1983). Criminal violence in a birth cohort. In K. Van Dusen and S. Mednick (Eds.), *Prospective studies of crime and delinquency.* Boston: Kluwer.

Hamparian, D. M., Davis, J. M., Jacobson, J. M., & McGraw, R. E. (1985). *The young criminal years of the violent few.* Washington, DC: U.S. Department of Justice.

Hanson, C. L., Henggeler, S. W., Haefele, W. F., & Rodick, J. D. (1984). Demographic, individual, family relationship correlates of serious and repeated crime among adolescents and their siblings. *Journal of Consulting & Clinical Psychology, 52*(4), 528–538.

Helfer, R. E., & Kempe, C. H. (Eds.). (1976). *Child abuse and neglect: The family and the community.* Cambridge, MA: Ballinger.

Hewitt, L. E., & Jenkins, R. L. (1946). *Fundamental patterns of maladjustment: The dynamics of their origin.* Michigan: Child Guidance Institute.

Hirschi, T. (1969). *Causes of delinquency.* Berkeley: University of California Press.

Holinger, P. C., & Offer, D. (1981). Perspectives in suicide in adolescence. *Research in Community and Mental Health, 2,* 139–157.

Holter, J., & Friedman, S. (1969). Etiology and management of severely burned children: Psychosocial considerations. *American Journal of the Disturbed Child, 118,* 680–686.

Hood, R., & Sparks, R. (1970). *Key issues in criminology.* London: Weindelfeld & Nicholson.

Husain, A., & Chapel, J. L. (1983). History of incest in girls admitted to a psychiatric hospital. *American Journal of Psychiatry, 140*(5), 591–593.

Jacobson, N. S., & Martin, B. (1976). Behavior marriage therapy: Current status. *Psychological Bulletin, 83,* 540–556.

James, K. L. (1977). Incest: The teenager's perspective. *Psychotherapy: Theory, Research and Practice, 14*(2), 146–155.

Johnson, B., & Morse, N. (1968). Injured children and their parents. *Children, 15,* 147–152.

Jones, R. J., & Azrin, N. H. (1973). An experimental application of a social reinforcement approach to the problem of job finding. *Journal of Applied Behavior Analysis, 6,* 345–353.

Julian, V., Mohr, C., & Lapp, J. (1980). Father-daughter incest: A descriptive analysis. In W. Holder (Ed), *Sexual abuse of children: Implications for treatment.* Denver, CO: American Humane Association.

Justice, B., & Justice, R. (1979). *The broken taboo: Sex in the family.* New York: Human Sciences Press.

Kaplan, H. B., & Robbins, C. (1983). Testing a general theory of deviant behavior in longitudinal perspective. In K. Van Dusen & S. Mednick (Eds.), *Prospective studies of crime and delinquency.* Boston: Kluwer.

Kaplan, H. B., Robbins, C., & Martin, S. (1983). Antecedents of psychological distress in young adults: Self-rejection, deprivation of social support and life events. *Journal of Health and Social Behavior, 24,* 230–244.

Kazdin, A. E. (1985). *Treatment of antisocial behavior in children and adolescents: Alternative interventions and their effectiveness.* Homewood, IL: Dorsey Press.

Kelly, J. A., Laughlin, C., Claiborne, M., & Patterson, J. (1979). A group procedure for teaching job interviewing skills to formerly hospitalized psychiatric patients. *Behavior Therapy, 10,* 299–210.

Kempe, C. H., & Helfer, R. E. (1972). *Helping the battered child and his family.* Philadelphia: J. B. Lippincott.

Kinard, E. M. (1980a). Emotional development in physically abused children. *American Journal of Orthopsychiatry, 50,* 686–696.

Kinard, E. M. (1980b). Mental health needs of abused children. *Child Welfare, 59*(8), 451–462.

Knittle, B. J., & Tuana, S. J. (1980). Group therapy as primary treatment for adolescent victims of intrafamilial sexual abuse. *Clinical Social Work Journal, 8*(4), 236–242.

Knudson, D. G. (1981). *Interpersonal dynamics and mothers' involvement in father-daughter incest in Puerto Rico.* Doctoral dissertation, Ohio State University, Columbus, Ohio.

Koch, M. (1980). Sexual abuse in children. *Adolescence, 15*(59), 643–648.

Koerlin, B. B. (1980). Child abuse and neglect: Changing policies and perspectives. *Child Welfare, 59*(9), 542–550.

Lamphear, V. S. (1985). The impact of maltreatment on children's psychosocial adjustment: A review of the research. *Child Abuse & Neglect, 9,* 251–263.

Lange, A. J., & Jakubowski, P. (1976). *Responsible assertive behavior.* Champaign, IL: Research Press.

Larry, G. (1970). The battered-child syndrome: Parental motivation, clinical aspects. *Bulletin of the New York Academy of Medicine, 46*, 676–685.

Lefkowitz, M., Eron, L., Walder, L., & Huesmann, L. R. (1977). *Growing up to be violent: A longitudinal study of the development of aggression.* New York: Pergamon.

Levitt, J. M. (1977). A family systems approach to treatment of child abuse. In *Child Abuse and Neglect: Issues on Innovation and Implementation, 2.* Proceedings of the Second National Conference on Child Abuse and Neglect.

Loeber, R. (1982). The stability of antisocial and delinquent child behavior: A review. *Child Development, 53*, 1434–1446.

Loeber, R., & Schmaling, K. B. (1985). The utility of differentiating between mixed and pure forms of antisocial child behavior. *Journal of Abnormal Child Psychology, 13*(2), 315–336.

Lubell, D., & Soong, W. T. (1982). Group therapy with sexually abused adolescents. *Canadian Journal of Psychiatry, 27*(4), 311–315.

Lukianowicz, N. (1971). Battered children. *Psychiatria Clinica, 4*, 257–280.

Lukianowicz, N. (1972). Attempted infanticide. *Psychiatria Clinica, 5*, 1–16.

Lystad, M. H. (1975). Violence at home: A review of the literature. *American Journal of Orthopsychiatry, 45*, 328–345.

Machotka, P., Pittman, F., & Flomenhaft, S. (1967). Incest as a family affair. *Family Process, 6*(1), 98–116.

Manis, J. G. (1974). Assessing the seriousness of social problems. *Social Problems, 22*, 1–15.

Martin, H. P. (1972). The child and his development. In C. Kempe & R. Helfer (Eds.), *Helping the battered child and his family.* Philadelphia: J. B. Lippincott.

Martin, H. P. (1976). Factors influencing the development of the abused child. In H. Martin (Ed.), *The abused child: A multidisciplinary approach to developmental issues and treatment* (pp. 139–162). Cambridge, MA: Ballinger.

Martin, H. P., Beezley, P., Conway, E. F., & Kempe, C. H. (1974). The development of abused children. *Advances in Pediatrics, 21*, 25–73.

Mastria, E. O. (1979). Treatment of child abuse by behavioral intervention: A case report. *Child Welfare, 58*(4), 252–262.

McCord, J. (1979). Some child-rearing antecedents of criminal behavior in adult men. *Journal of Personality and Social Psychology, 37*(9), 1477–1486.

Meiselman, K. (1978). *Incest: A psychological study of causes and effects with treatment recommendations.* San Francisco: Jossey-Bass.

Melnick, B., & Hurley, J. R. (1969). Distinctive personality attributes of child-abusing mothers. *Journal of Consulting and Clinical Psychology, 33*, 746–749.

Miller, D. (1981). Adolescent suicide: Etiology and treatment. In Feinstein, Looney, Schwartzberg, & Sorosky (Eds.), *Adolescent psychiatry: Developmental and clinical studies* (Vol. 9). Chicago: University of Chicago Press.

Milner, J. S., & Ayoub, C. (1980). Evaluation of "at risk" parents using the child abuse potential inventory. *Journal of Clinical Psychology, 36*(4), 945–948.

Milner, J. S., & Wimberley, R. C. (1981). Prediction and explanation of child abuse. *Journal of Clinical Psychology, 36*(4), 975–984.

Morse, C. W., Sahler, O. J., & Friedman, S. B. (1970). A three-year follow-up study of abused and neglected children. *American Journal of Diseases of Children, 120,* 439–446.

Nagi, S. Z. (1975). Child abuse and neglect programs: A national overview. *Children Today, 4,* 13–17.

Nasjleti, M. (1980). Suffering in silence: The male incest victim. *Child Welfare, 59*(5), 269–275.

National Center on Child Abuse and Neglect. (1976). *Intrafamily sexual abuse of children.* Washington, DC: National Center on Child Abuse and Neglect.

National Society for Autistic Children. (1978). National Society for Autistic Children definition of the syndrome of autism. *Journal of Autism and Childhood Schizophrenia, 8,* 162–167.

Newberger, E. H. (1977). Child abuse and neglect: Toward a firmer foundation for practice and policy. *American Journal of Orthopsychiatry, 47,* 374–376.

Nurse, S. M. (1964). Familial patterns of parents who abuse their children. *Smith College Studies of Social Work, 34,* 11–25.

O'Dell, S. (1974). Training parents in behavior modification: A review. *Psychological Bulletin, 81,* 418–433.

Ornitz, E. M., Guthrie, D., & Farley, A. H. (1977). The early development of autistic children. *Journal of Autism and Childhood Schizophrenia, 7,* 207–229.

Packard, V. (1983). *Our endangered children: Growing up in a changing world.* Boston: Little-Brown.

Panton, J. H. (1979). MMPI profile configurations associated with incestuous and nonincestuous child molesters. *Psychological Reports, 45*(1), 335–338.

Parke, R. D., & Collmer, W. (1975). Child abuse: An interdisciplinary analysis. In E. Heatherington (Ed.), *Child development research*

Patterson, G. R. (1982). *Coercive family process* (Vol. 3). Eugene, OR: Castalia.

Patterson, G. R., & Dishion, T. J. (1985). Contributins of families and peers to delinquency. *Criminology, 23*(1), 63–79.

Patterson, G. R., & Stouthamer-Loeber, M. (1984). The correlation of family management practices and delinquency. *Child Development, 55,* 1299–1307.

Perlmutter, L. H., Engsl, T., & Sagar, S. J. (1982). The incest taboo: Loosened sexual boundaries in remarried families. *Journal of Sex and Marital Therapy, 8*(2), 83–96.

Petzel, S., & Riddle, M. (1981). Adolescent suicide: Psychosocial and cognitive aspects. In Feinstein, Looney, Schwartzberg, & Sorosky (Eds.), *Adolescent psychiatry: Developmental and clinical studies* (Vol. 9). Chicago: University of Chicago Press.

Pollack, C. B., & Steele, B. F. (1972). A therapeutic approach to the parents. In C. Kempe & R. Helfer (Eds.), *Helping the battered child and his family.* Philadelphia: J. B. Lippincott.

Rentoul, E., & Smith, H. (Eds.). (1973). *Glaister's medical jurisprudence and toxicology* (13th ed.). Baltimore: Williams and Wilkins.

Rich, A. H., & Schroeder, H. E. (1976). Research issues in assertiveness training. *Psychological Bulletin, 83,* 1081–1096.

Riemer, S. (1940). A research note on incest. *American Journal of Sociology, 45,* 565–571.

Robins, L. N., & Ratcliff, K. S. (1979). Risk factors in the continuation of childhood antisocial behavior into adulthood. *International Journal of Mental Health, 7,* 96–116.

Rolston, R. H. (1971). The effect of prior physical abuse on the expression of overt and fantasy aggressive behavior in children. *Dissertation Abstracts International.* (University microfilms, Ann Arbor, MI, Number 71-29389).

Rosenberg, M. S., & Reppucci, N. D. (1985). Primary prevention of child abuse. *Journal of Consulting and Clinical Psychology, 53*(5), 576–585.

Rosenfeld, A. (1979). Incidence of a history of incest among 18 female psychiatric patients. *American Journal of Psychiatry, 136*(6), 791–795.

Rubel, R. J. (1980). Analysis and critique of HEW's *Safe school study report to Congress. Crime and Delinquency, 24,* 257–265.

Russell, D. E. H. (1983). The incidence and prevalence of intrafamilial and extrafamilial sexual abuse of female children. *Child Abuse and Neglect, 7*(2), 133–146.

Sarafino, E. P. (1979). An estimate of nationwide incidence of sexual offenses against children. *Child Welfare, 58,* 127–134.

Schinke, S. P., & Rose, S. D. (1976). Interpersonal skills training in groups. *Journal of Counseling Psychology, 23,* 442–448.

Schinke, S. P., Schilling, R. F., II, Kirkham, M. A., Gilchrist, L. D., Barth, R. P., & Blythe, B. J. (1986). Stress management skills for parents. *Journal of Child and Adolescent Psychotherapy, 3*(4), 293–298.

Schopler, E., & Sloan, J. L. (1983). Recent developments in the diagnosis and assessment of autism. In S. Ray, M. O'Neill, & N. Morris (Eds.), *Low incidence children: A guide to psychoeducational assessment* (pp. 8–65). Nachitoches, LA: Steven Ray.

Schultz, L. G. (1973). The child sex victims: Social, psychological and legal perspectives. *Child Welfare, 52*(3), 147–157.

Selig, A. L. (1976). The myths of the multiproblem family. *American Journal of Orthopsychiatry, 46,* 526–632.

Sgroi, S. M. (1982). Family treatment of child sexual abuse. *Journal of Social Work and Human Sexuality, 1,* 109–128.

Shapland, J. M. (1978). Self-reported delinquency in boys age 11 to 14. *British Journal of Criminology, 18*(3).

Silver, L. B. (1969). Does violence breed violence? Contributions from a study of one child abuse syndrome. *American Journal of Psychiatry, 3,* 126.

Smith, S. M. (1975). *The battered child syndrome.* Boston: Butterworth's.

Smith, S. M., Hanson, R., & Noble, S. (1974). Social aspects of the battered baby syndrome. *British Journal of Psychiatry, 125,* 568–582.

Specktor, P. (1979). *Incest: Confronting the silent crime.* Minneapolis: Minnesota Program for Victims of Sexual Abuse.

Spinetta, J., & Rigler, D. (1972). The child-abusing parent: A psychological review. *Psychological Bulletin, 77,* 296–304.

Spreat, S., Roszkowski, M., Isett, R., & Alderfer, R. (1980). Emotional disturbance in mental retardation: An investigation of differential diagnosis. *Journal of Autism and Developmental Disorders, 10,* 361–367.

Steele, B. F. (1970). Parental abuse of infants and small children. In E. Anthony & T. Benedek (Eds.), *Parenthood.* Boston: Little, Brown & Co.

Steele, B. F., & Pollack, C. B. (1968). A psychiatric study of parents who abuse infants and small children. In R. Helfer & C. Kempe (Eds.), *The battered child.* Chicago: University of Chicago Press.

Sturkie, K. (1983). Structured group treatment for sexually abused children. *Health and Social Work, 8*(4), 299–308.

Swanson, D. W. (1968). Adult sexual abuse of children. *Diseases of the Nervous System, 29*(10), 677–683.

Tabachnick, N. (1981). The interlocking psychologies of suicide and adolescence. In Feinstein, Looney, Schwartzberg, & Sorosky (Eds.), *Adolescent psychiatry: Developmental and clinical studies* (Vol. 9). Chicago: University of Chicago Press.

Taubman, S. (1984). Incest in context. *Social Work, 29*(1), 35–40.

Thomson, E. M., Paget, N. W., Bates, D. W., Mesch, M., & Putnam, T. I. (1971). *Child abuse: A community challenge.* New York: Henry Steward.

Thornberry, T. P., Moore, M., & Christenson, R. L. (1985). The effect of dropping out of high school on subsequent criminal behavior. *Criminology, 23*(1), 3–18.

Time Magazine. (1980). Attacking the last taboo. *Time, 115,* 72.

Tormes, T. (1968). *Child victims of incest.* Denver, CO: American Humane Association, Children's Division.

Tracy, J. J., & Clark, E. H. (1974). Treatment of child abusers. *Social Work, 19,* 338–343.

U.S. Department of Justice. (1979). *Uniform crime reports, 1979.* Washington, DC: U.S. Government Printing Office.

Vander, B. J., & Neff, R. L. (1982). Adult-child incest: A review of research and treatment. *Adolescence, 17*(68), 717–735.

Webb, K. W., & Friedman, F. G. (1976, March). *Child abuse and neglect: Methods for determining incidence.* Paper presented at the Annual Meeting of the Council on Social Work Education, Philadelphia, PA.

Weber, E. (1977). Incest: Sexual abuse begins at home. *Ms. Magazine, 5,* 64–67.

Weinberg, S. K. (1955). *Incest behavior.* New York: Citadel Press.

Weiner, I. (1962). Father-daughter incest: A clinical report. *Psychiatric Quarterly, 36,* 607–632.

Wenz, F. (1979). Self-inquiry behavior, economic status and the family anomic syndrome among adolescents. *Adolescence, 14*(54), 387–398.

Wilson, H. (1980). Parental supervision: A neglected aspect of delinquency. *The British Journal of Criminology, 20*(3).

Wodarski, J. S. (1981). Comprehensive treatment of parents who abuse their children. *Adolescence, 16*(64), 959–972.

Wodarski, J. S. (1982). Single parents and children: A review for social workers. *Family Therapy, 9*(3), 311–320.

Wolfgang, M. E., Figlio, R. M., & Sellin, T. (1972). *Delinquency in a birth cohort.* Chicago: University of Chicago Press.

Wolfgang, M. E., & Weiner, N. A. (Eds.). (1982). *Criminal violence.* Beverly Hills: SAGE Publications.

Young, L. (1964). *Wednesday's children.* New York: McGraw-Hill.

Zefran, J., Jr., Riley, H. F., Anderson, W. O., Curtis, J. H., Jackson, M., Kelly, P. H.,

McGury, E. T., & Suriano, M. K. (1982). Management and treatment of child sexual abuse cases in a juvenile court setting. *Journal of Social Work and Human Sexuality, 1,* 155–170.

Zigler, E. (1967). Familial mental retardation: A continuing dilemma. *Science, 155,* 292–298.

Chapter 8

ADOLESCENTS

Adolescence is characterized by a period of time with high changes in physical stature, cognitive ability, and the development of interpersonal relationships. Growing up in today's society, adolescents face many difficulties in terms of equipping themselves cognitively and socially to compete in the American market place. If adolescents do not develop these social and cognitive competencies, profound complications exist. No one would doubt that the adolescents in America are in trouble. We have the highest incidence of teenage pregnancy, runaways, substance abuse, and depression and subsequent suicide of any society. Children who engage in these activities face substantial consequences for life. This chapter will elaborate the issues of teenage pregnancy, unemployment, runaway children, substance abuse, and depression and suicide among adolescents. Major intervention foci in terms of peers and families will be presented.

Teenage Pregnancy

One of the critical social problems facing our society is the marked increase in the number of adolescents who have become parents, but are insufficiently mature, unable or unwilling to provide adequate care, protection, and nurture a child's needs (Crawford & Furstenberg, 1985). A recent report by Guttmacher Institute (1985) revealed that 40% of today's 14-year-old girls can expect to become pregnant by the time they are 20 years old. Each year roughly 600,000 babies are born to the one million teenage girls (Guttmacher Institute, 1985), approximately 378,500 are aborted and the remainder are recorded as stillbirths or miscarriages (Dryfoos, 1982a, 1982b; National Center for Health Statistics, 1978). Furthermore, more than half of these adolescent mothers will have a repeat pregnancy within two years after the birth of their first child (while they are still school age) which heightens their probability for societal dependency (Howard, 1978; Trussell & Menken, 1978).

173

These statistics speak plainly to the magnitude of the problem. Adolescents who become pregnant are ensuring for themselves and their babies a bleak future. A future marked by truncated education, inadequate vocational training, poor work skills, economic dependency and poverty, large single-parent households and social isolation (Barth & Schinke, 1983). As Campbell (1968) commented in our societal concern over this problem, 90% of an adolescent's life script is written when she becomes a mother, and the story is often an unhappy one.

Adolescent pregnancy is increasingly commonplace today and poses many difficulties for both the individuals involved and society as a whole. For programs to successfully address this problem, factors related to unintended pregnancies and consequences of teenagers' pregnancies must be identified and understood.

Factors Related to Teenage Pregnancies

Physical and Rate Changes

A decrease in the average age at which the menstrual cycle begins and increasing sexual activity among youths have resulted in an alarmingly high incidence of teenage pregnancy (Chilman, 1979; Flick, 1986; Schinke, 1978). Sexual activity most often begins before the 16th year. Many youths sexually debut before they are 13 (Baldwin, 1980). Forty percent more black than white teenagers have been sexually active (Zelnik & Kantner, 1980), but fewer blacks than whites have many partners and fewer blacks have intercourse very frequently (Zelnik & Kantner, 1977). Sexual activity is increasing most rapidly among white adolescents (Zelnik & Kantner, 1980).

Contraceptive Use

Contraceptive use has not kept pace with adolescents' coital activity. Many sexually active youths wait a year or more before requesting birth control information and/or services (De Amicis, Klorman, Hess, & McAnarney, 1981). Despite widespread availability of over-the-counter contraceptives such as condoms, foams, and sponges, only one out of three adolescents aged 15 to 19 uses contraceptives each time he or she has intercourse. Contraceptive use also seems to decrease with age (Zelnik

& Kantner, 1980). Developmentally, adolescents are at a cognitive stage in their lives that may make contraceptive use less likely, i.e., guilt is associated with premeditated birth control. To avoid pregnancy, adolescents must have the cognitive ability to think abstractly—to connect present with future consequences—and must be able to logically consider possible solutions and to recognize the risks involved in unprotected sexual experiences (Doctors, 1985; Urburg, 1982). Adolescents (especially the younger ones) have not achieved this level of cognitive ability (Cobliner, 1974).

Increased use of birth control is found in adolescents who have higher levels of communication between partners (Anderson, McPherson, Beeching, Weinberg, & Vessey, 1978; Cvetkovich & Grote, 1980), and higher levels of parent-child communication about sexual activities and birth control (Fox & Inazu, 1980; Herald & Samson, 1980). Adolescents who are successful users of contraception methods are more likely to have accurate information about sex and contraception, higher academic achievement and exhibit a stronger sense of individual and internal locus of control (Mindick & Oskamp, 1982).

Family Communication

Most Americans believe that it is desirable for parents to discuss sex and contraception with their children but such communication occurs so infrequently. Thus, families are logical places for investigating factors that lead adolescents toward and away from the risk of early pregnancies (Schinke, 1984). Data support assertions that children get little sex education at home. Many families head off the discussion of sexual matters through a "conspiracy of silence"—they may even suspect the worst is happening, but they'd rather hope for the best and keep silent (Lindemann, 1974; Pocs, Godow, Tolone, & Walsh, 1977, p. 56). Researchers of mother-daughter communication have suggested that a potential for positive familial influence on this subject matter has largely gone untapped (Cicirelli, 1980; Inazu & Fox, 1980; Olson & Worsbey, 1984; Sheehy, 1974). Cicirelli (1980) indicated that mother-daughter relations make a difference in strongly influencing adolescents' sexual behaviors. He contends that girls are strongly influenced by parents rather than boys, and there is evidence to suggest that mother are (can be) the major force in girls' lives. In support of Cicirelli's assertions, Fox and Inazu (1980) reported that the strongest predictor of sexual experience was the daughter's report of her relationship with her mother; the more favorable the relationship, the less likely was the daughter to engage in premarital sex (p. 98).

Peer Influence

Peer groups greatly influence sexual behavior which is not always helpful in shaping teenagers' sexual attitudes and behavior (Cvetkovich & Grote, 1980; Rosenberg, 1980; Zelnik & Shah, 1983). Rosenberg (1980) reported that teenagers are most likely to discuss sex and birth control with friends, with whom they may well have exchanged inaccurate information. Rosenberg further reported that peers accounted for the knowledge teenagers had on topics such as masturbation, ejaculation, petting, intercourse, prostitution, homosexuality and contraceptives. When it came to birth control information from friends, only one in five teenagers in Rosenberg's study was knowledgeable (Schinke, 1984). A high involvement with peers and strong resemblence of peer values and views as opposed to parents often overrides the effects of parental involvement for adolescent males and is also associated with early sexual behavior for both gender groups (Miller & Simon, 1974; Zelnik & Shah, 1983). Studies have also indicated that teenagers' perceptions of frequent coital activities by peers or awareness of peers who use birth control is strongly associated with greater sexual activity (Cvetkovich & Grote, 1980; Hansson, O'Conner, Jones, & Blocker, 1981; Jorgenson, King, & Torrey, 1980). Peer influences were also reported by female adolescents who had sex because they felt unable to say no, wanted to please their partners, or saw intercourse as expected at the end of a date, and were reported by teenage males who said they initiated coitus to prove their love (Cvetkovich & Grote, 1980; Field, 1981; Rogel & Zuehlke, 1982).

Adolescents at Risk

Adolescents who engage in sexual activities are also those who are most likely to be impulsive risk takers and to participate in deviant behavior such as alcohol or drug use or other delinquent behavior (Jessor & Jessor, 1985). They have lower grades in school, lower expectations of achievements, lower acceptance of parental controls and are more likely to see their parents and friends as being in conflict. Many adolescent mothers have a low sense of self-esteem and levels of competence, poor individual and internal locus of control, and are more inclined to be passive and hold traditional stereotypical views of male-female gender roles (Cvetkovich & Grote, 1980; Cvetkovich, Grote, Lieberman, & Miller, 1978; Jessor & Jessor, 1975, 1985; Miller & Simon, 1974). Regular church attendance and/or association with an established religion has also been negatively associated with sexual activities of adolescents (Chilman, 1981; Jessor & Jessor, 1975, 1985; Miller & Simon, 1974).

Consequences of Adolescent Pregnancy

Health

Teenage pregnancies are associated with substantially increased health risks for both the mother and child. Adolescent pregnancies that result in childbirth often result in severe, adverse consequences such as high incidences of pregnancy and childbirth complications, and high incidence of low birth weight babies which are often associated with developmental and mental disabilities and high infant mortality and morbidity rates (Bolton, 1980; Levering, 1983; Rutter, 1980). Low birth weight and infant death are twice as likely for adolescent mothers than those beyond their teen years. These babies are also two to three times more likely to die in their first year as compared to babies born to older women (Hunt, 1976). Pregnancy related health risks faced by adolescent girls may be attributed to biological immaturity, nutritionally insufficient diets and poor prenatal care (Klerman & Jekel, 1973; Septo, Keith, & Keith, 1975; Ventura & Hendershort, 1984).

Interpersonal

Children of adolescent mothers are at greater risk of abuse and neglect. Studies have indicated a significant negative correlation between the age of the mother and the potential for abuse and gross neglect of the child. Additionally, children of teenage mothers are more likely to become teenage mothers themselves and continuing this cycle of recurring abuse and early childbearing (American Humane Association, 1978; Bolton, Laner, & Kane, 1980; Herrenkohl & Herrenkohl, 1979). Social and psychological studies further indicate that behavior disorders, school problems, and low intellectual functioning are more probable for adolescents' offspring than children of nonadolescent mothers. Many of the social and psychological problems are largely attributable to the social and economic insecurities of these teenage mothers (Belmont, Stein, & Zybert, 1978; Finkelstein, Finkelstein, Christie, Roden, & Shelton, 1982; Gunta & La Barba, 1980).

Moreover, psychologically, the role change from teenager to mother can produce negative emotional experiences. The unwed pregnant teenager who decides to have and keep her baby is often unprepared for the ensuing isolation and extremely demanding role of motherhood (Chilman, 1981; Gilchrist & Schinke, 1983a, 1983b; Quay, 1981). Adolescent years are known for their "emotional turbulance." Teenagers are still developing the coping skills and maturity needed for a psychologically healthy life—which have not fully developed—but are necessary for positive parenting (Levering, 1983; Little & Kendall, 1979; Smith, Weinman, & Mumford, 1982). At its worst, emotional stresses, depression experienced by many adolescent mothers, lead to frustration and anger which could ultimately be vented through violence either to themselves or their children. Gabrielson and his colleagues (1970) reported a higher incidence of suicide among pregnant adolescents.

Employment Preparation

For young parents, adolescent pregnancy interrupts and/or terminates education, which results in reduced earning power and dependence on public assistance and the social welfare system (Levering, 1983; Moore & Caldwell, 1977; Trussell & Menken, 1978). Data from the Wodarski, Parham, Lindsey and Blackburn (1986) study entitled "Toward a Poverty Agenda" indicates that this may be one of the most significant factors involved in welfare dependency. Teenage parents encounter additional stresses of ill-considered marriages and an increased likelihood of marital problems and high divorce rates (Lorenzi, Klerman, & Jekel, 1977).

Pregnancy has a disruptive effect on education which in turn affects subsequent job opportunities and income levels. The new responsibilities as a parent also interfere with the young mother's ability to locate employment (Kamerman, 1985). The odds for an adolescent mother achieving a successful and rewarding life are significantly lower than for those women who postpone childbearing until they are at least 20 years old. The very young mother often falls into a "syndrome of failure" which is hard to stop. Her combined lack of education, skills and work experience makes a poor resume for future employment and often leads to economic dependency (Burden & Klerman, 1984; Dillard & Pol, 1982, p. 257).

Furthermore, adolescent mothers tend to have repeat pregnancies which only serve to perpetuate this "syndrome of failure" (Schinke, 1984). The odds of falling into this syndrome are great, especially since 80% or more of adolescent mothers, age 17 or younger, do not finish high school. What are her options? Welfare is one and marriage is another possibility. Sixty percent of women in single-headed households receive AFDC and had their first child while in their teens (Wodarski, Parham, Lindsey, & Blackburn, 1986). Adolescent mothers fall below federal poverty lines—twice the rate of women who initiate childbearing after their teen years (Barker, Loughlin, & Rudolph, 1979). Reducing the subsequent pregnancies among young mothers is one of the major factors in reducing long-term dependency (Bane & Ellwood, 1983, p. vii).

Certain of the immediate economic problems are solved when teenage mothers have a strong social support system, e.g., family and parents. Many of these teen mothers stay with their parents or relatives, at least for a period of time (Scheirer, 1983; U.S. Bureau of the Census, 1983). Thus, because poverty rates for teenage mothers who head their household is very high, most teenage mothers live as sub-families in the household of a relative, usually a parent (Kamerman, 1985). Because many teenage mothers come from families who are economically disadvantaged themselves, this too causes additional stress and strain that could cause family tension or dissolution (Howard, 1978).

Teenage Unemployment

One of the most poignant aspects of black unemployment is the astronomical level of joblessness among black youth. The U.S. Department of Labor put black teenage unemployment at about 40% throughout most of the 1970's (National Urban League, 1981). Many areas of the black community are currently in a state of depression with over 50% of young blacks being unemployed (Williams, 1983).

Despite high unemployment, the desire for jobs among youths in general, and among disadvantaged and minority youths in particular, remains strong (Briar, 1976). However, the job prospects for certain youth are so bleak that after exhaustive, unsuccessful job searches, they permanently drop out of the conventional labor force. They become alienated and disenfranchised from traditional social institutions. If not corrected early, unemployment can have an irreversible impact on employment aspirations, social attachment and mental health.

The problem of youth unemployment is not simply a sign of the *present* economic times. Social and economic indicators forecast that youth joblessness may be a chronic problem. For example, even if the upturn in the economy continues, youth who are particularly under-educated are competing for jobs with unemployed who were previously employed, and with women and immigrants who are new to the job market. Furthermore, the high birth rates in the black population will continue to result in an increasing pool of black young people seeking to move into the job market.

Data indicate two groups of young people who are at extreme risk for unemployment and the subsequent mental health, health and criminal problems that accompany joblessness. The groups consist of (1) male and female school dropouts from central cities with special emphasis on black youths; (2) disadvantaged male and female senior high school students from central cities who are about to graduate and who will attempt to enter the job market. School dropouts traditionally have been identified as a high risk population. However, with the present employment trends, disadvantaged high school graduates are also at risk.

Interpersonal

Although unemployment can precipitate a range of mental health problems, does work *per se* have a positive impact on one's psychological well-being? Briar (1976) reported that for most of the 150 youth in her study, employment brought improved psychological, social and economic changes into their lives. For instance, 66% felt less depressed, 60% less angry and frustrated, and 80% less dependent. They also reported improved interpersonal relationships. Glaser (1978) found that getting a job decreased delinquency. Shore (1977) discovered that a clinical-work program for antisocial youth resulted in better job adjustment and higher pay, positive personality changes such as in self-image and control of aggression, accelerated achievement in reading and arithmetic, and a reduction in antisocial behavior. A follow-up of the treated youths revealed that they had substantially lower crime rates than controls.

Although the literature indicates that work does enhance one's mental health, it also points out that many youths, particularly the disadvantaged, are motivated to work but lack "know-how" about how to accurately assess their own interests and abilities, plan for their careers, and find and hold jobs. Many youth, especially those with negative school experiences, may suffer from alienation from society and a lack of self-esteem. For youth to be successfully employed, data suggest that it is necessary to take a holistic approach which responds not only to the problem of getting a young person a job but also preparing the youth both psychologically and socially for the job market.

Social Skills

Research indicates that it is necessary to teach youths the work skills and attitudes necessary for them to successfully compete in the job market; handle current problems and stresses; anticipate and prevent future problems; and advance their mental health, social functioning and economic welfare. Initially, adolescents' vocational aptitude and work skills-attitudes should be assessed. Subsequently, they participate in a series of psychoeducational "courses" including vocational enrichment (Azrin, 1978); enhancing interpersonal relationships (Lange & Jakubowski, 1976); managing stress, building social responsibility (Schinke & Gilchrist, 1984); alternatives to aggression, dealing with feelings (Goldstein, Sprafkin, Gershaw, & Klein, 1980); and problem solving (D'Zurilla & Goldfried, 1971; Spivack & Shure, 1974). A variety of psychoeducational methods are employed in the "courses" including individual and group counseling, self assessments, live and videotape demonstrations, behavior rehearsal with counselor, peer and videotape feedback, written materials, positive reinforcement, individual and group contracts, buddy systems, and progress logs. Most of these therapeutic strategies are delivered through a group work approach (Feldman & Wodarski, 1975; Wodarski, 1981).

The psychoeducational approach is based on an amalgamation of Goldstein and his colleagues' structured learning model, "Skillstreaming the Adolescent" (1980); Gazda's (1982) life span development skills training approach; Schinke and Gilchrist's (1984) life skills counseling with adolescents program; and Gurney's (1977) relationship enhancement model. The emphasis is on imparting transferable work skills-attitudes rather than either specific vocational skills or basic skills such as reading and mathematics. There is "very little evidence to support the proposition that employers are handicapped by the fact that employees lack the basic skills" (Rodriguez, 1980, p. 26). Furthermore, vocational training teaches skills specific to one job; and frequently in today's rapidly expanding technology, these skills become quickly antiquated. Youths need life management skills which are transferable from one job to the next and from work to home (Dayton, 1978; Dew, 1983). However, skills training *per se* is not enough. To enable high risk unemployed youths to cope with present stresses and to facilitate their adolescent development, individual and group counseling are essential (Shore, 1977; Zalinger, 1969).

The group context of the psychoeducation program is intended to capitalize on the adolescent's dependence on peers. "Group identity and cohesion should be fostered within groups of adolescents. Group support can be mobilized to aid individuals at moments of particular difficulty" (Ross & Glaser, 1973). The group interaction situation typifies many kinds of daily living situations, and the group provides a context where new behaviors can be tested in a realistic atmosphere (Feldman & Wodarski, 1975).

Although numerous projects have been conducted to help young people deal with employment problems, requisite components should include the following. First, emphasis on prevention rather than remediation. Second, it should be comprehensive, that is, it is intended to not only facilitate adolescents' career planning and orientation to work but also to provide them with skills and attitudes for healthy living. Third, although previous programs have used a combination of counseling, education and work to assist unemployed youth, none have combined the recent development in life skills training as this program proposes to do. Finally, the problem of youth unemployment, especially for minority youth, will be with us for the foreseeable future. It is critical that the field of mental health address the problems now.

Runaway Children

One of the most perplexing and critical problems confronting mental health professionals is how to effectively treat families with runaway children. It is estimated that between 700,000 to one million boys and girls run away from their homes every year. Consequences for runaways are severe in terms of prostitution, drugs, and even their lives (Brennan,

Huizinga, & Elliott, 1978; Miller, Miller, Hoffman, & Duggan, 1980). The seriousness and complexity of this social problem represents a difficult task for the worker who must be prepared to deal competently with children and their families. Yet there are still to be developed comprehensive training programs to prepare these workers to provide essential services to children and parents if families are to remain intact. Most treatment programs provide only one service to runaway children and families even though research indicates the causes of the difficulties are multiple, implying that children and families need a variety of services.

Data indicate that parents whose children run away face multiple social and psychological difficulties. The clearest empirical finding with regard to runaways seems to be the lack of consistency by the parent or parents in the handling of their children and the consequent lack of effectiveness in managing the child's behavior in a manner that facilitates their psychological and social development. It has also been pointed out that another common feature of relationships between parents and runaway children is unrealistic expectations by the parents regarding what is appropriate behavior for their child. Data suggests parents do not know what to expect from their children, how to teach necessary social skills and tasks to their children, and to appropriately apply child management procedures (Amanat & Able, 1973; Blood & D'Angelo, 1974; D'Angelo, 1974; Goldmeir & Dean, 1973; Hildebrand, 1968; Stierlin, 1973); therefore, social workers should be prepared to help parents in these areas.

Another empirical finding of substance has been the high degree of strain evident in families. Family interaction patterns have been characterized as primarily negative; that is, parents engage in excessive amounts of criticism, threats, negative statements, physical punishment, and a corresponding lack of positive interaction such as positive statements, praise, positive physical contact, and so forth (Bock & English, 1973; Brandon & Folk, 1977; Brennan, Huizinga, & Elliott, 1978; Hildebrand, 1968; Robinson, 1978; Suddick, 1973; Vandeloo, 1977). Additional data characterize families as having inadequate communication skills, problem solving, and conflict resolution skills. In view of this finding, a comprehensive treatment approach should include appropriate interventions that teach communication skills, problem solving, and conflict resolution to family members.

Recent research isolates another major factor—that many runaway children are dissatisfied with interpersonal relationships with peers and adults in terms of the frequency of positive interactions and their perception of social adequacy and social relevance for their peers and families (Beyer, 1974; Brandon, 1975; Wolk & Brandon, 1977). Thus, inadequately met social needs often precipitate runaway behavior.

Social workers must be trained to identify social expectations and implement interpersonal skills training such as: social conversational skills in how to introduce oneself, initiate and maintain conversation and give and receive compliments; enhancement of appearance and nonverbal communication; development of assertive behaviors for appropriate situations; and acquisition of planning, goal setting, problem-solving, and negotiation skills.

The pooling of data from these different research foci indicates therefore that a comprehensive treatment program would involve provision of service in several areas. It has been suggested that the reason treatment programs have not produced significant results in treating runaway children is that they focus on only one of the factors that operate to produce runaway behavior, i.e., lack of child management skills, family dissatisfaction, or interpersonal dissatisfaction (Kehoe & Freer, 1977; Margolin, 1976).

To reduce or prevent runaway behavior it will be necessary to offer new ways of developing behaviors that will bring children reinforcement. The proposed program combines several means of effectively changing behavior for families whose children run away. Each aspect is chosen for the strong empirical base upon which it rests. It is logical that an effective treatment approach to runaways must view the problem as multidetermined and services should be structured in such a manner. Thus, the comprehensive treatment program should consist of the following:

1. Child Management Program
2. Family Enrichment Program
3. Interpersonal Enrichment Program

Programs to accomplish the acquisition of requisite skills in each area are chosen from the technology of applied behavioral analysis. Reviews of parent training programs (Berkowitz & Graziano, 1972; Graziano, 1977; O'Dell, 1974; Twardosz & Nordquist, 1987), family enrichment (Bagarozzi & Wodarski, 1977, 1978; Jacobson & Martin, 1976; Patterson & Fleischman, 1979), and interpersonal skills training (Lange & Jakubowski, 1976; Rich & Schroeder, 1976; Schinke & Gilchrist; Schinke & Rose, 1976) have shown that their effectiveness is substantial as compared to other treatment programs.

Substance Abuse

Adolescence has been identified as a time when experimentation with drugs may be most active (Gorsuch & Arno, 1978; Mayer & Filstead, 1980). The acute consequences of substance use and misuse include traffic accidents, death due to accidents, later life health problems, suicide, school-related problems, temporary sickness, and absenteeism (Barr, Antes, Ottenberg, & Rosen, 1984). In addition, several studies have delineated the possible consequences of adolescent substance abuse which manifest themselves in antisocial behaviors (Gropper, 1984; Kane & Patterson, 1972; MacKay, 1961). Long-range consequences of teenage substance misuse include the failure to formulate goals for the future (Goodstadt & Sheppard, 1983) and stigmitization following an arrest while under the influence of drugs. The labeling of an adolescent under these circumstances can result in the loss of status, opportunity, and personal self-esteem (Mayer & Filstead, 1980). Patterns of substance abuse also have significant health consequences (Prendergast & Schafer, 1974).

Adolescence is a time when individuals become more oriented toward their peers and less toward their parents (Botvin, 1983; Bronfenbrenner, 1974; Montemayor, 1982). Adolescents turn to peers in order to receive emotional support that inattentive and unconcerned parents fail to provide. Hill (1980) stresses the importance of the conflict between parent and adolescent which leads to the adolescent accepting or seeking the approval of peers. Substantial data are available to indicate that, relative to the pre-adolescent years, parent and adolescent perceptions of conflict increase, actual conflict increases, and effective communication decreases between parents and adolescents (Montemayor, 1982; Smith & Forehand, in press). Simultaneously, peers become increasingly influential (Montemayor, 1982), and therefore the relative importance of family and peers must be carefully considered in adolescent drug prevention programs. As Glynn (1981) has indicated, theoretical approaches to this issue range from those which view either family (Hirschi, 1969) or peers (Sutherland & Cressey, 1970) as the primary influence to those which view both family and peers as important but typically in different domains of behavior (Kandel, Kessler, & Margulies, 1978; Pentz, 1983).

Adolescence is a critical period for the development of social, cognitive, and academic skills. It is essential that appropriate intervention foci are found to decrease substance abuse during this developmental period. At present the best model for viewing family and peer influence on adolescent drug use is one developed by Kandel and her colleagues (Kandel, 1974a, 1974b, 1981; Kandel & Faust, 1975; Kandel et al., 1978). Among other influences, the influence of parents and peers on each of the following three stages of drug use is considered: (1) initiation to hard liquor, (2) then marijuana, and finally (3) other illicit drugs. Based on a review of the available research, Glynn (1981) concludes that parents are most influential in adolescent initiation into hard liquor use and in adolescent initiation into use of illicit drugs other than marijuana, whereas peers are the primary influence in marijuana use. Parental modeling of drug use and the parental relationship with his/her adolescent are the primary mechanisms identified in adolescent drug use, whereas modeling alone appears to be the primary mechanism for peer influence.

Our theoretical perspective, as is Kandel's, is anchored within a broad base of a social learning framework (Robin & Foster, 1984). From this viewpoint, the adolescent learns appropriate and inappropriate behavior from the context (that is, parents and peers) in which he/she functions by modeling and reinforcement (Bandura, 1969). That is, by observing the behaviors demonstrated by others and by receiving or not receiving reinforcement/punishment for engaging in such behaviors, adolescents acquire certain behavior patterns. Furthermore, and of particular importance, if an adolescent functions within a context in which good communication and/or adequate cognitive skills are lacking [e.g., he/she has inadequate knowledge and unrealistic beliefs, expectations or attributions (Robin & Foster, 1984)], he/she is more likely to engage in maladaptive behavior patterns through modeling and reinforcement. Such a developmental process does not provide the adolescent with the requisite behaviors for prosocial attachment to family members, peers, and social institutions and is a high risk factor for subsequent substance abuse.

While researchers are increasing their data base about teenage substance abuse and its consequences and are beginning to develop models for drug abuse, they know little about the effective prevention of substance misuse among teenagers. The solution to the problem of adolescent substance abuse among teens will require an all out effort by families, schools, peers and communities (Fors & Rojeck, 1983; Wodarski & Fisher, 1986).

As peers and parents are the best predictors of adolescent drug use (Adler & Kandel, 1982; Glynn, 1981), preventive programs are needed that include one or ideally both of these groups. Data now are emerging to suggest effective procedures for dealing with peers and parents in order to prevent substance abuse. Critical questions that must be addressed are the type of interventions and their subsequent foci.

A unique adolescent education program, Teams-Games-Tournaments (TGT), has been developed for use by school professionals to teach adolescents about alcohol and to prevent its misuse. TGT was developed through extensive research on games used as teaching devices, using small groups as classroom work units, and emphasizing the task-and-reward structures used in the traditional classroom. The TGT technique is an alternative teaching approach that fully utilizes structure emphasizing group, rather than individual, achievement and utilizes peers as teachers and supporters of prosocial norms (Feldman & Wodarski, 1975; Wodarski, 1981; Wodarski et al., 1980). Thus the TGT method capitalizes on peer influence and subsequently increases social attachment to peers. For an elaboration of the TGT technique refer to the prevention chapter of this text.

The other significant variable that influences an adolescent's drug use is the family. In particular, parents serve as models in drug and alcohol use (Kandel, 1980); that is, the probability of drug experimentation and use is increased when adolescents view parents exhibiting such behaviors. Furthermore, particular types of parenting behavior (lack of positive reinforcement, setting appropriate expectations, communication skills, and problem solving skills) can serve as predictors of adolescent drug use (Pulkkinen, 1983), and can discriminate between adolescent drug users and non-users (Rees & Wilborn, 1983). Therefore, it would appear that teaching parents to provide appropriate models and expectations, and improving parents' problem solving and communication skills would be critical ingredients of an adolescent drug prevention program for parents.

Basically, problem solving involves four steps: problem identification, generation of alternative solutions, decision making, and planning solution implementation (Robin & Foster, 1984). Communication involves skills which can be used during problem solving discussions and at other times. Robin and Foster (1984) have identified 20 behaviors that may interfere with effective communication. These include accusing, putting down, interrupting, getting off topics, dwelling on the past, and threatening. Robin, Foster, and their colleagues have conducted three well-controlled studies which support the effectiveness of a problem solving communication skills training program for parents. Relative to waiting list control groups and a family therapy approach, problem solving communication skills increase communication and decrease conflicts (Foster, Prinz, & O'Leary, 1983; Robin, 1981; Robin, Kent, O'Leary, Foster, & Prinz, 1977). Furthermore, at follow-ups improvements achieved with problem solving skills were maintained.

Adolescent Depression and Suicide

Within the past decade a considerable effort has been made to assimilate information and elucidate causes of one of the most difficult problems facing America today—adolescent suicide. Following accidents while intoxicated and homocides, suicide is the third leading cause of death in the 15–24 year old age group (National Center for Health Statistics, 1978). The adolescent population is at greatest risk in regard to suicide, and the risk is increasing (Frederick, 1978; Toolan, 1975). Between 1960–1980, the suicide rate rose from 5.2 to 12.3 per 100,000 for this age segment accounting for a 136% increase. The rate is increasing most rapidly for white males (Berman, 1984). Traditionally, adolescence has been portrayed as a carefree period in the life span, when enjoyable times are had by all. In reality, however, the transition from childhood to adulthood is fraught with psychological, sociological and physical changes (Elkind, 1984a, 1984b).

The epidemic of adolescent suicide closely resembles French sociologist Durkheim's (1951) definition of anomic suicide, which arises from a rapid change in the social order or social norms. Roberts (1975), in *Self-Destructive Behavior,* writes of anomic suicide: "The individual becomes uncertain of the appropriate behavior expected of him/her and experiences a state of anomic normlessness, an unbridgeable gap between aspirations and achievements where individual passions are out of control" (p. 27).

Childhood today is not in the same sphere as was growing up in the 1960's. In the past, a majority of children had the support system of relatively warm, caring families, stable school environments, and trusting adults. Contrary to this, a significant percentage of today's teenagers are maturing in a state of relative fear. Family breakups either are being experienced personally by the adolescent, or observed in the homes of their contemporaries (Wattenberg, 1986; Wodarski, 1982). Demographic trends have led to overcrowded schools where an impersonal atmosphere leads to a sense of alienation (Holinger & Offer, 1981; Packard, 1983; Wenz, 1979). Primary emphasis, however, can be placed on the inability of children and teenagers to form close, interpersonal relationships with adults at home and outside the family structure. The alienation experienced by both children and adolescents has long-term effects on the individual's outlook on both moral and social issues. Alienation itself breeds a lack of trust within the child (Arnold, 1983; Coles, 1983). Society in the 1980's tends to ally children with children and adults with adults in social settings. Felt rejection in the adolescent results from this lack of intergenerational interaction (Kaplan, Robbins, & Martin, 1983).

Helplessness and hopelessness characterize the environment envisioned by the suicidal adolescent (Berkovitz, 1981; Miller, 1981; Petzel & Riddle, 1981; Tabachnick, 1981). Davis notes that the suicidal adolescent suffers from a helpless feeling of "tunnel vision" where he/she fails to see other options when placed in highly intensive emotional situations, e.g., break-up with boy/girlfriend or conflict with mother/father (Davis, 1983). This constricted view affords the teenager the opportunity to deal only with difficulties in the present frame of reference (Berman, 1984). Topol and Reznikoff (1982) suggest that external locus of control on the part of the teenagers contributes to this sense of hopelessness.

Causal Factors in Adolescent Suicide

Suicidal behavior is the result of dysfunctional adjustment by the teenager to psychological and environmental circumstances. Aspects of depression and stress have been cited in research studies as prodromal clues in attempted and completed suicides (Davis, 1983). Evaluation of the role of the family and peer involvement have been examined in the same context.

Depression. Depression naturally occurs in all adolescents as part of the maturational process. However, the intensity and severity of this depression is a factor in the adolescent's psychological health (Nichtern, 1982). The suicidal individual's emotional state is indecisive, with the wish to live versus the wish to die playing at his/her emotions. Research on suicide attempters by Kovacs and Beck (1977) found this "internal debate" in over 50% of the participants tested, using a Wish to Live/Wish to Die Scale.

Intense depression has been found to be the most prevalent characteristic of suicidal youth (Calhoun, 1972; Carson, 1981; Friedman, Corn, Hurt, Fibel, Schulick, & Swirsky, 1984; Gibbs, 1981; Holinger & Offer, 1981; Marks & Haller, 1977; Miller, 1975; Tishler & McKenry, 1983). Vegetative symptoms of depression include mood variations, sleep disturbances, fatigue and loss of energy, and changes in appetite (Rosenblatt, 1981; Tishler & McKenry, 1983). In the school setting, depression is indicated by a decline in academic performance or a withdrawal from peers and extracurricular activities (DenHouter, 1981; Greuling & DeBlassie, 1980; Petzel & Riddle, 1981).

In an examination of their backgrounds, the "loner" adolescent, who presents him/herself with no significant friendships during these critical years, is especially vulnerable to depression and suicidal ideation. Miller (1981) and Hawton (1982) have found a number of adolescents to have been depressed for years either because of earlier deprivation or a profound sense of emptiness in their lives. Individuals who attempt suicide are characterized by a high degree of alienation in relation to peer group interaction (Madison, 1978).

Alcohol and drug abuse is recognized as a defense mechanism to combat depression. Severe alcohol ingestion may lead to a loss of control over suicidal impulses (Dorpat, 1975). Greuling and DeBlassie (1980) studied statistics from several large cities and found that over 50% of teenagers who had committed suicide had a history of moderate to severe drinking and abusive use of drugs prior to their deaths. Researchers are now noting that "acting out" behaviors and discipline problems exhibited by adolescents many times mask the depressive condition (Greuling & DeBlassie, 1980; Nielsen, 1983). The adolescent's suicide attempt has been viewed as a means of dealing with the depression and regaining control over his life (Getz, Allen, Myers, & Linder, 1983).

Stress. The debilitating physical and psychological effects of stress on the human body have been studied in depth. As compared with other cultures, Americans traditionally place themselves under an inordinate amount of stress due to extremely high expectations for themselves. This has gradually filtered down to the expectations placed upon children. McAnarney (1979) and Herbert (1984) suggest that this emphasis on achievement contributes to the suicidal crisis of today.

Testing and grading procedures in American school systems tend to label children according to the failure/success model at an early age. A correlation between school failure and suicide has been noted. However, school failure contributes significantly to the stressful, helpless feelings demonstrated by teenagers who have a background of poor school grades (Sartore, 1976). White males are viewed as particularly susceptible to performance pressures (Holinger & Offer, 1981; Smith, 1981). For example, the high suicide rates of Japanese adolescents are linked to the school examination system. In Japan, adolescents compete feverishly for the coveted selection into college (Farber, 1968; World Health Organization, 1975).

Stress is especially great for U.S. teenagers whose parents live vicariously through the achievements of their children (Madison, 1978). Overachievers as well as underachievers are at a distinct risk for suicide. Herbert (1984) found that the unusually high expectations of overachievers led to an unhealthy mental attitude, while a sense of futility burdened those adolescents who were labeled as being "learning disabled".

Stress can also be involved in situations where internal and external conflicts have not been resolved, such as inadequate separation from the parent (Nielsen, 1983). Suicide is seen as a form of conflict resolution for many disturbed adolescents (Miller, 1980).

Stress is also precipitated by drastic changes in the life situation of a teenager, e.g., death of parent, firing from a job, rejection by team/school. Significant others who are aware of these events should be alert to their impact on the teenager's life and be able to recognize certain behaviors as attempts to adjust to the particular circumstances (McBrien, 1983).

Family Influences. The family as the integral formation model has a distinct effect on the child. In the early years, foundations of trust and love are established for the child within the home structure. The functioning of the individual is largely determined by his/her psychological growth during this period.

The American family has been in a state of flux for the last twenty years. The growing incidence of family dissolutions, and the resulting single and/or female headed household with its attending life style, makes this an especially difficult period. Old patterns of child rearing are being put aside to make accommodations for new parenting situations. Sociological researchers tend to view the phenomenon of adolescent suicide as a reflection of this turmoil in American family living (Hawton, 1982; Petzel & Riddle, 1981; Swenson & Rabin, 1981). Hendin (1975) posits that there is a trend toward the devaluation of the family and children, and an atmosphere in which there is an absence of intimacy and affection. Experiences in environments which are non-supportive and overly hostile lend themselves to the development of personality characteristics of a suicidal nature.

Studies of suicide attempts by hospitalized patients and of actual suicides within an academic school year have demonstrated that family disruptions and disintegration played a significant role in the maladaptation of these individuals (Herbert, 1984; Topol & Reznikoff, 1982). Close to one-half (43%) of cases reviewed by Litt, Cuskey and Rudd (1983) reported that a family argument preceded a suicide attempt. A family environment where the possibility of divorce or separation was openly discussed was found to be especially troubling for teenagers and a factor in suicide attempts.

Peer Involvement. When the teenager attempts to form a separate identity from his parents, he/she commences earnest involvement with peers. At school adolescents begin to ascertain their strengths and limitations both academically and socially. Their ability to handle the rigors of this adjustment period rests heavily on their previous experiences. Sexual identification and the addition of a "significant other" to the life of the teenager create a push-pull effect, where the teenager is being pushed into adulthood while still desiring the basic security of childhood. Tabachnick (1981) has focused on the fear of the adolescent that "he/she cannot make it."

The ability of adolescents to interact with peers significantly influences their later social adjustment. Janes, Hesselbrock, Myers, and Penneman (1979), who studied boys initially in late childhood and early adolescence and twelve years later in a follow-up, concluded that failure to get along with peers is closely associated with a wide spectrum of dysfunctional adult behaviors.

It is in the search for the components of their personality that teenagers scrutinize those around them and determine their own self-worth. When a troubled youth is surrounded by seemingly well-functioning peers, this only tends to lower his self-esteem and leads to suicidal contemplation (Holinger & Offer, 1981).

Based on these data we posit using a life skills approach with adolescents in middle school grades. The theoretical rationales which form the empirical basis for the intervention are based on the literature indicating that teaching adolescent life skills through peer experiences which enhance learning and behavior change and families are important agents in supporting learning and behavior change. The comprehensive package has four components: information about depression and suicide; self-management skills related to depression with the following foci: problem solving, increasing interpersonal skills, and stress reduction through relaxation; social and family interactional skills; and the maintenance of knowledge and behavior. The program is targeted to provide essential knowledge and skills to adolescents for depression management and suicide prevention. The program utilizes a peer group experience to increase the likelihood of acquisition and maintenance of knowledge and behavior. In cases where an attempt has been made, professionals working with a distraught teenager must try to have the entire family respond to the crisis situation through intensive family therapy (Berman, 1984; Pfeffer, 1981; Rosenkrantz, 1978; Walker & Mehr, 1983).

Summary

This chapter has reviewed the magnitude of problems that adolescents face in terms of teenage pregnancy, runaway children, unemployment, substance abuse, and depression and suicide. We have centered in on the aspects that lead to these problems, particularly the lack of family communication and peer relationships. We have briefly evaluated the life skills model as a model that could facilitate adolescents' development and prevent substantial severe consequences from occurring. This model will be further elaborated in the next chapter.

REFERENCES

Adler, I., & Kandel, D. B. (1982). A cross-cultural comparison of socio-psychological factors in alcohol use among adolescents in Israel, France and the United States. *Journal of Youth and Adolescence, 11,* 89–113.

Amanat, E., & Able, S. (1973). Marriage role conflicts and child psychopathology. *Adolescence, 8*(32), 575–588.

American Humane Association. (1978). *National analysis of official child neglect and abuse reporting: An executive summary.* Englewood, CO: American Human Association.

Anderson, P., McPherson, K., Beeching, N., Weinberg, J., & Vessey, M. (1978). Sexual behavior and contraceptive practice of undergraduates at Oxford University. *Journal of Biosocial Science, 10*(3), 277–286.

Arnold, L. E. (1983). Unprevented alienation: Case illustration and group discussion. In L. Arnold (Ed.), *Preventing adolescent alienation.* Lexington, MA: D. C. Heath.

Azrin, N. H. (1978, November). *A learning approach to job finding.* Paper presented at the Association for Advancement of Behavior Therapy, Chicago.

Bagarozzi, D. A., & Wodarski, J. S. (1977). A social exchange typology of conjugal relationships and conflict development: Some implications for clinical practice, assessment, and future research. *Journal of Marriage and the Family, 39,* 53–60.

Bagarozzi, D. A., & Wodarski, J. S. (1978). Behavioral treatment of marital discord. *Clinical Social Work Journal, 6*(2), 135–154.

Baldwin, W. H. (1980). Adolescent pregnancy and childbearing: Growing concerns for Americans. *Population Bulletin, 31*(2), 1–37.

Bandura, A. (1969). *Principles of behavior modification.* New York: Holt, Rinehart & Winston.

Bane, M. J., & Ellwood, D. T. (1983). *The dynamics of dependence: The routes to self-sufficiency* (prepared for the Office of Income Security Policy, U.S. Department of Health and Human Services). Washington, DC: U.S. Government Printing Office.

Barker, S. R., Loughlin, J., & Rudolph, C. S. (1979). The long-term effects of adolescent childbearing: A retrospective analysis. *Journal of Social Service Research, 2*(4), 341–355.

Barr, H., Antes, D., Ottenberg, D., & Rosen, A. (1984). The mortality of treated alcoholics and drug addicts: The benefits of sobriety. *Journal of Studies on Alcohol, 45*(5), 440–452.

Barth, R. P., & Schinke, S. P. (1983). Coping with daily strain among pregnant and parenting adolescents. *Journal of Social Service Research, 7*(2), 51–63.

Belmont, L., Stein, Z., & Zybert, P. (1978). Child spacing and birth order: Effect on intellectual ability in two-child families. *Science, 202,* (4371), 995–996.

Berkovitz, I. H. (1981). Feelings of powerlessness and the role of violent actions in adolescents. In Feinstein, Looney, Schwartzberg & Sorosky (Eds.), *Adolescent psychiatry: Developmental and clinical studies* (Vol. 9). Chicago: University of Chicago Press.

Berkowitz, B. P., & Graziano, A. M. (1972). Training parents as behavior therapists: A review. *Behavior Research and Therapy, 10,* 297–317.

Berman, A. L. (1984, October). Testimony on behalf of the American Psychological Association before the Committee on the Judiciary, Subcommittee on Juvenile Justice. In *United States Senate hearing on teenage suicide.*

Beyer, M. (1974). The psychosocial problems of adolescent runaways (Doctoral dissertation, Yale University, 1974). *Dissertation Abstracts International, 35,* 2420–2421B. (University microfilms No. 74-25, 718B).

Blood, L., & D'Angelo, R. (1974). A progress research report on value issues in conflict between runaways and their parents. *Journal of Marriage and the Family, 36,* 486–491.

Bock, R., & English, A. (1973). *Got me on the run.* Boston: Beacon.

Bolton, F. G. (1980). *The pregnant adolescent: Problems of premature parenthood.* Beverly Hills, CA: SAGE Publications.

Bolton, F. G., Laner, R. H., & Kane, S. P. (1980). Child maltreatment risk among adolescent mothers: A study of reported cases. *American Journal of Orthopsychiatry, 50*(3), 489–504.

Botvin, G. J. (1983). Prevention of adolescent substance abuse through the development of personal and social competence. In *Preventing adolescent drug abuse: Intervention strategies* [NIDA Research Monograph No. 47, U.S. Department of Health and Human Services (ADM) 83-1280]. Washington, DC: U.S. Government Printing Office.

Brandon, J. S. (1975). The relationship of runaway behavior in adolescence to the individual's perceptions of self, the environment, and antecedents. *Dissertation Abstracts International, 36,* 646B. (University microfilms No. 2-B).

Brandon, J. S., & Folk, S. (1977). Runaway adolescents' perceptions of parents and self. *Adolescence, 12,* 175–187.

Brennan, T., Huizinga, D., & Elliott, D. S. (1978). *The social psychology of runaways.* Lexington, MA: D.C. Heath and Co.

Briar, K. H. (1976). *The effect of long-term unemployment on workers and their families.* DSW dissertation, The University of California at Berkely.

Bronfenbrenner, U. (1974). The origins of alienation. *Scientific American, 231,* 53–61.

Burden, D. S., & Klerman, L. V. (1984). Teenage parenthood: Factors that lessen economic dependence. *Social Work, 29*(1), 11–16.

Calhoun, J. F. (1972). *Abnormal psychology.* New York: Random House.

Campbell, A. (1968). The role of family in the reduction of poverty. *Journal of Marriage and the Family, 30*(2), 236–246.

Carson, G. A. (1981). The phenomenology of adolescent depression. In Feinstein, Looney, Schwartzberg, & Sarosky (Eds.), *Adolescent psychiatry: Developmental and clinical studies* (Vol. 9). Chicago: University of Chicago Press.

Chilman, C. S. (1979). *Adolescent sexuality in a changing American society: Social and psychological perspectives.* Washington, DC: U.S. Government Printing Office.

Chilman, C. S. (1981). Social and psychological research concerning adolescent childbearing: 1970–1980. *Journal of Marriage and the Family, 42*(4), 793–805.

Cicirelli, V. G. (1980). A comparison of college women's feelings toward their siblings and parents. *Journal of Marriage and the Family, 42*(1), 111–117.

Cobliner, W. G. (1974). Pregnancy in the single adolescent girl: The role of cognitive functions. *Journal of Youth and Adolescence, 3*(1), 17–29.

Coles, R. (1983). Alienated youth and humility for the professions. In L. Arnold (Ed.), *Preventing adolescent alienation.* Lexington, MA: D. C. Heath & Co.

Crawford, A. G., & Furstenberg, F. F. (1985). Teenage sexuality, pregnancy, and childbearing. In Laird & Hartman (Eds.), *A handbook of child welfare: Context, knowledge and practice* (pp. 532–559). New York: Free Press.

Cvetkovich, G., & Grote, B. (1980). Psychosocial development and the social problem of teenage illegitimacy. In C. Chilman (Ed.), *Adolescent pregnancy and childbearing: Findings from research* (pp. 15–41). [NIH Publication No. 81-2077]. Washington, DC: Department of Health and Human Services.

Cvetkovich, G., Grote, B., Lieberman, E., & Miller, W. (1978). Sex role development and teenage fertility-related behavior. *Adolescence, 13,* 231–236.

D'Angelo, R. (1974). *Families of sand: A report concerning the flight of adolescents from their families.* Columbus, OH: Ohio State University College of Social Work.

Davis, P. A. (1983). *Suicidal adolescents.* Springfield, IL: Charles C Thomas.

Dayton, C. W. (1978, March). The dimensions of youth unemployment. *Journal of Employment Counseling,* 3–27.

DeAmicis, L. A., Klorman, R., Hess, D. N., & McAnarney, E. R. (1981). A comparison of unwed pregnant teenagers and nulligravid sexually active adolescents seeking contraception. *Adolescence, 16*(61), 11–20.

DenHouter, K. V. (1981). To silence one's self: A brief analysis of the literature on adolescent suicide. *Child Welfare, 25,* 2–10.

Dew, A. (1983). Personal communication. University of Alabama at Birmingham, July 1.

Dillard, K. D., & Pol, L. G. (1982). The individual economic cost of teenage childbearing. *Family Relations, 31*(2), 249–259.

Doctors, S. R. (1985). Premarital pregnancy and childbirth in adolescence: A psychological overview. In Z. DeFries, R. C. Friedman, & R. Corn (Eds.), *Sexuality: New perspectives* (pp. 45–70). Westport, CT: Greenwood Press.

Dorpat, T. (1975). Dyscontrol and suicidal behavior. In A. Roberts (Ed.), *Self-destructive behavior.* Springfield, IL: Charles C Thomas.

Dryfoos, J. G. (1982a). Contraceptive use, pregnancy intentions and pregnancy outcomes among U.S. women. *Family Planning Perspectives, 14*(2), 81–94.

Dryfoos, J. G. (1982b). The epidemiology of adolescent pregnancy: Incidence, outcomes, and interventions. In I. Stuart & C. Wells (Eds.), *Pregnancy in adolescence: Needs, problems, and management* (pp. 27–47). New York: Van Nostrand Reinhold Company.

Durkheim, E. (1951). *Suicide: A study in sociology.* New York: Free Press.

D'Zurilla, T. J., & Goldfried, M. R. (1971). Problem solving and behavior modification. *Journal of Abnormal Psychology, 78,* 101–126.

Elkind, D. (1984a). *All grown up and no place to go.* Reading, MA: Addison Wesley.

Elkind, D. (1984b). *The hurried child.* Reading, MA: Addison Wesley.

Farber, M. L. (1968). *Theories of suicide.* New York: Funk & Wagnalls.

Feldman, R. A., & Wodarski, J. S. (1975). *Contemporary approaches to group treatment.* San Francisco: Jossey-Bass.

Field, B. (1981). Socio-economic analysis of out of wedlock births among teenagers. In K. Scott, T. Field, & E. Robertson (Eds.), *Teenage parents and their offspring* (pp. 15–33). New York: Grune and Stratton.

Finkelstein, J. W., Finkelstein, J. A., Christie, M., Roden, M., & Shelton, C. (1982). Teenage pregnancy and parenthood: Outcome for mother and child. *Journal of Adolescent Health Care, 3*(1), 1–7.

Flick, L. H. (1986). Paths to adolescent parenthood: Implications for prevention. *Public Health Report, 101*(2), 132–147.

Fors, S. W., & Rojek, D. G. (1983). The social and demographic correlates of adolescent drug use patterns. *Journal of Drug Education, 13,* 205–222.

Foster, S. L., Prinz, R. J., & O'Leary, K. D. (1983). Impact of problem-solving communication training and generalization procedures on family conflict. *Child and Family Behavior Therapy, 5,* 1–24.

Fox, G. L., & Inazu, J. K. (1980). Patterns and outcomes of mother-daughter communication about sexuality. *Journal of Social Issues, 36,* 7–29.

Frederick, C. J. (1978). Current trends in suicidal behavior in the United States. *American Journal of Psychotherapy, 32,* 172–200.

Friedman, F. C., Corn, R., Hurt, S. W., Fibel, B., Schulick, J., & Swirsky, S. (1984). Family history of illness in the seriously suicidal adolescent: A life cycle approach. *American Journal of Orthopsychiatry, 54*(3), 390–397.

Gabrielson, I. W., Klerman, L. V., Currie, J. B., Tyler, N. C., & Jekel, J. F. (1970). Suicide attempts in a population pregnant as teenagers. *American Journal of Public Health, 60*(12), 2289–2301.

Gazda, G. M. (1982). Life skills training. In E. Marshall & D. Kurtz (Eds.), *Interpersonal helping skills.* San Francisco: Jossey-Bass.

Getz, W. L., Allen, D. B., Myers, R. K., & Linder, K. C. (1983). *Brief counseling with suicidal persons.* Lexington, MA: D.C. Heath & Co.

Gibbs, J. T. (1981). Depression and suicidal behavior among delinquent females. *Journal of Youth and Adolescence, 10*(2), 159–166.

Gilchrist, L. D., & Schinke, S. P. (1983a). Coping with contraception: Cognitive and behavioral methods with adolescents. *Cognitive Therapy and Research, 7*(5), 379–388.

Gilchrist, L. D., & Schinke, S. P. (1983b). Counseling with adolescents about their sexuality. In C. S. Chilman (Ed.), *Adolescent sexuality in a changing American society* (pp. 230–249). New York: Wiley.

Glaser, K. (1978). The treatment of depressed and suicidal adolescent. *American Journal of Psychotherapy, 32*(2), 252.

Glynn, T. J. (1981). From family to peer: A review of transitions of influence among drug-using youth. *Journal of Youth and Adolescence, 10,* 363–383.

Goldmeir, J., & Dean, R. D. (1973). The runaway: Person, problem, or situation? *Crime and Delinquency, 19,* 539–544.

Goldstein, A. P., Sprafkin, R. P., Gershaw, N. J., & Klein, P. (1980). *Skillstreaming the adolescent.* Champaign, IL: Research Press.

Goodstadt, M. S., & Sheppard, M. A. (1983). Three approaches to alcohol education. *Journal of Studies on Alcohol, 44*(2), 362–380.

Gorsuch, R. L., & Arno, D. H. (1978). The relationship of children's attitudes toward alcohol to their value development. *Journal of Abnormal Child Psychology, 7*(31), 287–295.

Graziano, A. M. (1977). Parents as behavior therapists. In M. Hersen, R. Eisler, & P. Miller (Eds.), *Progress in behavior modification* (Vol. 4). New York: Academic Press.

Greuling, J., & DeBlassie, R. R. (1980). Adolescent suicides. *Adolescence, 15*(59), 589–601.

Gropper, B. A. (1984, November). *Probing the links between drugs and crime* (pp. 4–8). Washington, D.C.: National Institute of Justice.

Gunter, N. N., & La Barba, R. C. (1980). The consequences of adolescent childbearing on postnatal development. *International Journal of Behavioral Development,* *3*(2), 191–214.

Gurney, B. G. (1977). *Relationship enhancement.* San Francisco: Jossey-Bass.

The Alan Guttmacher Institute. (1985, March). *Report on adolescent pregnancy.* New York: Guttmacher Institute.

Hansson, R., O'Conner, M., Jones, W., & Blocker, T. (1981). Maternal employment and adolescent sex behavior. *Journal of Youth and Adolescence, 10*(1), 55–60.

Hawton, K. (1982). Attempted suicide in children and adolescence. *Journal of Child Psychology and Psychiatry and Allied Disciplines, 23*(4), 497–503.

Hendin, H. (1975). Growing up dead: Student suicide. *American Journal of Psychotherapy, 29,* 327–338.

Herald, E. S., & Samson, L. M. (1980). Differences between women who begin pill use before and after first intercourse: Ontario, Canada. *Family Planning Perspectives, 12*(6), 304–305.

Herbert, M. (1984, October). Addressing the issue of teenage suicide in a public school system. Statement for the U.S. Senate Committee on the Judiciary Subcommittee on Juvenile Justice.

Herrenkohl, E. C., & Herrenkohl, R. C. (1979). A comparison of abused children and their nonabused siblings. *Journal of the American Academy of Child Psychiatry, 18*(2), 260–269.

Hildebrand, J. A. (1968). Reasons for runaways. *Crime and Delinquency, 14*(1), 42–48.

Hill, J. P. (1980). The family. In M. Johnson (Ed.), *Toward adolescence: The middle school years.* Chicago: University of Chicago Press.

Hirschi, T. (1969). *Causes of delinquency.* Berkeley: University of California Press.

Holinger, P. C., & Offer, D. (1981). Perspectives in suicide in adolescence. *Research in Community and Mental Health, 2,* 139–157.

Howard, M. (1978). Yount parent families. In *Child welfare strategy in the coming years* (pp. 197–226) [DHEW Publication No. (OHDS) 78-30158]. Washington, DC: Office of Human Development Services, Administration for Children, Youth and Families.

Hunt, W. B. (1976). Adolescent fertility: Risk and consequences. *Population reports,* 157–176.

Inazu, J. K., & Fox, G. L. (1980). Maternal influence on the sexual behavior of teenage daughters. *Journal of Family Issues, 1*(1), 81–102.

Jacobson, N. S., & Martin, B. (1976). Behavior marriage therapy: Current status. *Psychological Bulletin, 83,* 540–556.

Janes, C. L., Hesselbrock, V. M., Myers, D. G., & Penneman, J. H. (1979). Problem boys in young adulthood: Teacher's ratings and the twelve year follow-up. *Journal of Youth and Adolescence, 8*(4), 453–472.

Jessor, S. L., & Jessor, R. (1975). Transition from virginity to nonvirginity among youth: A social-psychological study over time. *Developmental Psychology, 11,* 473–484.

Jessor, S. L., & Jessor, R. (1985). Structure of problem behavior in adolescence and young adulthood. *Journal of Consulting and Clinical Psychology, 53*(6), 890–904.

Jorgenson, S. R., King, S. L., & Torrey, B. A. (1980). Dyadic and social network influences on adolescent exposure to pregnancy risk. *Journal of Marriage and the Family, 42*(1), 141–155.

Kamerman, S. B. (1985). Young, poor, a mother alone: Problems and possible solutions. In H. McAdoo & T. M. Parham (Eds.), *Services to young families: Program review and policy recommendations* (pp. 1–38). Washington, DC: American Public Welfare Association.

Kandel, D. (1974a). Inter- and intra-generational influences on adolescent marijuana use. *Journal of Social Issues, 30,* 107–135.

Kandel, D. (1974b). Interpersonal influences on adolescent drug use. In E. Josephson & E. Carroll (Eds.), *Drug use: Epidemiological and sociological approaches.* Washington, DC: Hemisphere.

Kandel, D. (1980). Developmental stages in drug involvement. In D. Lettieri (Ed.), *Theories of drug abuse* [NIDA Research Monograph Series, No. 30, DHHS Publication No. (ADM) 80-967]. Washington, DC: U.S. Government Printing Office.

Kandel, D. (1981). Adolescent marijuana use: Role of parents and peers. *Science, 181,* 1067–1070.

Kandel, D., & Faust, R. (1975). Sequences and stages in patterns of adolescent drug use. *Archives of General Psychiatry, 32,* 923–932.

Kandel, D., Kessler, R., & Margulies, R. (1978). Adolescent initiation into stages of drug use: A developmental analysis. In D. Kandel (Ed.), *Longitudinal research on drug use: Empirical findings on methodological issues.* Washington, DC: Hemisphere-Wiley.

Kane, R. L., & Patterson, E. (1972). Drinking attitudes and behavior of high school students in Kentucky. *Quarterly Journal of Studies on Alcohol, 33*(3), 635–646.

Kaplan, H. B., Robbins, C., & Martin, S. (1983). Antecedents of psychological distress in young adults: Self-rejection, deprivation of social support and life events. *Journal of Health and Social Behavior, 24,* 230–244.

Kehoe, C. J., & Freer, R. (1977). Cooperative services for runaway youth. *Juvenile Justice, 28*(1), 35–39.

Klerman, L., & Jekel, J. (1973). *School-age mothers: Problems, programs and policy.* Hamden, CT: Linnett.

Kovacs, M., & Beck, A. (1977). The wish to die and the wish to live in attempted suicide. *Journal of Clinical Psychology, 33*(3), 361–365.

Lange, A. J., & Jakubowski, P. (1976). *Responsible assertive behavior.* Champaign, IL: Research Press.

Levering, C. S. (1983). Teenage pregnancy and parenthood. *Childhood Education, 59*(3), 182–185.

Lindemann, C. (1974). *Birth control and unmarried young women.* New York: Springer.

Litt, I. F., Cuskey, W. R., & Rudd, S. (1983). Emergency room evaluation of the adolescent who attempts suicide: Compliance with follow-up. *Journal of Adolescent Health Care, 4*(2), 106–108.

Little, V. L., & Kendall, P. C. (1979). Cognitive-behavioral interventions with delinquents: Problem solving, role taking, and self-control. In P. Kendall &

S. Hallon (Eds.), *Cognitive-behavioral interventions: Theory, research and procedures.* New York: Academic Press.

Lorenzi, M. E., Klerman, L. V., & Jekel, J. F. (1977). School-aged parents: How permanent a relationship? *Adolescence, 12*(45), 13–22.

MacKay, J. R. (1961). Clinical observations on adolescent problem drinkers. *Quarterly Journal of Studies on Alcohol, 22,* 124–134.

Madison, A. (1978). *Suicide and young people.* New York: Seabury Press.

Margolin, M. H. (1976). Styles of service for runaways. *Child Welfare, 55*(3), 205–215.

Marks, P. A., & Haller, D. L. (1977). Now I lay me down for keeps: A study of adolescent suicide attempts. *Journal of Clinical Psychology, 33,* 390–400.

Mayer, J. E., & Filstead, W. J. (1980). Adolescence and alcohol: A theoretical model. In J. Mayer & W. Filstead (Eds.), *Adolescence and alcohol.* Cambridge, MA: Ballinger Publishing Co.

McAnarney, E. R. (1979). Adolescent and young adult suicide in the United States: A reflection of societal unrest? *Adolescence, 14*(56), 765–774.

McBrien, R. J. (1983). Are you thinking of killing yourself? Confronting students' suicidal thoughts. *School Counselor, 31*(1), 75–82.

Miller, D. (1980). The treatment of severely disturbed children. In Feinstein, Looney, Schwartzberg & Sorosky (Eds.), *Adolescent psychiatry: Developmental and clinical studies* (Vol. 8). Chicago: University of Chicago Press.

Miller, D. (1981). Adolescent suicide: Etiology and treatment. In Feinstein, Looney, Schwartzberg & Sorosky (Eds.), *Adolescent psychiatry: Developmental and clinical studies* (Vol. 9). Chicago: University of Chicago Press.

Miller, D., Miller, D., Hoffman, F., & Duggan, R. (1980). *Runaways—Illegal aliens in their own land: Implications for service.* New York: Praeger.

Miller, J. (1975). Suicide and adolescence. *Adolescence, 10,* 13–23.

Miller, P., & Simon, W. (1974). Adolescent sexual behavior: Context and changes. *Social Problems, 22*(1), 58–76.

Mindick, B., & Oskamp, S. (1982). Individual differences among adolescent contraceptors: Some implications for intervention. In I. Stuart & C. Wells (Eds.), *Pregnancy in adolescence: Needs, problems and management* (pp. 140–176). New York: Van Nostrand Reinhold.

Moore, & Caldwell,. (1977). *Out of wedlock childbearing.* Washington, DC: Urban Institute.

Montemayor, R. (1982). The relationship between parent-adolescent conflict and the amount of time adolescents spend alone with parents and peers. *Child Development, 53,* 1512–1519.

National Center for Health Statistics. (1978, March 29). Final natality statistics, 1976: Advance report. *Monthly Vital Statistics Report, 26*(12), 1–26. [DHEW Publication No. (PHS) 78-1120].

National Urban League. (1981). *The state of black America.* Washington, DC: National Urban League.

Nichtern, S. (1982). The sociocultural and psychodynamic aspects of the acting-out and violent adolescent. In Feinstein, Looney, Schwartzberg, & Sorosky (Eds.),

Adolescent psychiatry: Developmental and clinical studies (Vol. 10). Chicago: University of Chicago Press.

Nielsen, G. (1983). *Borderline and acting out adolescents.* New York: Human Sciences Press.

O'Dell, S. (1974). Training parents in behavior modification: A review. *Psychological Bulletin, 81,* 418–433.

Olson, C. F., & Worsbey, J. (1984). Perceived mother-daughter relations in a pregnant and nonpregnant adolescent sample. *Adolescence, 119*(76), 781–794.

Packard, V. (1983). *Our endangered children: Growing up in a changing world.* Boston: Little Brown.

Patterson, G. R., & Fleischman, M. J. (1979). Maintenance of treatment effects: Some considerations concerning family system and follow-up. *Behavior Therapy, 10*(2), 168–185.

Pentz, M. A. (1983). Prevention of adolescent substance abuse through social skill development. In T. Glynn, C. Leukefeld, & J. Ludford (Eds.), *Preventing adolescent drug abuse: Intervention strategies* (NIDA Research Monograph 47). Rockville, MD: DHHS.

Petzel, S., & Riddle, M. (1981). Adolescent suicide: Psychosocial and cognitive aspects. In Feinstein, Looney, Schwartzberg, & Sorosky (Eds.), *Adolescent psychiatry: Developmental and clinical studies* (Vol. 9). Chicago: University of Chicago Press.

Pfeffer, C. (1981). The family system of sucidal children. *American Journal of Psychotherapy, 35*(3),

Pocs, D., Godow, A., Tolone, W., & Walsh, R. (1977). Is there sex after 40? *Psychology Toady, 11*(1), 54–56, 87.

Prendergast, T. J., & Schafer, E. F. (1974). Correlates of drinking and drunkenness among high school students. *Quarterly Journal of Studies on Alcohol, 35,* 232–242.

Pulkkinen, L. (1983). Youthful smoking and drinking in a longitudinal perspective. *Journal of Youth and Adolescence, 12,* 253–283.

Quay, H. C. (1981). Psychological factors in teenage pregnancy. In K. G. Scott, T. Fields, & E. Robertson (Eds.), *Teenage parents and their offspring* (pp. 73–90). New York: Grune and Stratton.

Rees, C. D., & Wilborn, B. L. (1983). Correlates of drug abuse in adolescents: A comparison of families of drug users with families of non-drug users. *Journal of Youth and Adolescence, 12,* 55–63.

Rich, A. H., & Schroeder, H. E. (1976). Research issues in assertiveness training. *Psychological Bulletin, 83,* 1081–1096.

Roberts, A. R. (1975). *Self-destructive behavior.* Springfield, IL: Charles C Thomas.

Robin, A. L. (1981). A controlled evaluation of problem-solving communication training with parent-adolescent conflict. *Behavior Therapy, 12,* 593–609.

Robin, A. L., & Foster, S. L. (1984). Problem-solving communication training: A behavioral family systems approach to parent-adolescent conflict. In P. Karoly & J. Steffen (Eds.), *Adolescent behavior disorders: Foundations and contemporary concerns.* Lexington, MA: Lexington Books.

Robin, A. L., Kent, R., O'Leary, K. D., Foster, S., & Prinz, R. (1977). An approach to teaching parents and adolescents problem-solving communication skills: A preliminary report. *Behavior Therapy, 8,* 639–643.

Robinson, P. A. (1978). Parents of 'beyond control' adolescents. *Adolescence, 13*(49), 109–119.

Rodriguez, J. F. (1980). Youth employment: A needs assessment. In *A review of youth employment problems, programs and policies: The youth employment problem* (Vol. 1). Washington, DC: U.S. Government Printing Office.

Rogel, M., & Zuehlke, M. (1982). Adolescent contraceptive behaviors: Influences and implications. In I. Stuart & C. Wells (Eds.), *Pregnancy in adolescence: Needs, problems and management* (pp. 194–218). New York: Van Nostrand Reinhold Co.

Rosenberg, P. B. (1980). Communication about sex and birth control between mothers and their adolescent children. *Population Environment, 3*(1), 35–50.

Rosenblatt, J. (1981). Youth suicide. *Editorial Research Reports, 1,* 431–438.

Rosenkrantz, A. L. (1978). A note on adolescent suicide: Incidence, dynamics, and some suggestions for treatment. *Adolescence, 13*(50), 209–213.

Ross, H., & Glaser, E. (1973). Making it out of the ghetto. *Professional Psychology, 4*(3), 347–356.

Rutter, M. (1980). *Changing youth in a changing society.* Cambridge, MA: Harvard University Press.

Sartore, R. L. (1976). Students and suicide: An interpersonal tragedy. *Theory into Practice, 15*(5), 337–339.

Scheirer, M. A. (1983). Household structure among welfare families: Correlates and consequences. *Journal of Marriage and the Family, 45*(4), 761–771.

Schinke, S. P. (1978). Teenage pregnancy: The need for multiple casework services. *Social Casework, 59*(7), 406–410.

Schinke, S. P. (1984). Preventing teenage pregnancy. In M. Hersen, P. Eisler, & P. Miller (Eds.), *Progress in behavior modification* (Vol *16,* pp. 31–64). Orlando, FL: Academic.

Schinke, S. P., & Gilchrist, L. D. (1984). *Life skills counseling with adolescents.* Baltimore: University Park Press.

Schinke, S. P., & Rose, S. O. (1976). Interpersonal skill training in groups. *Journal of Counseling Psychology, 23,* 442–448.

Septo, R., Keith, L., & Keith, D. (1975). Obstetrical and medical problems. In J. Zackler & W. Bradstadt (Eds), *The teenage pregnant girl* (pp. 83–133). Springfield, IL: Charles C Thomas.

Sheehy, G. (1974). *Passages.* New York: E. P. Dutton & Co., Inc.

Shore, M. F. (1977). Evaluation of a community-based clinical program for antisocial youth. *Evaluation, 4,* 104–107.

Smith, E. J. (1981). Adolescent suicide: A growing problem for the school and family. *Urban Education, 16*(3), 279–296.

Smith, K. A., & Forehand, R. (in press). Parent-adolescent conflict: Comparison and prediction of the perceptions of mothers, fathers, and daughters in a non-clinic sample.

Smith, P. B., Weinman, M. L., & Mumford, D. M. (1982). Social and affective factors associated with adolescent pregnancy. *Journal of School Health, 52*(2), 90–93.

Spivack, G., & Shure, M. B. (1974). *Social adjustment of young children.* San Francisco: Jossey-Bass.

Stierlin, H. (1973). A family perspective on adolescent runaways. *Archives of General Psychiatry, 29,* 56–62.

Suddick, D. (1973). Runaways: A review of the literature. *Juvenile Justice, 24,* 46–54.

Sutherland, E., & Cressey, D. (1970). *Criminology.* New Jersey: Lippincott.

Swenson, B., & Rabin, P. (1981). Teenage suicide attempts and parental divorce. *New England Journal of Medicine, 304*(17), 1048.

Tabachnick, N. (1981). The interlocking psychologies of suicide and adolescence. In Feinstein, Looney, Schwartzberg, & Sorosky (Eds.), *Adolescent psychiatry: Developmental and clinical studies* (Vol 9). Chicago: University of Chicago Press.

Tishler, C. L., & McKenry, P. C. (1983). Intrapsychic symptom dimensions of adolescent suicide attempters. *Journal of Family Practice, 16*(4), 731–734.

Toolan, J. M. (1975). Suicide in children and adolescents. *American Journal of Psychotherapy, 29*(3), 339–344.

Topol, P. & Reznikoff, M. (1982). Perceived peer and family relationships, hopelessness and locus of control as factors in adolescent suicide attempts. *Suicide and Life Threatening Behavior, 12*(3), 141–150.

Trussell, J., & Menken, J. (1978). Early childbearing and subsequent fertility. *Family Planning Perspectives, 10*(4), 209–218.

Twardosz, S., & Nordquist, V. M. (1987). Parent training. In M. Hersen & V. Van Hasselt (Eds.), *Behavior therapy with children and adolescents: A clinical approach* (pp. 75–105). New York: Wiley.

U.S. Bureau of the Census. (1983). *Households and family characteristics — March, 1983* (Series P-20, No. 388, Current Population Reports). Washington, DC: U.S. Government Printing Office.

Urburg, K. (1982). A theoretical framework for studying contraception use. *Adolescence, 17*(67), 527–540.

Vandeloo, C. (1977). A study of coping behavior of runaway adolescents as related to situational stresses. *Dissertation Abstracts International, 38,* 2387–2388B. (University microfilms No. 5-B).

Ventura, S., & Hendershort, G. (1984). Infant health consequences of childbearing by teenagers and older mothers. *Public Health Reports, 99*(2), 138–146.

Walker, B. A., & Mehr, M. (1983). Adolescent suicide — A family crisis: A model for effective intervention by family therapists. *Adolescence, 18*(70), 285–292.

Wattenberg, E. (1986). The fate of baby boomers and their children. *Social Work, 31,* 20–28.

Wenz, F. (1979). Self-inquiry behavior, economic status and the family anomic syndrome among adolescents. *Adolescence, 14*(54), 387–398.

Williams, R. (1983). Critical issues: An endangered people. *Planning and Changing, 14*(1), 5–14.

Wodarski, L. A., Adelson, Tidball, & Wodarski, J. S. (1980). Teaching nutrition by teams-games-tournaments. *Journal of Nutrition Education, 12*(2), 61–65.

Wodarski, J. S. (1981). *Role of research in clinical practice.* Baltimore: University Park Press.

Wodarski, J. S. (1982). Single parents and children: A review for social workers. *Family Therapy, 9*(3), 311–320.

Wodarski, J. S., & Fisher, A. (1986). The alteration of adolescent DUI: A macro approach. *Alcoholism Treatment Quarterly, 3*(2), 153–162.

Wodarski, J. S., Parham, T. M., Lindsey, E. W., & Blackburn, B. (1986). Reagan's AFDC policy changes: The Georgia experience. *Social Work, 31*(4), 273–279.

Wolk, S., & Brandon, J. (1977). Runaway adolescents' perceptions of parents and self. *Adolescence, 12,* 175–187.

World Health Organization. (1975). *World health statistics annual 1972: Volume I: Vital statistics and causes of death.* Geneva: World Health Organization.

Zalinger, A. D. (1969). Job training programs: Motivational and structural dimensions. *Poverty and Human Resources Abstracts, 4*(3), 5–13.

Zelnik, M., & Kantner, J. (1977). Sexual and contraceptive experiences of young unmarried women in the U.S.: 1971–1976. *Family Planning Perspectives, 9*(2), 55–71.

Zelnik, M., & Kantner, J. (1980). Sexual activity, contraceptive use and pregnancy among metropolitan area teenagers: 1971–1979. *Family Planning Perspectives, 12*(5), 230.

Zelnik, M., & Shah, F. (1983). First intercourse among young Americans. *Family Planning Perspectives, 15*(2), 64–70.

Chapter 9

PREVENTIVE SERVICES FOR CHILDREN AND ADOLESCENTS: AN IDEA WHOSE TIME HAS COME

The prevention approach to intervention has implications for the traditional role of the social worker and to the timing of the intervention. The prevention approach places major emphasis on the teaching components of the intervention process (Wodarski & Bagarozzi, 1979b). Social workers attempt to help clients learn how to exert control over their own behaviors and over the environments in which they live. Practitioners do not take a passive role in the intervention process. Instead they use their professional knowledge, expertise and understanding of human behavior theory and personality development in the conceptualization and implementation of intervention strategies. Since their training equips them to evaluate scientifically any treatment procedure they have instituted, there is continual assessment of the treatment process.

Prevention is especially appropriate to dealing with the problems of the adolescent. It provides an early developmental focus for intervention which may forestall development of future problems. These problems usually intensify later and become harder to alter. Prevention provides a view of the person that is optimistic. The approach is mass-oriented rather than individual-oriented, and it seeks to build health from the start rather than to repair.

Problem behaviors of the young and their undesirable consequences are extensive and well documented. Teenagers' experimentation with drugs and alcohol can lead to overindulgence and abuse. Serious short- and long-term effects include risk-taking and daredevil behavior that increases risks to mental and physical health, including accidents, a leading cause of death among adolescents. Likewise, they may increase the incidence of irresponsible sexual activity which eventuates in venereal disease, unwanted pregnancy, and premature parenthood. Preven-

205

tion during the childhood and adolescent developmental periods would reduce these serious physical and social problems.

Initially, the chapter defines prevention and reviews the three approaches to prevention: primary, secondary and tertiary. From a life span developmental approach, skills an adolescent must master, such as social, cognitive and academic, should provide the focus for intervention. The life skills approach is proposed as the treatment of choice. This approach has rationale and elements in common with other prevention programs that are based on a public health orientation. These consist of three essential components: health education, skills training, and practice applying skills. The teams-games-tournaments (TGT) model consists of the same components except that in addition it uses peers as parallel teachers.

The chapter reviews data available to support the life skills and TGT model. It concludes with issues related to implementation of prevention strategies for adolescents, including cognitive aspects of prevention, social and family networks, intervention components in terms of where, by whom, why, how long, and on what practice level, and research foci.

Prevention Defined

Whereas a major preoccupation of adolescent mental health programs across the country appears to be crisis intervention and direct therapy, a more serious approach to reducing recurring problems, and to detecting signs of future problems, is coming into focus. Proposed programs, aimed at prevention, may be the key to mental health in the 1980's (Wodarski, 1983). Prevention is defined as the act of discouraging a problematic behavior or illness before it actually happens or before it becomes a problem. As there is a gradual shift away from the band-aid, after-the-fact, approach to mental health, programs designed to prevent more serious consequences of present and/or future mental health problems or to prevent the recurrence of mental dysfunctioning are beginning to emerge in rural as well as in urban areas. Since it is more cost-effective to prevent or reduce social problems, these programs proposed during a period of tight funds are sure to continue gaining appeal.

Social problems are the by-product of undesirable or ineffective behaviors. These behaviors frequently are the result of the adolescent's failure to attempt to cope with life's problems or to obtain desirable results when attempts are made (D'Zurilla & Goldfried, 1971). Predisposing factors include economic distress, peer rejection, academic failure, inadequate socialization, lack of problem solving skills, racism, and rapid physical changes (Whittman, 1977). These factors should be taken into account and dealt with as part of the problem gestalt.

Approaches to Prevention

Preventive programs should focus on those adolescents who will require services in the future if no ameliorating activities occur. The ultimate objective of preventive programs should be to eliminate or reduce the known predisposing factors within the community and thus reduce the number of adolescents at risk (Gottesfield, 1972). Preventive programs must teach alternate ways of dealing with environmental conditions (alternatives to undesirable behavior). For example, programs might focus on the development of social skills, or on acquisition of cognitive and emotional skills for reducing stress in one's own life (Rae-Grant, Gladwin, & Bower, 1966; Schinke & Blythe, in press). Essentially, preventive service programs must achieve two objectives. Each program must develop knowledge of factors that predispose the child and adolescent, and it must organize the community support systems to use this specific knowledge in its programs aimed toward altering such factors. Prevention of social distress encompasses, therefore, an array of programs, services and information.

Primary prevention is concerned with methods of reducing the overall incidence of social problems. Two foci of primary prevention which reduce the probability of interpersonal problems include teaching individuals to cope with stress and reducing stress in the actual environment (Gottesfield, 1972). Good examples of primary prevention of physical need deficits could be testing newborns for PKU to prevent mental retardation and providing adolescent parents information regarding child rearing. Primary prevention of psychosocial need deficits could focus on acquisition of studying skills.

Secondary prevention takes on a different approach to the issue of social problems. Secondary prevention necessitates the organization of a helping system for selected candidates within the community (Caplan, 1974). Medication prescriptions for adolescents known to be distressed is an example of secondary prevention from a physical perspective. Secondary sociocultural prevention is present in school systems in the form of psychological testing and counseling services, and in mental health centers in the form of educational classes or groups to prevent suicide among high risk adolescents (Wodarski & Harris, 1985).

Tertiary prevention deals with adolescents who have had previous social problems. The goal is to maintain the individual in the community and to prevent problems from recurring. The effort here is to reduce the recidivism rate for adolescents who have been institutionalized. Community organization and planning is essential for tertiary prevention programs (Gottesfield, 1972). Tertiary prevention programs try to ensure that those who have recovered will be aided, not hampered, by the community to which they return (Caplan, 1961). Continued medication and referrals for additional services are examples of physical tertiary prevention services. Aftercare counseling, follow-ups, and day treatment programs are all types of psychosocial tertiary prevention.

Life Span

Adolescent Developmental Tasks

The adolescent is preoccupied with rapid physical and intellectual maturation, heightened emotional sensitivity, and acceptance by social groups. Abstract thinking is possible and the adolescent is capable of conceptualizing changes that may occur in the future. The adolescent can anticipate the consequences of behavior and is especially sensitive to consistent and inconsistent parental behavior. Membership in peer groups that are more structured and organized than they were in earlier stages are extremely important. Group membership is most frequently based on physical attractiveness. The adolescent also begins engaging in heterosexual relationships. Parents and significant adults influence the child's identity and self-esteem less than the all-important peers.

The psychosocial crisis at this stage is "group identity versus alienation." The adolescent receives pressure from parents, peers, and school to identify with a group. A positive resolution of the crisis results in the individual allying with a group that is perceived as meeting social needs and providing a sense of belonging. A negative resolution results in the adolescent experiencing a sense of isolation and continually feeling uneasy in the presence of peers. The central process is peer pressure (Newman & Newman, 1979).

Peer Influence

The peer group serves as a transitional world for the adolescent. Data suggest that participation in extracurricular activities is the most important determination of the adolescent's status with peers (Feldman, Caplinger, & Wodarski, 1983). The self-concept of the adolescent is very susceptible to status fluctuations that occur with family transiency and high school transitions. The worker should encourage the adolescent undergoing such transitions to become involved in extracurricular activities because they can provide support.

For teenagers, actions detrimental to health frequently occur in situations involving peers. The influence of peer groups on adolescent behavior is well known (Sherif & Sherif, 1964) and, for many teenagers, strong social pressure provokes participation in peer sanctioned behaviors such as smoking, drinking, and sexual intercourse. Although teenagers may understand health risks involved in these activities, this understanding is insufficient to counter the social significance of indulging. Recent research (McAlister, Perry, & Maccoby, 1979) conducted jointly at Stanford and Harvard Universities underscores this point:

> Behaviors detrimental to health are embedded in a complex milieu of social forces that often overwhelms educated rationality . . . Even if a young person develops a negative attitude toward unhealthy behaviors, she or he may not possess the skills to resist strong social pressures to conform with peers who do not share that attitude (p. 650).

Specific cognitive and behavioral skills are needed to resist external pressures and to successfully negotiate interpersonal encounters where pressure occurs. Adolescents often lack these skills not because of individual pathology but for developmental reasons. Age brings increased opportunity to engage in previously unknown or prohibited activities. Lack of experience and prior learning opportunities hampers youths' ability to deal with new situations and new behavioral requirements. Sexual experimentation provides an example. A significant number of 15 to 17 year olds in a recent national survey reported becoming sexually involved because it seemed "expected" of them and they did not know how to refuse (Cvetkovich & Grote, 1976). Lack of interpersonal skill is also implicated in teenagers' frequent nonuse of contraception (Kovar, 1979; Zelnick & Kantner, 1977). Recent research links failure to use contraception with failure to acquire critical assertive and communication skills (Campbell & Barnlund, 1977; Mindick, Oskamp, & Berger,

1978). These findings suggest teenagers may know about and value birth control, but, embarrassed and lacking skill, they may be unable to obtain it or to negotiate its use with sexual partners.

Similar inability to resist external pressure and lack of skill in handling critical interpersonal situations has been associated with onset of cigarette smoking (Newman, 1970) and drug and alcohol misuse (Roy & Shields, 1979; Smart, Gray, & Bennett, 1978). In short, a growing body of work suggests that teachers can profitably focus prevention and health promotion efforts on teaching youth skills for coping with risk-related interpersonal situations.

Progress in preventing health-impairing behavior is painfully slow (McAlister et al., 1979). Confusion exists as to what constitutes adequate prevention education (Matus & Neuhring, 1979). Therefore, primary educational prevention programs are poorly supported through policy and funding (Broskowski & Baker, 1977). In addition, because preventive educational intervention is frequently poorly designed, with vague goals compounding difficulties, prevention program effects are hard to evaluate, further diminishing the likelihood of public and legislative support. A new conceptualization is required if prevention and health promotion services are to become effective components of service systems.

There is an accurate data base to provide rationale and empirical support for the development of prevention and health education programs for children and adolescents. This is based on the Skills Training Interventive Model and the use of Teams-Games-Tournaments (TGT), a teaching method with a successful empirical history.

Skills Training Interventive Model[1]

The skills training model described here has rationale and elements in common with other preventive approaches based on a public health orientation (Caplan, 1964) and are variously called "graded pre-exposure" (Epstein, 1967), "immunization" (Henderson, Montgomery, & Williams, 1972), "psychological inoculation" (McGuire, 1964), "behavioral prophylaxis" (Poser, 1970, 1979), and "stress inoculation" (Meichenbaum, 1975). Whatever the label, the interventive goal is skill building to strengthen adolescents' resistance to harmful influences in advance of their impact. Three components comprise this preventive model: health education, skills training, and practice applying information and skills in troublesome situations.

Health Education. That adolescents need accurate information to make informed choices is clear. Equally clear is the inadequacy of simply exposing teenagers to facts about unhealthy consequences of certain behavior. One fault with past health education programs is their assumption that exposure to training materials guarantees learning. Information-only programs have had few long-lasting effects (Haggerty, 1977). Accurate perception, comprehension, and storage of new information is a complex process dependent on individual receptivity and on the nature of the information presented (Mahoney, 1974). Particularly among younger adolescents, perceptual errors—selectively ignoring, misreading, or mishearing certin facts or selectively forgetting information—can create discrepancies between facts presented and facts received and remembered. The model proposed here addresses this potential problem by asking teenagers to periodically summarize presented content in written and verbal quizzes. Correct responses are then reinforced and errors detected and clarified. Also, peers are used as teachers thus enhancing their commitment to healthy behaviors.

A second critical issue overlooked in traditional health education programs is helping youths relate specific facts and observable risks to themselves and to their own lives. Called "relational thinking" (Mahoney, 1974), this is the process by which abstract information becomes part of an individual's everyday reality. This relational or personalization process is best accomplished by actively involving adolescents in gathering and assimilating information. Examples include special information-collecting assignments (interviewing community resources and conducting mini-surveys) and experimental exercises requiring verbalization of facts and choices in personal terms ("Each time I have sex and don't use birth control, I risk pregnancy"). Also helpful for information personalization are direct discussions of illusions and faulty thinking patterns used to conveniently ignore important health facts (i.e., "It can't happen to me;" "I can quit anytime I want to;" "I never have an orgasm so I don't have to worry about getting pregnant;" and the like).

Skills Training. Even personalized information is of little value if adolescents lack the skills to use it. Translating health information into everyday decision making and behavior involves cognitive and behavioral skills. The model thus emphasizes skills for making effective short- and long-term decisions and assertive and communication skills needed to implement decisions.

Cognitive skills training is adapted from research on problem solving

(D'Zurilla & Goldfried, 1971; Spivack, Platt, & Shure, 1976). Especially for adolescents, problem behavior is associated with peer norms and expectations. Realistic decisions about how to act must, therefore, consider responses of significant others. The ability to anticipate both interpersonal and health consequences of behavior, generate alternative action strategies, and arrive at the best choice are all crucial to health-promotive decision making. Again, training focused on sexual behavior provides an example. Following discussion of birth control advantages and disadvantages, adolescents anticipate possible difficulties using this information in social situations; for instance, not knowing when or how to initiate discussion of birth control with dating partners. The problem is examined in detail and major issues identified, such as selecting appropriate times and places for discussion, handling personal embarrassment, and dealing with partner reactions. Adolescents generate several possible plans specifying when, where, and how the discussion could occur. They predict the probable outcome of each plan, and select the one most feasible.

Training also focuses on behavioral skills necessary to transform decisions into action. Based on established assertive and communication skills-training procedures (Lange & Jakubowski, 1976; Schinke, Gilchrist, Smith, & Wong, 1976; Schinke & Rose, 1976), training presents verbal and nonverbal aspects of good communication to help adolescents learn to initiate difficult interactions, to practice self-disclosure of positive and negative feelings, to refuse unreasonable demands, to request changes in another's behavior, to ask others for relevant information and feedback, and to negotiate mutually acceptable solutions.

Practice Applying Skills. In the final and most important phase of the model, adolescents practice applying skills in a variety of potentially risky interpersonal situations. Extended role-played interactions provide adolescents with opportunities to recall and make use of health information, decision-making techniques, and communication skills as in the following vignette. You are at a party with someone you've been dating for about six months. The party is at someone's house; their parents are gone for the weekend. There is a lot of beer and dope and couples are going into the upstairs bedrooms to make out. Your date says, "Hey, Lisa and Tom have gone upstairs. It's real nice up there—let's go—come on."

In role-playing, teenagers practice responding to increasingly insistent demands receiving feedback, instructions, and praise to enhance performance. Practice applying skills also takes the form of "homework" assignments involving written contracts to perform certain tasks outside the training environment such as meeting with a family planning counselor and initiating discussion of birth control with a dating partner.

Another example of applying skills is contained in the drug refusal training aspects of the comprehensive health curriculum. The basic aim of drug refusal training is to help students develop more effective ways of dealing with social pressures to consume drugs. Specific situations are practiced where individuals apply pressure to persuade others to consume excessive amounts of drugs. Students practice reactions to statements like: "One drink won't hurt you;" "What kind of friend are you;" or "Just have a little one, I'll make sure you won't have any more."

Components of appropriate reactions are taught such as: (1) to look directly at the pusher when responding; (2) to speak in a firm, strong tone with appropriate facial expressions and body language; (3) to offer an alternative suggestion such as "I don't care for a beer but I'd love a Coke"; (4) to request that the pushers refrain from continued persuasion; and (5) to change the subject by introducing a different topic of conversation.

Although all phases of the interpersonal skills training model can be conducted with individuals, groups provide the most efficient and effective training context for this final practice phase. Group settings allow teenagers to try out skills with various partners, give feedback and encouragement to each other, and learn from a variety of models.

Teams-Games-Tournaments Model

The most important socialization agent in an adolescent's life is his/her peers with schools providing a natural environment for peer influence. Virtually all attempts to educate teenagers about health topics have taken an educational lecture model approach aimed at general education of all teenagers. Nearly all instruction in educational techniques are aimed at the individual pupil, ignoring the potential usefulness of the peer group in motivating students to learn and to acquire new skills or behaviors. Evaluative data indicate, however, the effectiveness of such an approach is minimal. Over the past three decades, a substantial amount of research has been conducted on learning groups. This research has suggested that learning teams in classrooms have uniformly positive effects on students.

The TGT technique, developed through two decades of research at the Johns Hopkins University Center for Social Organization of Schools, is an innovative, small group teaching technique. The method is grounded in current theory, applies to diverse problems, populations, and settings, and provides clear criteria for evaluating program effects. The technique alters the traditional classroom structure and gives each student an equal opportunity to achieve and to receive positive reinforcement from peers by capitalizing on team cooperation, the popularity of games, and the spirit of competitive tournaments. Group reward structures set up a learning situation wherein the performance of each group member furthers the overall group goals. This has been shown to increase individual members' support for group performance, to increase performance itself under a variety of similar circumstances, and to further increase the group's goals. There is significance in using the group reward structure with adolescents in that it capitalizes on peer influence and reinforcement, which are considered to be two of the most potent variables in the acquisition, alteration, and maintenance of behavior in youth (Buckholdt & Wodarski, 1978). Moreover, it facilitates the learning of low academic achievers, a group that is at greater risk to develop health problems. Data indicate that TGT is a viable mode for providing adolescents education about health related concerns. It has been found to be successful in helping children and adolescents acquire and retain knowledge in such areas as reading, arithmetic and social studies, and in the health related areas of nutrition and alcohol abuse.

Peer relationships play a significant role in the adolescent's socialization and health behavior. Thus, the information is provided in a group context to help students practice necessary social skills to develop adequate health behavior. Moreover, it capitalizes on the power of peers to influence the acquisition and subsequent maintenance of behavior which data indicate is the most potent influencing factor in an adolescent's life. It capitalizes on peers as teachers and this changes the normative peer structure to support healthy behavior (Buckholdt & Wodarski, 1978).

Components of TGT Model. The components of the education program are as follows.

(1) *Education.* This aspect includes facts about enhancing interpersonal relationships, alcohol and drugs, coping with sexuality, managing stress and depression, promoting health including good nutrition, securing employment, and accepting social responsibility.

(2) *Self-Management.* The comprehensive educational program provides instruction in self-management. This component is based on social learning theory concepts. For example, students learn how certain stim-

uli cue drinking behavior such as parties, peer statements, emotional upset, and loneliness. Through assertiveness training, students are taught how to refuse alcohol in a socially acceptable manner. Additionally, they learn how to reward themselves for not drinking and for developing skills that will, in the future, bring them reinforcement.

Specific Preventive Activities

Many types of preventive activities can be undertaken. For example, in planning programs for adolescents the following topics can be included: (1) nutrition education; (2) social skills training; (3) adequate health care, i.e., smoking, sexuality, consumption of alcohol; (4) job securement and maintenance; (5) resolving parental conflict; (6) problem solving techniques; and (7) increasing self-esteem to reduce adolescent suicide. Programs are available to facilitate implementation of all the above. For excellent reviews see Gilchrist (1981), Schinke and Blythe (in press), Schinke, Blythe and Gilchrist (1981), Schinke, Gilchrist and Blythe (1980), Wodarski et al. (1980), Wodarski (in press, a & b), and Wodarski and Harris (1985).

In a more specific example, adolescents identified as high risk in terms of coping with the daily problems of living are taught a problem solving approach based on the work of D'Zurilla and Goldfried (1971), Goldfried and Goldfried (1975), Shinke and Gilchrist (1984), and Spivack and Shure (1974). The general components emphasized are:

1. How to generate information
2. How to generate possible solutions
3. How to evaluate possible courses of action
4. Ability to choose and implement strategies through the following procedures:
   a) General introduction to how the provision of certain consequences and stimuli can control problem solving behavior
   b) Isolation and definition of a behavior to be changed
   c) Use of stimulus control techniques to influence rates of problem solving behavior
   d) Use of appropriate consequences to either increase or decrease a behavior
5. Verification of the outcome of the chosen course of action.

Cognitive Anger Control

One consistent finding is that the violent adolescent lacks means to control anger (LeCroy, 1983; May, 1986). Professionals must be prepared to help at-risk adolescents develop the following behaviors:

1. Identification of stresses which can provoke anger and subsequent violent behavior
2. Development of cognitive relaxation skills to reduce the effects of stresses
3. Learning how to receive assertions and deal with others' anger
4. Development of appropriate communication and assertion skills
5. Practicing alternate behavior, such as stimulus removal, in anger-provoking situations.

Employment Programs

Adolescents having difficulty in securing employment and social interaction could benefit from the two programs outlined below.

Vocational Enrichment Program. The vocational program is based on the work of Azrin (1978), Azrin, Flores and Kaplan (1975), and Jones and Azrin (1973). The general components emphasized are:

1. Group discussions involving strong motivation for vocational enrichment. These discussions involve mutual assistance among job seekers, development of a supportive buddy system, family support, sharing of job leads, and widening the variety of positions considered.

2. Employment securing aids, such as searching want ads, role playing, interview situations, instructions in telephoning for appointments, procedures for motivating the job seeker, developing appropriate conversational competencies, ability to emphasize strong personal attributes in terms of dress and grooming, and securing transportation for job interviews.

Social Enrichment Program. This program is based on the work of Lange and Jakubowski (1976) and involves interpersonal skills training and development of assertive behavior for appropriate situations. Specific elements that are emphasized include:

1. How to introduce oneself
2. How to initiate conversations and continue them
3. Giving and receiving compliments

4. Enhancing appearance
5. Making and refusing requests
6. Spontaneous expression of feelings
7. Appropriate use of nonverbal distance, body language, face, hand and foot movement, and smiling.

Issues

Cognitive Foci

Cognitive theories propose, in their stages of development, that a child is in a concrete operations stage early in school and moves into more abstract, formal operational thought during adolescence. By utilizing cognitive-behavioral methods the worker is able to adjust the service mode according to the child's cognitive developmental stage. The ultimate goal of most cognitive intervention methods is to increase the individual's ability to control his/her own outcomes, with self-control being viewed as a developmental achievement that follows external control (Bugenthal et al., 1977). For adolescents, the achievement of adequate cognitive process is essential to their development of adequate self-concept and self-esteem.

Cognitive theorists have proposed several major approaches, many of which overlap. These approaches focus both on particular sets of cognitive deficits or ways in which thinking may deviate from the logical and on the methods by which these errors or deficits may be corrected. The ultimate aim in cognitive intervention is to produce change in the negative attitudes an adolescent has, thus reducing cognitive blocks to appropriate behavior.

Cognitive theorists' investigation of the client's thinking is based on two premises. First, clients think in an idiosyncratic way (that is, they have a systematic negative bias in the way they regard themselves, their world, and their future). Second, the way clients interpret events maintains their cognitive distortions.

Cognitive therapists view cognition in the treatment process as either the "behavior" that needs to be modified or as an area that is indirectly changed when the overt behavior is treated (Meichenbaum, 1975). The cognitive therapist attempts to alter what the adolescent thinks in order to effect a change in behavior. The belief is that therapy should aim at reducing the frequency of the cognitions that elicit the undesirable behaviors (Hulbert & Sipprelle, 1978). The focus is on the cognitive self-statements the client makes, and faulty self-statements are viewed as a result of a faulty belief system and thinking pattern (Meichenbaum, 1975).

Cognitive theorists believe there to be four types of cognitive distortions:

1. Arbitrary inference: the process of drawing a conclusion when evidence is lacking or is actually contrary to the conclusion.

2. Overgeneralization: the process of making an unjustified generalization on the basis of a single incident.

3. Magnification: the propensity to exaggerate the meaning or significance of a particular event.

4. Cognitive deficiency: the disregard of an important aspect of a life situation. Clients with this deficit ignore, fail to integrate, or do not utilize information derived from experience, and consequently behave as though they have a defect in their system of expectations (Beck, 1970).

To address these distortions, the worker may have the client utilize problem-solving skills that are used throughout his/her life (Beck, 1976). In addition, a number of behavioral therapy procedures can be adapted to modify the cognitive self-statements (Meichenbaum, 1975). For example, cognitive theorists have emphasized the following cognitive aspects of depression. Beck (1976) assigned a primary position to a cognitive triad consisting of a very negative view of the self, of the outside world, and of the future. This triad is seen as the key to the consequences of depression, such as the lack of motivation, the affective state, and other ideational and behavioral manifestations. The depressed person's cognitions lead to misinterpretations of experiences, hence many of the secondary responses are logical sequences of such misinterpretations. The depressed person is locked in an insoluable situation, the result of which is further despair (Calhoun, Adams, & Mitchell, 1974). Thus, cognitive responses that can be altered by the therapist are: (1) sense of hopelessness, (2) self-condemnation and self-defeating thoughts, (3) low self-esteem, (4) tension, (5) death wishes, and (6) sense of helplessness.

Significant interactive effects have been found to exist between the intervention approach and the person's attributional style (Bugenthal et al., 1977; Prager-Decker, 1980). The individual's expectations and assumptions will play a significant role in the success he/she will experience in therapy (Goldfried & Goldfried, 1975). In relation to success in therapy, Bandura et al. (1977) noted that regardless of the methods used, treatments implemented through the individual's actual performance achieve consistently superior results to those based on symbolic forms of the same approach.

Social Networks

Data suggest that adolescents are at less social risk to develop mental distress if they are socially connected to other peers, i.e., social supports buffer stress, support and help individuals through crisis periods, promotes good physical health, and facilitates the acquisition and maintenance of relevant social competencies (Heller & Swindle, 1983).

One of the most perplexing yet critical problems confronting social work professionals interested in prevention is the effective use of networking for adolescents at risk. Questions that need to be resolved include the following. How can adolescents be tied to the networks available in their peer communities? What peer characteristics may be matched with adolescent attributes to facilitate networking and enhancement of the individuals' functioning? What support systems such as the church, extended family, and friends are available to enhance the adolescent's networks?

This aspect of prevention would involve development of programs to utilize efficacious and cost effective assessment procedures to isolate physical, psychological and social factors that lead to networking. Possible procedures include (1) assessment of adolescent's attributes such as homogeneity of peers, social cohesion, and services available; (2) enlistment of social networks and support groups such as family, peers, ministers and significant adult models to provide necessary support; (3) preparation of the adolescent in terms of emphasizing appropriate social behaviors that will be rewarded and will facilitate integration into the social structure of their peer community; (4) educating the adolescent about support services available and whom to contact and gradually introducing the individual to appropriate available support systems; and (5) developing appropriate preventive intervention.

Family Prevention

One empirically supported theoretical perspective is anchored within a broad base of a social learning framework (Robin & Foster, 1984). From this viewpoint, the adolescent learns appropriate and inappropriate behavior from the context (that is, parents and peers) in which he/she functions by modeling and reinforcement (Bandura, 1969). That is, by observing the behaviors demonstrated by parents who receive or do not receive reinforcement/punishment for engaging in such behaviors, adolescents acquire certain behavior patterns. Furthermore, and of particular importance, if an adolescent functions within a context in which good communication and/or adequate cognitive skills are lacking (e.g., he/ she has inadequate knowledge and unrealistic beliefs, expectations or attributions), he/she is more likely to engage in maladaptive behavior patterns through modeling and reinforcement (Robin & Foster, 1984).

One of the critical variables that influence an adolescent's development is the family. The particular types of parenting behavior (lack of positive reinforcement, communication skills, and problem-solving skills) can serve as predictors of adolescent problems (Pulkkinen, 1983), and can discriminate between adolescents at high risk of developing subsequent interpersonal difficulties (Rees & Wilborn, 1983).

Basically, problem solving involves four steps: problem identification, generation of alternative solutions, decision making, and planning solution implementation (Robin & Foster, 1984). Communication involves skills which can be used during problem solving discussions and at other times. Robin and Foster (1984) have identified 20 behaviors that may interfere with effective communication. These include accusing, putting down, interrupting, getting off topics, dwelling on the past, and threatening. Robin, Foster and their colleagues have conducted three well-controlled studies which support the effectiveness of a problem solving communication skills training program for parents. Relative to waiting list control groups and a family therapy approach, problem solving communications skills increase communication and decrease conflicts (Foster, Prinz, & O'Leary, 1983; Robin, 1981; Robin, Kent, O'Leary, Foster, & Prinz, 1977). Furthermore, at followups improvements achieved with problem solving skills were maintained. Therefore, it would appear that teaching parents to provide appropriate models and improving parents' problem solving and communication skills would be critical ingredients of an adolescent prevention program.

Research Foci

Few would deny the controversy surrounding the efficacy of current social work preventive services aimed at changing adolescents' behavior. Issues pertain to where services should be provided and by whom, what is proper duration of services, and what are appropriate criteria for evaluation. The legal emphasis on providing effective services to clients and the expressed desire to provide social services on an empirical and rational basis are motivating factors in the development of a sound theoretical base (Reid & Hanrahan, 1982; Wodarski, 1981; Wodarski & Bagarozzi, 1979a, 1979b).

Critical questions center on the following issues. What are the relevant human behavior variables that can provide a solid basis for structuring prevention services to adolescents? What guidelines can be furnished for structuring services from an organizational perspective? What criteria can be utilized in the evaluation of services? How can one delineate the level of intervention on the micro-macro level continuum? Results and products culminating from a number of research projects over the last decade indicate rationale for a more elaborate comprehensive theory of prevention.

It is evident that more elaborate theories of human behavior are needed to provide the rationale for complex therapeutic intervention systems that are based on principles derived from empirical knowledge, with the goal being to prevent adolescent dysfunctioning. These theories must consider biological, sociological, economic, political, and psychological factors as they interact in the human matrix to cause behavior (Wodarski, 1985). It is a definite challenge for any theory of human behavior to isolate those components that lead to prevention, such as the specific aspects of an intervention package in terms of expectations for change, role of cognitive processes, particular client and social worker characteristics, interventions, context of intervention, and so forth. Once this knowledge is developed, the choice of prevention techniques can be made on such criteria as client and worker characteristics, context of intervention, and type of intervention.

Recent evidence suggests that in order for prevention to be successful, macro-level intervention variables have to be considered. An adequate theory of prevention will isolate the social system variables (i.e., legal, political, health, financial, social services, educational, housing, employment, etc.) and their effects on human behavior. Moreover, these variables have to be addressed in a manner that focuses on the attainment of prevention and maintenance of behavior. Current theories fall far short of this goal.

Summary

A major challenge to the community mental health approach is the question of the timing of intervention. Prevention places great emphasis on the teaching components of the interventive process with social workers attempting to help clients learn how to exert control over their own behaviors and the environments in which they live.

In recognition of the critical role of prevention in improving the mental health of all citizens, it has been suggested that a special staff be set up in each mental health center just for prevention programs (Rae-Grant et al., 1966). Such a set-up would be costly, but the impact in the long run would be substantial. The initial cost no doubt would be great but relative to the cost of remedial programs, prevention should prove a bargain.

Endnote

1. The Skills Training Model was developed by Steven Schinke and colleagues at the University of Washington School of Social Work. For an elaboration see Schinke, S., & Gilchrist, L. D. (1984). *Life skills counseling with adolescents.* Baltimore, MD: University Park Press.

REFERENCES

Azrin, N. H. (1978, November). *A learning approach to job finding.* Paper presented at the Association for Advancement of Behavior Therapy, Chicago.

Azrin, N. H., Flores, T., & Kaplan, S. J. (1975). Job-finding club: A group-assisted program for obtaining employment. *Behavior Research and Therapy, 13,* 17–27.

Bandura, A. (1969). *Principles of behavior modification.* New York: Holt, Rinehart & Winston.

Bandura, A., Adams, N., & Beyer, J. (1977). Cognitive processes mediating behavioral change. *Journal of Personality and Social Psychology, 35,* 125–139.

Beck, A. (1970). Cognitive therapy: Nature and relation to behavior therapy. *Behavior Therapy, 1,* 184–200.

Beck, A. (1976). *Cognitive therapy and the emotional disorders.* New York: International Universities Press.

Broskowski, A., & Baker, F. (1977). Professional, organizationa, and social barriers to primary prevention. *American Journal of Orthopsychiatry, 44,* 707–719.

Buckholdt, D. R., & Wodarski, J. S. (1978). The effects of different reinforcement systems on cooperative behaviors exhibited by children in classroom contexts. *Journal of Research and Development in Education, 12,* 50–68.

Bugenthal, D. B., Whalen, C. K., & Hienker, B. (1977). Causal attributions of hyperactive children and motivation assumptions of two behavior change approaches: Evidence for an interactionist position. *Child Development, 48,* 874–884.

Calhoun, K. S., Adams, H. E., & Mitchell, K. M. (1974). *Innovative treatment methods in psychopathology.* New York: Wiley.

Campbell, B. K., & Barnlund, D. C. (1977). Communication patterns and problems of pregnancy. *American Journal of Orthopsychiatry, 47,* 134–139.

Caplan, G. (1961). *Prevention of mental disorders in children.* New York: Basic Books.

Caplan, G. (1964). *Principles of preventive psychiatry.* New York: Basic Books.

Caplan, G. (1974). *Support systems in community mental health: Lectures on concept development.* New York: Behavioral Publications.

Cvetkovich, G., & Grote, B. (1976, May). *Psychosocial development and the social problem of teenage illegitimacy.* Paper presented at the Conference on Determinants of Adolescent Pregnancy and Childbearing, Elkridge, Maryland.

D'Zurilla, T. J., & Goldfried, M. R. (1971). Problem solving and behavior modification. *Journal of Abnormal Psychology, 78,* 101–126.

Epstein, S. (1967). Toward a unified theory of anxiety. In B. Mahar (Ed.), *Progress in experimental personality research* (Vol. 4). New York: Academic Press.

Feldman, R. A., Caplinger, T. E., & Wodarski, J. S. (1983). *The St. Louis conundrum: The effective treatment of antisocial youths.* Englewood Cliffs, NJ: Prentice-Hall.

Foster, S. L., Prinz, R. J., & O'Leary, K. D. (1983). Impact of problemsolving communication training and generalization procedures on family conflict. *Child and Family Behavior Therapy, 5,* 1–24.

Gilchrist, L. D. (1981). Social competence in adolescence. In S. Schinke (Ed.), *Behavioral methods in social welfare* (pp. 61–80). New York: Aldine.

Goldfried, M., & Goldfried, A. (1975). Cognitive change methods. In F. Kanfer & A. Goldstein (Eds.), *Helping people change.* New York: Pergamon.

Gottesfield, J. (1972). *The critical issues of community mental health.* New York: Behavioral Publications.

Haggerty, R. J. (1977). Changing lifestyle to improve health. *Preventive Medicine, 6,* 276–280.

Heller, K., & Swindle, R. W. (1983). Social networks, perceived social support, and coping with stress. In R. Felner, L. Jason, J. Moritsugu, & S. Farber (Eds.), *Preventive psychology: Theory, research and practice.* New York: Pergamon.

Henderson, A. S., Montgomery, I. M., & Williams, C. L. (1972). Psychological immunization: A proposal for preventive psychiatry. *Lancet, 13,* 1111–1112.

Hulbert, R. T., & Sipprelle, C. N. (1978). Random sampling of cognitions in alleviating anxiety attacks. *Cognitive Therapy and Research, 2*(2), 165–169.

Jones, R. J., & Azrin, N. H. (1973). An experimental application of a social reinforcement approach to the problem of job finding. *Journal of Applied Behavior Analysis, 6,* 345–353.

Kovar, M. G. (1979). Some indicators of health-related behavior among adolescents in the United States. *Public Health Reports, 94,* 109–118.

Lange, A. J., & Jakubowski, P. (1976). *Responsible assertive behavior.* Champaign, IL: Research Press.

LeCroy, C. W. (1983). Social-cognitive group work with children. *Behavior Group Therapy, 5*(1), 9–12.

Mahoney, M. J. (1974). *Cognition and behavior modification.* Cambridge, MA: Ballinger.

Matus, R., & Neuhring, E. M. (1979). Social workers in primary prevention: Action and ideology in mental health. *Community Mental Health Journal, 15,* 33–40.

May, J. M. (1986). Cognitive processes and violent behavior in young people. *Journal of Adolescence, 9,* 17–27.

McAlister, A. L., Perry, C., & Maccoby, N. (1979). Adolescent smoking: Onset and prevention. *Pediatrics, 63,* 650–658.

McGuire, W. J. (1964). Inducing resistance to persuasion: Some contemporary approaches. In L. Berkowitz (Ed.), *Advances in experimental social psychology* (Vol. 1). New York: Academic Press.

Meichenbaum, D. (1975). Self-instructional methods. In F. Kanfer & A. Goldstein (Eds.), *Helping people change.* New York: Pergamon.

Mindick, B., Oskamp, S., & Berger, D. E. (1978, May). *Prediction of adolescent mental health.* Paper presented to the American Psychological Association, Toronto, Canada.

Newman, B. M. (1970). Peer pressure hypothesis for adolescent cigarette smoking. *School Health Review, 1,* 15–18.

Newman, B. M., & Newman, P. R. (1979). *Development through life: A psychosocial approach.* Homewood, IL: Dorsey.

Poser, E. G. (1970). Toward a theory of "behavioral prophylaxis." *Journal of Behavior Therapy and Experimental Psychiatry, 1,* 39–43.

Poser, E. G. (1979). Issues in behavioral prevention: Empirical findings. *Advances in Behavior Research and Therapy, 2,* 1–25.

Prager-Decker, I. J. (1980). The efficacy of muscle relaxation in combatting stress. *Health Education, 11,* 40–42.

Pulkkinen, L. (1983). Youthful smoking and drinking in a longitudinal perspective. *Journal of Youth and Adolescence, 12,* 253–283.

Rae-Grant, Q. A. F., Gladwin, T., & Bower, E. M. (1966). Mental health, social competence, and war on poverty. *American Journal of Orthopsychiatry, 36,* 652–664.

Rees, C. D., & Wilborn, B. L. (1983). Correlates of drug abuse in adolescents: A comparison of families of drug users with families of nondrug users. *Journal of Youth and Adolescence, 12,* 55–63.

Reid, W. J., & Hanrahan, P. (1982). Recent evaluations of social work: Grounds for optimism. *Social Work, 27*(4), 328–340.

Robin, A. L. (1981). A controlled evaluation of problem-solving communication training with parent-adolescent conflict. *Behavior Therapy, 12,* 593–609.

Robin, A. L., & Foster, S. L. (1984). Problem-solving communication training: A behavioral family systems approach to parent-adolescent conflict. In P. Karoly & J. Steffen (Eds.), *Adolescent behavior disorders: Foundations and contemporary concerns.* Lexington, MA: Lexington Books.

Robin, A. L., Kent, R., O'Leary, K. D., Foster, S., & Prinz, R. (1977). An approach to teaching parents and adolescents problem-solving communication skills: A preliminary report. *Behavior Therapy, 8,* 639–643.

Roy, T., & Shields, R. (1979). Alcohol education in school social work. *Social Work in Education, 1,* 43–53.

Schinke, S. P., & Blythe, B. J. (in press). Cognitive-behavioral prevention of childrens' smoking. *Child and Behavior Therapy.*

Schinke, S. P., Blythe, B. J., & Gilchrist, L. D. (1981). Cognitivebehavioral prevention of adolescent pregnancy. *Journal of Counseling Psychology, 28,* 451–454.

Schinke, S. P., & Gilchrist, L. D. (1984). *Life skills counseling with adolescents.* Baltimore: University Park Press.

Schinke, S. P., Gilchrist, L. D., & Blythe, B. J. (1980). Role of communication in the prevention of teenage pregnancy. *Health and Social Work, 5,* 54–59.

Schinke, S. P., Gilchrist, L. D., Smith, T. E., & Wong, S. E. (1976). Group interpersonal skills training in a natural setting: An experimental study. *Behavior Research and Therapy, 17,* 149–154.

Schinke, S. P., & Rose, S. D. (1976). Interpersonal skills training in groups. *Journal of Counseling Psychology, 23,* 442–448.

Sherif, M., & Sherif, C. W. (1964). *Reference groups: Exploration into conformity and deviation of adolescents.* New York: Harper & Row.

Smart, R. G., Gray, G., & Bennett, C. (1978). Predictors of drinking and signs of heavy drinking among high school students. *The International Journal of the Addictions, 13,* 1079–1094.

Spivack, G., Platt, J. J., & Shure, M. B. (1976). *The problem-solving approach to adjustment.* San Francisco: Jossey-Bass.

Spivack, G., & Shure, M. B. (1974). *Social adjustment of young children.* San Francisco: Jossey-Bass.

Whittman, M. (1977). Application of knowledge about prevention in social work education and practice. *Social Work and Health Care, 3,* 37–47.

Wodarski, J. S. (1981). *Role of research in clinical practice.* Austin, TX: PRO–ED.

Wodarski, J. S. (1983). *Rural community mental health practice.* Austin, TX: PRO–ED.

Wodarski, J. S. (1985). *Introduction to human behavior.* Austin, TX: PRO–ED.

Wodarski, J. S. (in press, a). A social learning approach to teaching adolescents about alcohol and driving: A multiple variable evaluation. *Journal of Social Service Research.*

Wodarski, J. S. (1987, b). Teaching adolescents about alcohol and driving. *Journal of Alcohol and Drug Education.*

Wodarski, J. S., & Bagarozzi, D. (1979a). *Behavioral social work.* New York: Human Sciences Press.

Wodarski, J. S., & Bagarozzi, D. (1979b). A review of the empirical status of traditional modes of interpersonal helping: Implications for social work practice. *Clinical Social Work Journal, 7*(4), 231–255.

Wodarski, J. S., & Harris, P. (1985). Adolescent suicide: A review of influences and the means for prevention. In *Practice Applications, 2*(4). St. Louis, MO: Washington University Center for Adolescent Mental Health.

Wodarski, L. A., Adelson, C., Tidball, M., & Wodarski, J. S. (1980). Teaching nutrition by teams-games-tournaments. *Journal of Nutrition Education, 12*(2), 61–65.

Zelnick, M., & Kantner, J. F. (1977). Sexual and contraceptive experience of young unmarried women in the United States, 1976 and 1971. *Family Planning Perspectives, 9,* 55–71.

Chapter 10

SUMMARY: EMERGING PRACTICE TRENDS

All practice theories have provided theoretical relevance for social work practice, i.e., a rationale on which interventions may be based. The literature indicates that there is a wealth of such theories; however, each captures only a part of the phenomena of social work practice with children and adolescents. There are very few examples in the literature where theories are presented as complete and logical systems; rather one finds bits and pieces throughout. Manuscripts and texts tend to focus solely on a specific concept derived from a larger theory while failing to relate its significance to the larger theory. Thus, we have failed to attain the goal of integrating human behavior theory for the assessment of client functioning, for the derivation of subsequent interventions, and for the inclusion of research data on appropriate outcomes (Sechrest, White, & Brown, 1979).

In the development of practice theory, differences have been appropriate and necessary, but what is needed now is a more encompassing theory of human behavior. This chapter addresses issues in the development of relevant theoretical frameworks for practice with children and adolescents.

Gender and Ethnic-Racial Variables

Human behavior can best be understood in the context of the individual's total life experience. However, all theories of human behavior developed thus far have excluded gender and ethnic-racial life experience factors. For example, how does growing up black effect a child (Cairns & Valsiner, 1984; Pettigrew, 1985; Yinger, 1985). A number of theories place primary blame for the client's affliction on the client (Brown, 1974; Glenn & Kunnes, 1973). A review of the available literature reveals no widely used theory that adequately conceptualizes how the social system might be responsible for individual afflictions; if such conceptual frameworks do indeed exist, they are not extensively utilized

227

in the profession (Crompton, 1974; Shaffer, 1972; Tidwell, 1971; Turner, 1972). Such theoretical emphasis results in the specification of the individual as the target of intervention. Moreover, it precludes the development of knowledge pertaining to how the institutions of the social system affect human behavior, it encourages racism and sexism, and it does not lead to specification of what strategies could be used to modify these institutions (Schneiderman, 1972).

Thus, theories utilized in the professions are at a distinct disadvantage to structure appropriate interventions for the alleviation of institutional racism and sexism (Hopkins, 1980; Nelson, 1978). Schools of social work must explore in depth how the various institutions of the social system— legal, political, educational, and economic—contribute to racist and sexist practices (Burgest, 1973; Harding, Proshansky, Kutner, & Chein, 1969; Mathis, 1975). For example, theories describing negative attributes of nonwhites, such as those based on the research of Coleman (1966), Jensen (1972, 1973), and Moynihan (1968), must be supplanted by theories that emphasize the strengths of the various minorities (Bertelson, Marks, & May, 1982; Cooper, 1973; Gynther, Lachar, & Dahlstrom, 1978; Hopkins, 1972; McAdoo, 1977; Reynolds & Paget, 1981; Taber, 1970; Thomas, 1976; Thomas & Sillen, 1972; Tuck, 1971; Warheit, Holzer, & Arey, 1975).

An extensive research effort should be undertaken that would isolate the critical variables involved in changing the sexist and racist attitudes of various groups. Moreover, such research should examine sexist and racist policies of various institutions, isolate how they support sexism and racism, prepare recommendations for policy changes, develop mechanisms for implementation of change strategies, evaluate the strategies, and, if successful, generate a model of change (Herrick, 1978; Herzog, 1971; Jackson, 1975; Nelson, 1978; Smith, 1973). Thus, practitioners would be equipped to deal more effectively with variables that are affecting their clients' lives.

Human behavior course content should be geared toward helping students understand the social, political, and economic contexts of children and adolescents, examining the distinctive living patterns that result from historical experiences. Characteristics to be elaborated are the isolation of clients, poverty, lack of transportation to secure the limited services available, the declining employment base resulting in limited incomes, high stress attributes of living environments, and the lack of educational opportunities and its effect on individuals (Brenner,

1977; Bullough, 1972; Dunkle, 1978; Eisenberg, 1981; Hopkins, 1980; Sue, McKinney, Allen, & Hall, 1974; Weinert, 1982). Personal attributes of children and adolescents should be emphasized to help students see how the emphasis on self-reliance will affect the acceptance of services; it should also be noted that networks such as peers, extended family and friends, and institutional structures such as hospitals, community mental health centers, hotlines, and so forth can be used to facilitate the acceptance of services (Froland, Pancoast, Chapman, & Kimboko, 1981; Ginsberg, 1971; Hendricks, Howard, & Gary, 1981; Whittaker & Garbarino, 1983). How personal attributes influence who should be the primary provider of services should be reviewed. In many instances the professional is not of the same gender, age range, and/or ethnic-racial group; the acceptance of subsequent effectiveness of services provided may thus be reduced (Dunkle, 1978; Sue, 1976; Sue et al., 1974; Thompson & Cimbolic, 1978).

Medical Model of Mental Illness

The concept of mental illness undoubtedly will change in the future. In the early stages of the development of social work practice, the adoption of a medical model of mental illness had positive effects upon the budding profession (Achenbach & Edelbrock, 1984). It offered social workers referent power by their association with the already established and prestigious medical profession and gave the practitioner a legitimate rationale for therapeutic intervention. Unfortunately, many clinical social workers have held tenaciously to this antiquated model of mental illness in spite of mounting scientific evidence indicating that much of the dysfunctional behavior exhibited by children and adolescents does not have its roots in organic pathology (Eysenck, Wakefield, & Friedman, 1983; Mischel, 1968; 1973a, 1973b; Redlich, 1974; Ullman & Krasner, 1965). The failure to discard outmoded theory has prevented practitioners from utilizing those models of human behavior that are based solidly on empirical research and are more effective in producing behavior change in clinical practice. Clinical social work has instead remained on the fringe of the social and behavioral sciences and out of touch with the more recent scientific developments that provide the foundation and rationale for a more effective and empirically based practice.

In the future, mental illness will probably be conceptualized from a behavioral point of view; that is, behaviors that are considered deviant will be specified by the larger social group. The Diagnostic and Statistical Manual of Mental Disorders (American Psychiatric Association, 1980) illustrates the magnitude of the behaviors considered to be deviant. When these behaviors violate acceptable levels, the social group decides that it is necessary to do something about them, and therefore mechanisms are employed for their alteration. A comprehensive theory of human behavior must delineate the nature of such control processes. Included must be a specification of why and how children and adolescents are selected for remedial work.

Life Span Development

We will see an emphasis in human behavior theory on the life span development approach to working with children and adolescents in practice. As mentioned in Chapter 5, this approach looks at an individual from the time of birth to the time of death, and indicates what types of critical tasks must be completed at each developmental stage. If these tasks are not completed, certain deficits in the organism occur and the difficulties of exhibiting appropriate behaviors are increased. For example, school failure does not prepare an individual with skills that will facilitate the securement of an adequate job (Sechrest et al., 1979). Much of clinical practice is concerned with helping children and adolescents achieve relevant tasks.

Also, in the future there will probably be less emphasis on variables that were operating early in a person's life. For example, research by Fanshel and Maas (1970) and Kadushin (1967) indicated that traumas that were supposedly associated with adoption can be altered, and that a separation from one's biological parents does not have a lasting effect on an individual's personality as previously believed. Recent research indicates that we should look much closer in time for variables that are currently affecting the individual's behavior.

Biological Variables

Accumulated data show that poor nutrition leads to retarded intellectual development, in some instances plays a role in hyperactive behavior, and may play a significant role in how individuals feel about themselves (Buchsbaum & Haier, 1983; Uytdenhoef, Linkowski, & Mendlewicz, 1982; Warren, 1973). Likewise, hereditary factors are being considered in terms of biological predispositions to schizophrenia, suicide, hypertension, and depression. Research indicates that, when individuals who have such predispositions are exposed to a highly stressful environment, the probability is increased substantially that they will succumb to such conditions. If the biological factors cannot be altered, more emphasis must be placed on helping susceptible individuals develop behaviors to forestall disease. Pioneer efforts have begun in the alleviation of alcohol abuse, smoking, noncompliance in medical treatment plans, obesity, and hypertension (Miller, 1983).

The view of the individual as an organism proceeding through life, a genetic endowment interacting with environmental processes, is fast becoming central in human behavior investigation (Erlenmeyer-Kimling, 1977). As biological research in psychiatry is gaining public attention, there is an emerging consensus that future advances in human behavior and mental disorder will come about through work done in genetics, biochemistry, and the neurosciences (Peele, 1981). Marriages are occurring between traditional fields, forming new multidisciplines such as psychobiology, behavioral medicine, sociobiology, biological psychiatry, and neuropsychiatry. The most optimistic regard this trend as a breakthrough.

Recent research has centered on inheritance patterns, studies of responses to medications, and brain chemistry with certain particularly promising findings. Discoveries related to drug actions have greatly enhanced our understanding of the biology of behavior. Perhaps the most rewarding outcome of biobehavioral research will be the elucidation of subtypes of mental illness, which could lead to the isolation of pure study groups. Much of the research has focused on manic-depressive disorders and schizophrenia, particularly in the area of genetics. To a lesser degree, suicide, alcoholism, certain personality disorders, and several personality variables are gaining attention in biological terms.

Learning

The process of learning has occupied a central position in the analysis of human behavior. That learning phenomena are relevant to the causation of behavior is considered a given. The focus is on specifying the exact conditions that are relevant to the learning process and determining how learning interacts with other psychosocial variables to alter behavior.

We will see an integration of the respondent, operant, and social learning theories, and it will be determined how conditions can be maximized for relevant learning of behaviors. The precise role of learning variables in the manifestation of human behavior will be elaborated and a more comprehensive theory will be developed. For instance, the role of memory in the choice of behavioral outcome and the individual's ability to evaluate different available outcomes will be delineated and the use of peer learning structures.

Peer learning structures create a learning situation in which the performance of each group member furthers the attainment of overall group goals. This increases individual members' support for group performance, strengthens performance under a variety of similar circumstances, and further enhances the aggainment of group goals. Group reward structures capitalize on peer influence and peer reinforcement. These are considered to be some of the most potent variables in the acquisition, alteration, and maintenance of prosocial norms among youths (Buckholdt & Wodarski, 1978).

Very little emphasis in social work practice has been placed on how a client's peers or significant others in his/her environment interact to affect behavior in terms of norms and reward structures. We will see more emphasis on group-level variables, such as social facilitation, comparison, and cohesion theories, in terms of how they affect the individual's behavioral development. Group membership theory will be enlarged to include the role models available, the type of organizations that the individual interacts with during the day, particularly in his/her environment, and the rewards provided for appropriate behaviors, other social organizations that affect behavior, and cultural background.

Concept of Self

A major element of all human behavior theories is the conceptualization of the individual as one striving to fulfill his/her potential. Goals of this striving are the individual's will being freed, ultimate self-development, self-actualization, and maximizing outcomes from the environment. These attributes are conceptualized as the individual having purpose in behavior. Critical to understanding the individual as having drives to fulfill certain biological, love, and security needs and the ability to self-actualize is the role of the self. How does the individual view him/herself? What are the factors involved in formulating cognitions about oneself? How do these cognitions influence one's behavior? Does the child or adolescent believe he/she can attain desired outcomes?

Cognitive variables have been conceptualized historically as unconscious determinants of behavior. However, much research now seems to indicate that what clients are saying to themselves has a distinct influence on behavior. The expectations a client has about success likewise will influence behavioral phenomenon; that is, cognitively, whether individuals believe that they can exhibit the appropriate behaviors will influence the occurrence of such behaviors. Moreover, how much effort the individual believes needs to be exerted in order to attain the desired outcomes influences the goals he/she strives to achieve.

How do clients view themselves and their abilities to operate in their environments and to secure desired outcomes? How do the individuals construct their psychological world in terms of perceptual maps, and to what extent can they process information correctly? What are the relevant processes in helping individuals overcome inaccurate perceptions? The cognitive focus will be a central variable in a comprehensive theory of human behavior. Research questions in the future will center on how children and adolescents can gain a feeling of mastery over their environments (Trotter, 1987).

Self-Control

The coming years will witness increased emphasis on the use of self-control techniques. Sufficient data from social psychology indicate that when clients participate in the choice of therapeutic procedures and their implementation, their motivation and commitment to change is increased, a condition indicated by research to be necessary for behavioral change (Brehm, 1976; Feldman & Wodarski, 1975; Hersen & Van Hasselt, 1986; Secord & Backman, 1964). The typical 55-minute interview with clients wherein therapeutic procedures are implemented and behavioral changes are exhibited does not allow for the generalization or maintenance of behavior. Although behavior may change in the therapeutic context, the process does not facilitate the generalization of behavior to other environments or assure its maintenance once it is achieved. When intervention techniques are applied only in the therapeutic context of an office, all of the stimuli of the office building, including the therapist's characteristics, become discriminative stimuli for the occurrence of the altered behavior (Stokes & Baer, 1977; Waters & McCallum, 1973). If children and adolescents can be taught how to covertly reinforce themselves through use of cognitive procedures, that is, offering themselves appropriate consequences, they can actually practice the alteration of their behavior in their homes, on the playground, or any other relevant context. Furthermore, if clients can practice anger control not only at the therapist's office, but at school, in peer contexts and their homes, the probability of generalization and maintenance increases. The increase in the number of practice trials results in greater learning and enlarges the number of discriminative stimuli that control the behavior thereby increasing the probability of the client actually exhibiting the behavior in the desired context (Staats, 1975).

A variety of issues concerning self-control techniques must be addressed. For example, who can apply them and what variables influence the self-control process? Variables to be investigated might include age, verbal, intellectual, and cognitive abilities of clients, e.g., internal and external focus of control, expectations about the therapeutic process, and self-consistency. Similar questions can be asked about the therapists. What are the essential characteristics of the therapists who can apply self-control techniques? Is there a certain type of therapist who likes to work with children and adolescents in this way and who is effective? Possibly the therapist who does not have to be very authoritative to function effectively with children and adolescents, who is flexible, and who believes in the ability of the clients to control their own behavior may find self-control techniques easy to implement in their practice. We also must ask what self-help groups can be used to help children and adolescents acquire essential life skills and how they can produce and maintain behavioral change.

Macro Level Variables

With additional evidence to indicate that behavior can be changed through the application of techniques based on social learning theory, more emphasis is likely to be placed on the maintenance of behavior change and generalization of the behavior to relevant contexts (Koegel & Rincover, 1977; Stokes & Baer, 1977; Waters & McCallum, 1973). No one can argue that interventions based on social learning theory do not alter behavior. The data show that these techniques are appropriate with a wide variety of populations: autistic, retarded, hyperactive, and antisocial children; inner city children who have deficient reading, verbal, and arithmetic skills; and adolescents who have been traditionally classified as neurotic and psychotic, antisocial, and retarded. We have the technology available to change behavior. Now we must investigate and develop procedures that ensure maintenance and generalization of behavior to relevant contexts.

Achievement of generalization and maintenance will necessitate the incorporation of macro level variables into any interventive approach. The generalization question will have to focus more on how the social system and state and national policies determine and maintain behavior. Brenner (1977) illustrated how fluctuations in the economy are associated with suicide rates, unemployment, crime rates, and other factors. We will have to look at these variables very critically. How do policies reinforce children and adolescents in terms of frequency and amount of rewards? Once behavior is modified, is the social worker ethically bound to ensure that the social system provide a sufficient level of reinforcement to maintain it?

Various procedures that can be implemented to ensure generalization have been discussed in this volume (See Chapter 6). We can apply the basic principles of variable schedules of reinforcement toward the end of therapy, fading procedures (that is, trying to incorporate the natural consequences of the environment to facilitate the behavior coming under their control), and practicing the behavior in various contexts to increase the number of stimuli that control it (Kazdin, 1975; Wodarski, 1980a). The role of social workers in the process of ensuring generalization and maintenance will be substantial. We are the professionals who are in the best position to program the individual's environment to ensure that sufficient reinforcements are provided and to help the individual practice the requisite behavior in the desired contexts.

Future questions will involve an analysis of social system variables in terms of their effect on the generalization and maintenance of behavior (Wodarski, 1977, 1980a). It is likely that future research will begin to unravel the complex relationship between societal experience and human behavior. The means by which we can construct a society with macro level interventions as opposed to individual interventions to prevent or facilitate certain behavior has been virtually ignored by the field. However, we have witnessed already how we can develop social policies with provision of incentives for adolescents who can work to secure and maintain employment, design physical environments in such a manner that learning is facilitated for the developmentally disabled, and provide interactional structures that facilitate cooperation rather than competition. The focus on generalization and maintenance of behavioral change will characterize sophisticated and effective intervention programs. The crucial questions center on how to structure environments that will support behavioral change achieved through interpersonal approaches, that is, provide enough reinforcers to maintain prosocial behavior, and what behaviors can be altered directly through macrolevel intervention (Kelly, Snowden, & Munoz, 1977). We also need to develop a whole technology for treatment termination. While much is said about termination in the social work literature, no criteria exist that can guide the process of terminating an intervention. We need to establish appropriate criteria for determining what are appropriate levels of frequency and quality of behaviors to facilitate the decision making process of termination.

Deinstitutionalization

One of the most perplexing yet critical problems confronting social work professionals is the effective implementation of deinstitutionalization procedures. Which children and adolescents can be placed in the community? What services are necessary to provide children in the community? What socialization processes are necessary? What community characteristics may be matched with individuals' attributes to facilitate placement and enhancement of the individuals' functioning? And what support systems are available to enhance placement? All are questions to be resolved before the placement of clients in the open community. Yet the community mental health social worker is ill prepared to address these issues, largely due to lack of research knowledge on the issues. Well developed assessment tools based on empirical knowledge from relevant social science disciplines and made available to social workers would help prepare these workers to implement deinstitutionalization procedures.

Development of these tools is essential to enable community mental health practitioners to utilize efficacious and cost-effective procedures to isolate physical, psychological, and social factors leading to successful placements in terms of the following items:

1. Assessment of individual attributes, such as dependence, social skills, and economic resources and community attributes, such as homogeneity of population, social cohesion, and employment possibilities

2. Preparation of the community through enlistment of social networks such as family, peers, ministers, and public employees to provide necessary support
3. Preparation of the individual in terms of emphasizing appropriate social behaviors that will be rewarded and will facilitate integration into the social structure of the community
4. Educating the individual about support services available and whom to contact, and gradually introducing the individual to the new living context and to appropriate available social support systems
5. Maintaining placement: monitoring placement and making necessary alterations to facilitate successful placement through the use of relevant diagnostic aids; that is, determining whether the individuals are maintaining themselves physically and socially in terms of attending school, working, receiving appropriate medical care, and experiencing frequent social interactions to prevent social isolation and depression (Brook, 1976; Fields, 1975; Keskiner, 1977; Lamb, 1976; Levine & Kozloff, 1978; Miller, 1977; Meyerson & Herman, 1983; Segal, 1978; Swann, 1973; Wood, 1976).

Empirically Based Concepts of Human Behavior

We will witness in social work the incorporation of new concepts of human behavior. The traditional S–R theory, or the classical Skinnerian paradigm which posits that one only responds to external stimuli, will have to be modified in the future to include cognitive processes, such as what clients are saying to themselves, what they perceive, what they expect, and how such processes affect behavior (Guttman, 1977; Lazarus, 1977; Mahoney, 1977). The inclusion of cognitive variables will see an increased emphasis on a theory of learning that relates coherently to the following items: how does the individual select stimuli; how does the organism process stimuli; how does the individual determine what response it will exhibit; how does one evaluate the rewards and costs for exhibiting or learning new behaviors; and how does this appraisal of behavior and its consequences affect behavior change? Thus, to be an effective theory of human behavior change, the theory will have to incorporate new empirically based knowledge of human cognition and information processing theories.

As discussed above, new variables must be isolated and new types of theories will have to be developed in order for us to effectively alter complex human behavior. Another development for social work practitioners will have to be the incorporation of not only learning theory in social work practice, but additional theories of human behavior and behavior change that are empirically based, such as the work of Truax and Carkhuff (1967a, 1967b) on accurate empathic understanding, nonpossessive warmth, and genuineness. Many graduate programs in social work will incorporate into their curricula current theories of interpersonal attraction, attribution, and relationship formation, game theory and decision theory, and theories on how organizations affect behavior, nonverbal communication, and so on.

In the past, employment opportunities for social workers in the following fields were uncontested: criminal justice, family counseling, child welfare, and human services. If social workers are to compete with other nontraditional human services programs that are also preparing individuals with such empirically based knowledge to enter the helping professions, the curricula of schools of social work will have to incorporate knowledge bases of social psychology that will provide an empirical base for practice techniques (Wodarski, 1979).

Evaluation of Practice

More emphasis will be placed on assessment of practice interventions with children and adolescents. Practitioners will continue to incorporate research skills that will add to the development of practice technology and conceptual advancement in the understanding of human behavior. Data systems will be developed by agencies to facilitate the execution of research pertinent to their needs (Orcutt & Mills, 1979; Reid, 1979). More sophisticated research questions will be posited. There will be a move away from polemic questions such as "Is casework effective?" to "What technique, with what type of worker and client, and what treatment contexts interact to produce the greatest client change?" The main question will be, "Did the services offered the client really make a difference in his/her life?" (Hadley & Strupp, 1977).

Component analyses of successful treatment packages will take place. For example, in task-centered casework (Paul, 1969) essential aspects of the model will be identified, such as structure, expectations, enhancing commitment procedures, planning task implementation, analyzing obstacles, modeling, rehearsal, guided practice and summarizing with the goal being to elicit specific client behaviors.

Research should help resolve critical legal dilemmas regarding practice that plague the profession at this time. If left unresolved by the profession, it will be up to the courts to set guidelines. For instance, what are the traditional acceptable standards of clinical practice? What is adequate treatment? Where should it be provided? What qualities should the change agent possess? How long should treatment be provided? What happens if there is no change in the client? (Bernstein, 1978; Johnson, 1975; Wodarski, 1980a).

Moreover, if data continue to accumulate to attest to the efficacy of particular treatment approaches, those treatment technologies that restrict the client's civil liberties the least and demonstrate superior effectiveness over the other approaches will have to be utilized. Under the legal doctrines of equal protection and least restrictive environment, constitutionally all individuals are entitled to the same privileges, or the same social services. Thus, if two or more technologies are available that achieve the same results, the technology restricting the child's or adolescent's liberties the least in terms of personal resources such as money, time, and energy must be used. These two criteria have been used in legal cases in the past and judges have based their rulings concerning treatment issues on this basis (Martin, 1974, 1975; Wodarski, 1976).

Competency Criteria

Initial Levels of Competence

More concrete criteria must be developed as to when students are ready to practice in terms of knowledge, interpersonal skills, and practice skills levels. Levels of competence should be differentiated, such as the ability to initiate field work, readiness for graduation, and independent practice. The prepractice training experiences reviewed in Chapter 1 alleviated one of the major difficulties of practicum at the different agencies, that is, the variety of practice techniques in which trainees have to exhibit competency. Differentiation of competencies for bachelor's and master's degrees will ensure that quality services are provided to clients by indicating what levels of supervision and consultation should be provided a worker.

Theoretical knowledge and acquisition of necessary practice skills should be assessed and demonstrated to be adequate through appropriate testing techniques before field practice. Before beginning an interventive process with a client, the worker should review a tape of a client or read a contrived case, make a diagnosis, design a corresponding intervention plan with specified outcomes and related means to measure said outcomes, and specify how the success of the plan will be evaluated. These should be accomplished to the satisfaction of the practicum instructor (Wodarski, 1980b).

Practitioner Competence

As the demand for social workers increases, the training of such practitioners will have to be formalized and competency criteria will have to be developed. Few places in the country offer concrete training. We will have to streamline existing training programs since interpersonal technologies are becoming extremely complex to apply and substantial time is needed to develop requisite skills for implementing the procedures in a comprehensive and competent manner. We must determine where to train practitioners and what level of skills must be acquired at each educational degree level in terms of a continuum of competencies. That is, what are the basic training functions at the undergraduate level, at the master's level, and the doctoral level? We will need to develop entrance criteria for students who will become social workers as well as appropriately defined objectives for training. Also, testing procedures will have to be developed and incorporated into training programs to ensure that students meet appropriate standards. Such an assessment process will ensure that the individuals are in fact competent to practice the techniques (Arkava & Brennen, 1975; Armitage & Clark, 1975; Peterson, 1976).

Building Human Behavior Theory

We are agreed that we need a general theory of human behavior enabling us to describe and predict human behavior. However, the argument will continue regarding what is the best way to develop a complex therapeutic intervention system based on principles derived from empirical knowledge and having the goal of helping children and adolescents achieve behavior change and its maintenance. Should it be built like learning theories, where simplistic assumptions about human behavior are tested in the laboratory, and subsequently data be collected to validate these assumptions? Or should it be built like general systems theories that conceptualize the whole, but do not include the necessary experimental work upon which theories may be empirically grounded? It is too early to predict which approach will lead to successful conceptualization of human behavior.

The complexity of any adequate human behavior theory is evidenced in the illustrations regarding the application of the rather elementary procedures based on the principles of positive reinforcement. In conjunction with the client, the social worker must decide what positive reinforcers will be used, who will administer them, where and with what frequency they will be employed, and what additional techniques are needed to change the behavior. The difficulty in applying comprehensive therapy techniques will necessitate the development of criteria regarding who can adequately implement the technology. Likewise, criteria to establish competencies at different levels of the educational process are necessary to streamline the preparation process. Only when these criteria are delineated can we protect the public against the misuse of complex intervention systems by inadequately trained practitioners who jeopardize the integrity of the field.

Summary

The complexity of human behavior will involve interdisciplinary theories, and sociologists, psychologists, psychiatrists, and nutritionists will have to come together to conceptualize the critical variables that impinge on human behavior (Lloyd, Cate, & Conger, 1983). The issue of the control of human behavior versus the understanding of human behavior will continue to be relevant. The requisites of experimentally isolating all the variables that might permit the understanding of behavior are substantial. Moreover, even if we understand behavior, there is no established link between understanding and the ability to alter it. Thus, it is probable that there will be a greater emphasis on controlling behavior with a lesser emphasis on understanding it.

We will witness in social work the incorporation of new concepts of human behavior. The traditional stimulus-response theory, or the classical Skinnerian paradigm that posits that one responds only to external stimuli, will have to be modified in the future to include congitive processes—that is, what clients are saying to themselves, what they perceive and what they expect, and how such processes affect behavior (Guttman, 1977; Lazarus, 1977; Mahoney, 1977). The inclusion of cognitive variables will see an increased emphasis on a theory of human behavior that addresses the following questions: How does the individual select stimuli? How does the individual process stimuli? How does one evaluate the rewards and costs for exhibiting or learning new behaviors? How does this appraisal of behavior and its consequences affect behavior change? Thus, to be an effective theory of human behavior change, social work practice will have to incorporate new, empirically based knowledge of human cognition and information-processing theories.

The incorporation in social work practice of not only social learning theory, but additional theories of human behavior and behavior change that are empirically based, such as the work of Truax and Carkhuff (1967a, 1967b) on accurate empathic understanding, nonpossessive warmth, and genuineness, must take place. In the future graduate programs in social work will incorporate into their curricula current theories of interpersonal attraction, attribution, and relationship formation; game theory and decision theory; theories on how organizations affect behavior; and so on. As this emphasis on investigation, discovery, implementation, and evaluation of new concepts gains impetus, social work will move forward in achieving the goal of managing the complexity of human behavior phenomena.

REFERENCES

Achenbach, T. M., & Edelbrock, C. S. (1984). Psychopathology of childhood. In M. Rosenzweig & L. Porter (Eds.), *Annual review of psychology* (Vol. 35). Palo Alto, CA: Annual Reviews Inc.

American Psychiatric Association. (1980). *Diagnostic and statistical manual of mental disorders* (3rd ed.). Washington, DC: APA.

Arkava, M. L., & Brennen, E. C. (1975). Toward a competency examination for the baccalaureate social work. *Journal of Education for Social Work, 11*(3), 22–29.

Armitage, A., & Clark, F. W. (1975). Design issues in the performance based curriculum. *Journal of Education for Social Work, 11*(1), 22–29.

Bernstein, B. E. (1978). Malpractice: An ogre on the horizon. *Social Work, 23*(2), 106–112.

Bertelson, A. D., Marks, P. A., & May, G. D. (1982). MMPI and race: A controlled study. *Journal of Consulting and Clinical Psychology, 50*(2), 316–318.

Brehm, S. S. (1976). *The application of social psychology to clinical practice.* New York: Wiley.

Brenner, M. H. (1977). Personal stability and economic security. *Social Policy,* May/June.

Brook, B. (1976). Community families: An alternative to psychiatric hospital intensive care. *Hospital and Community Psychiatry, 27,* 195–197.

Brown, P. (1974). *Toward a Marxist psychology.* New York: Harper Colophon.

Buchsbaum, M. S., & Haier, R. J. (1983). Psychopathology: Biological approaches. In M. Rosenzweig & L. Porter (Eds.), *Annual review of psychology* (Vol. 34). Palo Alto, CA: Annual Reviews.

Buckholdt, D. R., & Wodarski, J. S. (1978). The effects of different reinforcement systems on cooperative behaviors exhibited by children in classroom contexts. *Journal of Research and Development in Education, 12*(1), 50–68.

Bullough, B. (1972). Poverty, ethnic identity and preventive health care. *Journal of Health and Social Behavior, 13*(4), 347–359.

Burgest, D. R. (1973). Racism in everyday speech and social work jargon. *Social Work, 18*(4), 20–25.

Cairns, R. B., & Valsiner, J. (1984). Child psychology. In M. Rosenzweig & L. Porter (Eds.), *Annual review of psychology* (Vol. 35) (pp. 553–577). Palo Alto, CA: Annual Reviews Inc.

Coleman, J. S. (1966). *Equality of educational opportunity.* Washington, DC: U.S. Government Printing Office.

Cooper, S. (1973). A look at the effect of racism on clinical work. *Social Casework, 54*(2), 76–84.

Crompton, D. W. (1974). Minority content in social work education—Promise or pitfall? *Journal of Education for Social Work, 10*(1), 9–18.

Dunkle, R. E. (1978). Racial differences in the confidant relationship. *Journal of Sociology and Social Welfare, 5*(6), 863–871.

Eisenberg, L. (1981). Cross-cultural and historical perspectives on child abuse and neglect. *Journal of Child Abuse and Neglect, 5,* 299–308.

Erlenmeyer-Kimling, L. (1977). Issues pertaining to prevention and intervention of genetic disorders affecting human behavior. In G. Albee & J. Joffe (Eds), *Primary prevention of psychology.* Hanover, NH: University Press of New England.

Eysenck, H. J., Wakefield, J. A., & Friedman, A. F. (1983). Diagnosis and clinical assessment: The DSM–III. In M. Rosenzweig & L. Porter (Eds.), *Annual review of psychology* (Vol. 34). Palo Alto, CA: Annual Reviews.

Fanshel, D., & Maas, H. (1970). *Factorial dimensions of the characteristics of children in placement and their families.* New York: Child Welfare League of America. (ERIC Document Reproductive Service No. ED 039-284).

Feldman, R. A., & Wodarski, J. S. (1975). *Contemporary approaches to group treatment.* San Francisco: Jossey-Bass.

Fields, S. (1975). Breaking through the boarding house blues. *Innovation, 16,* 2–10.

Froland, C., Pancoast, D. L., Chapman, N. J., & Kimboko, P. J. (1981). *Helping networks and human services.* Beverly Hills: SAGE.

Ginsberg, L. H. (1971). Rural social work. *Encyclopedia of Social Work, 2,* 1138–1144.

Glenn, M., & Kunnes, R. (1973). *Repression or revolution.* New York: Harper Colophon.

Guttman, N. (1977). On Skinner and Hull: A reminiscence and projection. *American Psychologist, 32,* 321–328.

Gynther, M. D., Lachar, D., & Dahlstrom, W. G. (1978). Are special norms for minorities needed? Development of an MMPI F scale for blacks. *Journal of Consulting and Clinical Psychology, 46*(6), 1403–1408.

Hadley, S. W., & Strupp, H. H. (1977). Evaluations of treatment in psychotherapy: Naivete or necessity? *Professional Psychology, 8*(4), 478–490.

Harding, J., Proshansky, H., Kutner, B., & Chein, I. (1969). Prejudice and ethnic relations. In G. Lindzey & E. Aronson (Eds.), *The handbook of social psychology* (2nd ed., Vol. 5). Reading, MA: Addison-Wesley.

Hendricks, L. E., Howard, C. S., & Gary, L. R. (1981). Help-seeking behavior among urban black adults. *Social Work, 26*(2), 161–163.

Herrick, J. E. (1978). The perpetuation of institutional racism through ethnic and racial minority content in the curriculum of schools of social work. *Journal of Sociology and Social Welfare, 5*(4), 527–537.

Hersen, M., & Van Hasselt, V. B. (1986). Developments and emerging trends. In M. Hersen & V. Van Hasselt (Eds.), *Behavior therapy with children and adolescents: A clinical approach* (pp. 3–28). New York: Wiley.

Herzog, E. (1971). Who should be studied? *American Journal of Orthopsychiatry, 41*(1), 4–12.

Hopkins, T. J. (1972). The role of community agencies as viewed by black fathers. *American Journal of Orthopsychiatry, 42*(3), 508–516.

Hopkins, T. J. (1980). A conceptual framework for understanding the three "isms"— Racism, ageism, sexism. *Journal of Education for Social Work, 16*(2), 63–70

Jackson, J. J. (1975). Some special concerns about race and health: An editorial finale. *Journal of Health and Social Behavior, 16*(4), 342; 428–429.

Jensen, A. R. (1972). *Genetics and education.* New York: Harper & Row.

Jensen, A. R. (1973). *Educability and group differences.* New York: Harper & Row.

Johnson, F. M. (1975). Court decisions and the social services. *Social Work, 20,* 343–347.

Kadushin, A. (1967). Reversibility of trauma: A follow-up study of children adopted when older. *Social Work, 12*(4), 33–42.

Kazdin, A. E. (1975). *Behavior modification in applied settings.* Homewood, IL: Dorsey.

Kelly, J. G., Snowden, L. R., & Munoz, R. F. (1977). Social and community intervention. In M. Rosenzweig & L. Porter (Eds.), *Annual review of psychology.* Palo Alto, CA: Annual Reviews.

Keskiner, A. (1977). Determinants of placement outcomes in the foster community project. *Diseases of the Nervous System, 38,* 439–443.

Koegel, R. L., & Rincover, A. (1977). Research on the differences between generalization and maintenance in extra-therapy responding. *Journal of Applied Behavior Analysis, 10,* 1–12.

Lamb, H. (Ed.). (1976). *Community survival for long-term patients.* San Francisco: Jossey-Bass.

Lazarus, A. A. (1977). Has behavior therapy outlived its usefulness? *American Psychologist, 32,* 550–554.

Levine, S., & Kozloff, M. A. (1978). The sick role: Assessment and overview. In R. Turner, J. Coleman, & R. Fox (Eds.), *Annual review of sociology* (Vol. 4). Palo Alto: Annual Reviews.

Lloyd, S. A., Cate, R. M., & Conger, J. (1983). Family violence and service providers: Implications for training. *Social Casework, 64*(7), 431–435.

Mahoney, M. M. (1977). Reflections on the cognitive-learning trend in psychotherapy. *American Psychologist, 32,* 5–13.

Martin, R. (1974). *Behavior modification: Human rights and legal responsibilities.* Champaign, IL: Research Press.

Martin, R. (1975). *Legal challenges to behavior modification.* Champaign, IL: Research Press.

Mathis, T. P. (1975). Educating for black social development: The politics of social organization. *Journal of Education for Social Work, 11*(1), 105–112.

McAdoo, H. (1977). Family therapy in the black community. *American Journal of Orthopsychiatry, 47*(1), 75–79.

Meyerson, A., & Herman, G. (1983). What's new in aftercare? A review of the literature. *Hospital and Community Psychiatry, 34*(4), 333–342.

Miller, M. (1977). A program for adult foster care. *Social Work, 22,* 275–279.

Miller, N. E. (1983). Behavioral medicine: Symbiosis between laboratory and clinic. In M. Rosenzweig & L. Porter (Eds.), *Annual review of psychology* (Vol. 34). Palo Alto, CA: Annual Reviews.

Mischel, W. (1968). *Personality and assessment.* New York: Wiley.

Mischel, W. (1973a). Facing the issues. *Journal of Abnormal Psychology, 82,* 541–542.

Mischel, W. (1973b). On the empirical dilemmas of psychodynamic approaches: Issues and alternatives. *Journal of Abnormal Psychology, 82,* 335–344.

Moynihan, D. P. (1968). *The negro family: The case for national action.* New York: Bantam.

Nelson, K. (1978). Children in female-headed families: A comparison of blacks and whites in California. *Journal of Social Service Research, 1*(4), 373–389.

Orcutt, B. A., & Mills, P. R., Jr. (1979). The doctoral practice laboratory. *Social Service Review, 53,* 633–643.

Paul, G. L. (1969). Behavior modification research. In C. Franks (Ed.), *Behavior therapy: Appraisal and status.* New York: McGraw-Hill.

Peele, S. (1981). Reductionism in the psychology of the 80's. *American Psychologist, 36,* 807–808, 818.

Peterson, G. W. (1976). A strategy for instituting competency based education in large colleges and universities: A pilot program. *Educational Technology, 16*(12), 30–34.

Pettigrew, T. F. (1985). New black-white patterns: How best to conceptualize them? In R. Turner & J. Short (Eds.), *Annual review of sociology* (Vol. 11) (pp. 329–346). Palo Alto, CA: Annual Reviews Inc.

Redlich, F. (1974). Psychoanalysis and the medical model. *Journal of the American Academy of Psychoanalysis, 2,* 147–157.

Reid, W. J. (1979). The social agency as a research machine. *Journal of Social Service Research, 2*(4), 11.

Reynolds, C. R., & Paget, K. D. (1981). Factor analysis of the revised Children's Manifest Anxiety Scale for blacks, whites, males, and females with a national normative sample. *Journal of Consulting and Clinical Psychology, 49*(3), 352–359.

Schneiderman, L. (1972). Racism and revenue-sharing. *Social Work, 17*(3), 44–49.

Sechrest, L., White, S. O., & Brown, E. D. (Eds.). (1979). *The rehabilitation of criminal offenders: Problems and prospects.* Washington, DC: National Academy of Sciences.

Secord, P. F., & Backman, C. W. (1964). *Social psychology.* New York: McGraw-Hill.

Segal, S. (1978). *The mentally ill in community based sheltered care: Study of community care and social integration.* New York: Wiley-Interscience.

Shaffer, A. (1972). Community organization and the oppressed. *Journal of Education for Social Work, 8*(3), 65–75.

Smith, N. F. (1973). Who should do minority research? *Social Casework, 54*(7), 393–397.

Staats, A. W. (1975). *Social behaviorism.* Homewood, IL: Dorsey.

Stokes, T. F., & Baer, D. M. (1977). An implicit technology of generalization. *Journal of Applied Behavior Analysis, 12,* 349–367.

Sue, S. (1976). Client's demographic characteristics and therapeutic treatment: Differences that make a difference. *Journal of Consulting and Clinical Psychology, 44*(5), 864.

Sue, S., McKinney, H., Allen, D., & Hall, J. (1974). Delivery of community mental health services to black and white clients. *Journal of Consulting and Clinical Psychology, 42*(6), 794–801.

Swann, R. (1973). A survey of a boarding-home program for former mental patients. *Hospital and Community Psychiatry, 24,* 485–486.

Taber, R. H. (1970). A systems approach to the delivery of mental health services in black ghettos. *American Journal of Orthopsychiatry, 40*(4), 702–709.

Thomas, A., & Sillen, S. (1972). *Racism and psychiatry.* New York: Brunner/Mazel.

Thomas, M. J. (1976). Realism and socioeconomic status (ses) of occupational plans of low ses black and white male adolescents. *Journal of Counseling Psychology, 23*(1), 46–49.

Thompson, R. A., & Cimbolic, P. (1978). Black students' counselor preference and attitudes toward counseling center use. *Journal of Counseling Psychology, 25*(6), 570–575.

Tidwell, B. J. (1971). The black community's challenge to social work. *Journal of Education for Social Work, 7*(3), 59–65.

Trotter, R. J. (1987, February). Stop blaming yourself. *Psychology Today,* pp. 30–39.

Truax, C. B., & Carkhuff, R. R. (1967a). New directions in clinical research. In B. Berenson & R. Carkhuff (Eds.), *Sources of gain in counseling and psychotherapy.* New York: Holt, Rinehart and Winston.

Truax, C. B., & Carkhuff, R. R. (1967b). *Toward effective counseling and psychotherapy: Training and practice.* Chicago: Aldine-Atherton.

Tuck, S., Jr. (1971). Working with black fathers. *American Journal of Orthopsychiatry, 41*(3), 465–472.

Turner, J. B. (1972). Education for practice with minorities. *Social Work, 17*(2), 112–118.

Ullman, L. P., & Krasner, L. (1965). *Case studies in behavior modification.* New York: Holt, Rinehart & Winston.

Uytdenhoef, P., Linkowski, P., & Mendlewicz, J. (1982). Biological quantitative methods in the evaluation of psychiatric treatment: Some biochemical criteria. *Neuropsychobiology, 8,* 60–72.

Warheit, G. J., Holzer, C. E., III, & Arey, S. A. (1975). Race and mental illness: An epidemiologic update. *Journal of Health and Social Behavior, 16*(3), 243–256.

Warren, N. (1973). Malnutrition and mental development. *Psychological Bulletin, 80*(4), 324–328.

Waters, F. W., & McCallum, R. N. (1973). The basis of behavior therapy: Mentalistic or behavioralistic? A reply to E. A. Locke. *Behavior Research and Therapy, 11,* 157–163.

Weinert, B. A. (1982). A dialogue for change: Policy, politics and advocacy. *Administration in Social Work, 6*(2/3), 125–137.

Whittaker, J., & Garbarino, J. (1983). *Social support networks.* New York: Aldine.

Wodarski, J. S. (1976, June). *Recent supreme court legal decisions: Implications for social work practice.* Paper presented at the 102nd Annual Meeting of the National Conference on Social Welfare, Washington, DC.

Wodarski, J. S. (1977). The application of behavior modification technology to the alleviation of selected social problems. *Journal of Sociology and Social Welfare, 4*(7), 1055–1073.

Wodarski, J. S. (1979). Critical issues in social work education. *Journal of Education for Social Work, 15*(2), 5–13.

Wodarski, J. S. (1980a). Procedures for the maintenance and generalization of achieved behavioral change. *Journal of Sociology and Social Welfare, 7*(2), 298–311.

Wodarski, J. S. (1980b). Requisites for the establishment and implementation of competency based agency practice. *Arete, 6*(1), 17–28.

Wood, P. (1976). A program to train operators of board-and-care homes in behavioral management. *Hospital and Community Psychiatry, 27,* 767–770.

Yinger, J. M. (1985). Ethnicity. In R. Turner & J. Short (Eds.), *Annual review of sociology* (Vol. 11) (pp. 151–180). Palo Alto, CA: Annual Reviews Inc.

AUTHOR INDEX

Benward, J., 154, 161
Berenson, B. G., 37, 50, 246
Berger, D. E., 209, 224
Bergin, A. e., 9, 31, 32, 33, 73, 94, 96
Bergman, P., 153, 164
Berkovitz, I. H., 137, 161, 189, 194
Berkowitz, B. P., 37, 50, 125, 133, 148, 162, 184, 194
Berkowitz, L., 224
Berliner, L., 162
Berliner, R., 149, 152, 153, 162
Berman, A. L., 188, 189, 193, 194
Bernstein, B. E., 239, 242
Bernstein, D. A., 59, 71, 75
Bertelson, A. D., 228, 243
Bess, B. E., 153, 162
Beyer, J., 218, 222
Beyer, M., 184, 194
Bijou, S. W., 43, 49, 50, 54, 56, 58, 72
Binswanger, L., 81, 96
Black, J. L., 42, 51
Blackburn, B., 178, 179, 204
Bladholm, S., 108, 116
Blocker, T., 176, 198
Blood, L., 183, 194
Blumberg, M. L., 146, 162
Blyth, D. A., 154, 162
Bluthe, B. J., 110, 117, 143, 169, 215, 225
Bock, R., 183, 194
Bolton, F. G., 177, 194
Boren, J., 120, 133
Borgatta, E. F., 35, 51
Borges, M., 62, 73
Borkan, E. L., 153, 162
Borkovec, T. D., 59, 72
Botvin, G. J., 185, 195
Bower, E. M., 222, 224
Bradstadt, W., 202
Brandon, J. S., 183, 184, 195, 204
Brehm, S. S., 2 33, 243
Breitenbucher, M., 144, 163
Brennan, T., 182, 183, 194
Brennen, E. C., 240, 242
Brenner, M. H., 114, 115, 228, 235, 243
Briar, K. H., 113, 114, 116, 179, 180, 195
Briar, S., 94, 96
Brieland, D., 5, 31, 77, 96
Brim, O. G., 99, 115, 116
Bronfenbrenner, U., 185, 195
Brook, B., 243

Brooks, B., 153, 162
Brown, C. E., 35, 50
Brown, E. D., 227, 230, 246
Brown, P., 227, 243
Brown, S., 160, 61
Bruck, M., 80, 81, 95, 96
Buchsbaum, M. S., 230, 243
Buck, C., 152, 163
Buckholdt, D., 25, 31, 44, 48, 52, 93, 98, 127, 133, 214, 223
Buckholdt, D. R., 232, 243
Bugenthal, D. B., 217, 218, 223
Bullough, B., 229, 243
Burden, D. S., 179, 195
Burgess, A. W., 151, 162
Burgest, D. R., 228, 243
Burton, L., 151, 162
Bush, D., 154, 162
Butcher, J. N., 19, 32
Buttenwieser, E., 64, 74
Buttenfield, W. H., 57, 72
Butz, G., 70, 72

C

Cain, L. p., 148, 162
Cairns, R. B., 227, 243
Caldwell, 178, 200
Calhoun, J. F., 190, 195
Calhoun, K. S., 218, 223
Campbell, A., 174, 195
Campbell, B.K., 209, 223
Canter, R. J., 158, 163
Caplan, G., 208, 210, 223
Caplinger, T. E., vii, viii, 35, 50, 83, 96, 108, 116, 155, 163, 207, 223
Carkhuff, R. R., 37, 50, 51, 238, 242, 246
Carroll, E., 186, 199
Carson, G. A., 190, 195
Carson, R., 6, 32
Case, l. P., 53, 72
Cate, R. M., 241, 245
Cautela, J. R., 60, 72
Cavallin, H., 149, 162
Chalmers, M. A., 64, 74
Chandler, S. M., 151, 162
Chapel, J. L., 149, 165
Chapman, N. J., 229, 243
Chein, I., 228, 244
Chelune, Gordon, 49

Pocs, D., 175, 201
Pol, L. G., 179, 196
Polansky, N. A., 64, 74
Pollack, C. B., 147, 168, 170
Porter, L., viii, 31, 116, 242, 243, 244, 245
Poser, E.G., 210, 224
Potter, H.W., 101, 116
Power, E., 148, 164
Prager-Decker, I. J., 218, 224
Prendergast, T. J., 185, 201
Prinz, R. J., 188, 196, 201, 220, 223, 225
Proshansky, H., 228, 244
Prue, D. M., 119, 134
Pulkkinen, L., 127, 134, 187, 201, 220, 224
Putnam, T. I., 147, 170

Q

Quay, H. C., 178, 201

R

Rabin, P., 191, 203
Rae-Grant, Q.A.F., 222, 224
Ratcliff, K. S., 159, 168
Ray, S., 169
Razin, A., 50
Rebelsky, R. G., 107, 116
Redlich, F., 229, 245
Reed, P.L., 53, 74
Rees, C.D., 127, 134, 187, 201, 220, 224
Reese, S., 121, 133
Reid, J. W., 35, 51
Reid, W. J., 12, 26, 27, 32, 33, 60, 68, 74, 85, 95, 97, 221, 224, 238, 246
Rentoul, E., 151, 168
Reppucci, N. D., 143, 169
Reynolds, C.R., 228, 246
Reznikoff, M., 189, 192, 203
Rich, A. H., 148, 168,184, 201
Riemer, S., 151, 168
Rigler, D., 147, 169
Riley, H. F., 149, 150, 152, 153, 170
Riley, M. W., 99, 117
Rincover,A., 119, 133, 234, 244
Rinn, R. C., 126, 134
Risley, T. R., 54, 58, 71
Robbins, C., 137, 157, 166, 189, 199
Roberts, A. R., 188, 196, 201
Robertson, E., 196, 201

Robin, A. L., 186, 187, 188, 201, 219, 220, 224, 225
Robins, L. N., 53, 74, 159, 168
Robinson, J. D., 8, 32
Robinson, P. A., 183, 202
Roden, M., 178, 196
Rodick, J. D., 157, 158, 165
Rodman, H., 101, 117
Rodriguez,J. F., 182, 202
Roe, A., 53, 74
Rogel, M., 176, 202
Rogers, C., 53, 74
Rojek, D. G., 187, 196
Rolston, R. H., 146, 196
Rose, S. D., 25, 33, 123, 134, 148,169, 184, 202, 212, 225
Rosen, A., 185, 194
Rosen, S., 6, 33
Rosenberg, D., 144, 163
Rosenberg, M. S., 108, 117, 143, 169
Rosenberg, P. B., 176,202
Rosenblatt, A., 49, 51
Rosenblatt, J., 190, 202
Rosenfeld, A., 152, 169
Rosenhan, D. L., 53, 74, 75
Rosenkrantz, A. L., 193, 202
Rosenthal, R., 37, 51
Rosenzweig, M., viii, 31, 116, 242, 243, 244, 245
Rosnow,R. L., 37, 51
Ross, A., 164
Ross, H., 182, 202
Roszkowski, M., 142, 169
Rotter, J. B., 53, 65, 74
Roy, T., 210, 225
Rubel, R. J., 154, 161, 169
Rudd, S., 192, 199
Rudolph, C. S., 179, 194
Rusilko, S., 30, 33
Russell, D. E., 149, 169
Rutter, M., 177, 202
Ryan, W., 24, 33
Rychtarik, R. G., 119, 134

S

Sagar, S. J., 152, 168
Sahler,O. J., 146, 167
Salzinger, K., 18, 33
Samson, J., 163

SUBJECT INDEX

263